for the

lov

Joanna Bates.

About the Author

The author worked for a bank and made children's clothes in an earlier life.

She lives in Essex with her husband and helps him with their engineering business. She enjoys times with her children, who are still her best friends, and six grandchildren.

She enjoys entertaining and travelling.

Dedication

Dedicated to Paul, who was and is my inspiration, and Sam, Alex and Rafi, who I hope enjoy the anecdotal scraps within.

To my mother, who always encouraged me to write, and the grandmother I never knew, who lent me her name.

Joanna Bates

TRUST ME, I'M A SURVEYOR

AUSTIN MACAULEY
PUBLISHERS LTD.

A CIP catalogue record for this title is available from the British Library.

ISBN 9781786295330 (Paperback)
ISBN 9781786295347 (Hardback)
ISBN 9781786295354 (E-Book)

www.austinmacauley.com

First Published (2017)
Austin Macauley Publishers Ltd.
25 Canada Square
Canary Wharf
London
E14 5LQ

Chapter 1

Two take an office

I was in charge of the last-minute things, like telephones, getting the gas on and the whole organisational stuff really. He was out doing the important things like looking at cracked and distorted buildings.

So here I was in the ground floor office, previously a junk shop, trying to be calm as everything was being finalised today. At last. The carpet fitters from Forest Gate were turning up as soon as they could get away. I didn't ask where from. The carpet was going to be a surprise. That was the trouble when everyone wanted to "do you a deal", you were obliged to accept their choice. I had specified white paintwork everywhere to ensure it didn't clash with the carpet. I hoped it wasn't patterned or garish or nylon that would give me shocks as I walked on it.

A client with carpet shops had had a problem with his landlord, the local council and Chris had intervened. I wasn't sure what actually happened as I was freshly roped in on the enterprise but the council backed off, the leaking drains were fixed and the grateful proprietor promised to sort out our flooring. As time went on I grew to learn that most people really didn't want to pay their bills. Even very grateful ones found it difficult to prise open their wallets or put pen to cheque book. Instead they passed our name around and brought us gifts. Occasionally these were useful, like the carpet. It was in this way that over time we built up an eclectic mix of clients and their cohorts, families, various professionals and associates. We learned that responsible individuals or those who held responsible positions could no more be trusted than the hard-up scrounger; ordinary salt of the earth folks were usually trustworthy and very successful ones were often complete scumbags. This included council operatives who we were obliged to deal with often and found ourselves in a plethora of situations, some dangerous and life threatening.

My name is Christina Prentice and I am married to Chris. For some time, we have been juggling part time jobs with our joint enterprise. Chris is a structural surveyor to give him a title and this includes site surveying, drawing plans, rescuing hostages and solving crimes. I usually traipse along with him and generally hold the tape and take notes. When our loft and spare bedroom became full of equipment and records and paraphernalia and we had trouble walking around the storage boxes we decided to expand and found a perfect small office which we agreed to rent. After a while as we became established the landlord suggested that we buy it so our bank arranged the finance and we employed our solicitor.

'I'm in a hurry, Chris,' Mr Clooney the landlord said. 'Can we exchange and complete on the same day?'

'OK,' Chris agreed as there seemed no reason to delay.

We arrived on the due date as usual and while we stood outside with a small van and endless boxes of papers and stuff scattered over the pavement Chris took a call from the said landlord, cancelling the sale. Not only that, he wanted the office back for himself so we had one day to move out too. The flexible renting agreement was apparently cancelled.

Larry in the junk shop next door peered out curiously through his dirty windows and realised what had happened. He pushed aside a heap of jumble and called us in.

'I'm goin' up for sale, Mr Prentice, sodding off to Clacton, to my caravan,' he said breathlessly. 'Move in 'ere, don't let that bastard get you down.'

So, they chatted for a few minutes and the deal was done. A few square metres of space was cleared in front of the window, a drawing board set up, one desk and a chair installed and a wonky bin found from somewhere, dusted out, knocked into shape and placed unceremoniously down by the desk. Feeling (and looking) completely exposed, Chris worked in the window for several months while Larry sorted out his caravan in Clacton and we began again with the solicitor and the bank. Completely surrounded by fourth hand furniture, shabby rugs, faded pictures, odd crockery and assorted household goods our business flourished. The curious window display which changed daily may have had something to do with the initial attraction. During the next couple of months, as the legal teams idled their way through the process and Larry's gear was slowly sold off around him, Chris sat like a working model in Selfridges Christmas displays. He almost lost his surveying case twice, the waste basket disappeared and he came back from a site meeting in time to retrieve his desk as it waltzed out the door.

The office was taking shape now, closely watched by the immediate locals.

The area was quite a poor one but over time we made many friends and East End warmth enveloped us. Larry had run his emporium for forty years until his arthritis and love of booze had faded his enthusiasm, let alone capacity. Now his caravan and alcohol had revived his raison d'etre and he craved the sea breeze and a deck chair. The locals knew of his double affliction but he thought he'd hidden his secrets as well as the empty bottles and cans which we unearthed with each transaction. Every drawer and cupboard held bottles and cans. We gained a few pretty Victorian bits and bobs as well as a skip full of tat. If the shop itself was an Aladdin's cave the huge ramshackle shed at the back was worse. By completion date only the area around Chris's centre stage was clear, leaving the upstairs chaos intact.

'I'll leave the rest of the stuff here, start you off.' With that, he got into a black cab and drove out of our lives. Good grief.

Many trips to the refuse dump, pavement sales and charity donations later and we were clear to go.

The painters backed out of the door taking their brushes and pots. The torn and stained dust sheets had been gathered up revealing the desks and bare concrete floor and Sid, the local handyman, started to assemble the packs of bookcases which we had found out in the shed.

The windows now gleamed, the joinery was fresh black and the sign over said Chris Twice Surveyors and 'plans drawn' in smaller letters to the side with the pending phone number stencilled beneath.

The carpet fitters arrived at exactly the same time as the phone engineers and they played a game of seeing who could be the most awkward and obstructive when their positions coincided. I had to intervene when some wires got caught in the rolls and were accidentally sliced with an overzealous Stanley knife and a glue pot sucked up a screwdriver. I've always found a mug of tea helps in these situations and became just for a few minutes a helpless blonde bimbo threatening to panic so they stopped their childish antics and endeavoured to win approval. I can simper with the best of them when needs must and could see a few people approaching the door.

The postman brought the first utility bills and a couple of good luck cards, a bank statement showing a healthy red balance and a stack of mail for Larry. A couple of nosy locals trod all over the new grey cord flooring while looking around at our plans and books and Mrs Chin brought us chips. Starting my diet as I didn't mean to go on, I smothered them in salt and vinegar and dug straight in. Chris walked through the door as if on cue.

'Thanks, Mrs Chin, very welcome.' The first of our freebies. We would repay her a hundredfold in due course.

We had been trading from home for a while until we found the empty office in the parade but Larry taking pity on us was heaven sent, although we became for him a readymade buyer. All our contacts had been advised of the impending move, and we had to bribe the postman with sweets to bring wrongly addressed envelopes to our door instead. The reneging landlord installed his wife in the smaller office next door selling DVDs but she ran off with a local plumber and he was left tenantless and wifeless. We didn't laugh when he turned up in tears at our door, not so that he'd notice anyway. God has his little ways, as Reverend McDonald says.

We munched our chips and read our mail. I made a new file for the site he had visited, wrote all the notes up and we collided mid room in our eagerness to answer the phone.

''Ello, can I speak to Mr Chris please? I got 'is number from a mate.'

'Chris Prentice speaking, how can I help?'

'My brother's mate's in trouble and you need to come straight away. It's awkward but we don't know anyone else to sort him out.'

'Right. Well, I only moved into this office today really and just got back from a meeting, so I need you to explain the problem, please, Mr eh? Who did you say you are?'

'Well I never said but it don't matter. It's Shylock.'

'Really? What has happened, Mr Shylock?'

'My - um – acquaintance, as it were, needs a secure place to 'old his private collection, see, so he decided to dig a basement under his 'ouse.'

A small silence preceded the next sentence and he continued, 'So he's been bashing away and doing alright. There's a tidy 'ole under the floor, made a good space an' all but the front wall's fell out. It's all over the garden and everyone going by on the bus can see right in.'

Well I have to hand it to Chris because I had to clamp my jumper into my mouth to smother my scream of horror and mirth and he kept a straight face and took down the details. Once the phone was down and safely disconnected, he laughed.

It was Guy Fawkes day and we had promised the children fireworks and now a visit to an unsafe ruin, caused by thoughtless excavation, would take preference. Luckily it was Friday, so we picked them up from school and drove straight over to the disaster site. All of us. Chris rang a scaffolding team who arrived at the same time as we did and they lost no time installing emergency props and shores. The front of the roof hung by sarking felt on flimsy battens and facia and guttering swung loose. The shocked family sat in the kitchen, smoking. Mr Shylock's mate swigged whiskey as he marched up and down.

'Mr Chris, I can't fank you enough. I'm Jeffrey Gold. Call me Jeff. Gawd wot a mess. When I fink! We could've been killed. Wot a bleedin' state. Don't worry about money! Woteva you need, it's yours! Just make my 'ouse good. OK? Make my 'ouse good. Its Jonny Pearson wot told us about you. Diamond geezer he is, so I said to 'im, "if he's a mate of yours, Jonny he's gotta be OK."'

Mm, well Jonny Pearson wasn't exactly a mate, all his introductions seemed to be people who built illicit extensions or unlawful loft conversions and Chris ended up sorting out the retrospective applications to fend off the council enforcement teams and organising builders with scant knowledge of English or current building practice.

Chris explained that the emergency propping would be expensive in itself and all the work would have to be inspected and approved by the local council, which alarmed Mr Gold. He tried to railroad him into by-passing the department to save time and red tape. It would cost us our professional indemnity cover if we failed to follow the rules. Chris explained that we could prepare him plans for a properly constructed basement and help him through the building work, but to achieve it safely and legally would take time. His firm voice when he explained this made me shiver with pride and his thunderous face left no doubts. Jeffrey Gold agreed. He had no choice because Chris was gathering up his papers and equipment to leave. Our client disappeared upstairs to a rear room and came back with a wodge of banknotes which he pushed at Chris. 'That's a start, Chris. I can't fank you enuf. I'm sorry, I just need to get on. No offence mate. Do it your way. Just fast as you can.'

He looked then at me and our openly grinning children and shouted at his terrified wife to get her coat on. We all trooped out through the side garden to the common where someone lit the bonfire and the communal firework display began. Jonny Pearson the surveyor who had been introduced to Chris by a pair of gay estate agents arrived with his family and handed round sparklers to the children and Mrs Gold reappeared. She gave us each a box wrapped in newspaper and about thirty of us ate fish and chips while the local Round Table collected coins in buckets and kept the display going.

The children thought the whole trip was cool and their dad the hero. We wondered what we had let ourselves in for when we saw Jeffrey Gold sneaking back across the common. A black Range Rover with darkened windows had slowed and stopped outside his house, idling until he reached it; the off side back window lowered and a threatening face leered out at him. We pretended not to notice when he returned and Chris said the scaffolding had saved the roof and the timber boarding would secure the gaping front.

'I'll be in touch, Jeffrey, give me a couple of weeks but you can't rush. Me or the process,' and we all trooped back to our car and sang songs all the way home.

That was the first day working together in our new office and the destruction of my diet, having chips twice in one day.

The weekend saw Chris working with sketches and schemes for underpinning the front and side walls and forming retaining walls so the basement could be dug out in sequence then he went on to preparing the engineering calculations for the council to check.

It was brilliant that someone had paid us but we had an uneasy feeling about it.

Chapter 2

Reverend McDonald swept through the door, showering us with religious leaflets and toothpaste bright smiles. He ran a mission here in the area and operated it in conjunction with a sister concern somewhere in the West Indies. Between them his congregation supplied him with the means to jet backwards and forwards to both of his havens and enough willing ladies to look after his house and happiness. Even when he knew for certain that we never followed religion in any form he didn't give up. He stopped by with regular scraps of paper bearing mottoes of the day and his words of wisdom to gain everlasting happiness and peace through prayer. All the while he preached these breezy sermons he was handing us A4 sheets to copy for him in various colours, 'Just ten of these in green, my darling child. And your generous kindness will lead you on the right path. Thank you and God bless. See you again soon. Just keep love in your heart and give my warmest wishes to your dear husband.'

And out he would sweep. Afterwards I realised that he'd done it again. This was a psychological malfunction somewhere in my make-up because he cheered me up so much with his scraps of wisdom dispersed on paper probably supplied by me and cheeky audacity to preach lovingly as he helped himself to our supplies that I allowed him to do it.

One of the black sheep of his flock found his way to our office just after it became ours and came in every day to say hello and have a tea or coffee. One day he brought doughnuts to share. Denzil Black was as black as the ace of spades and we loved him for his irrepressible humour and loyalty. His persistence won through eventually when we finally said, 'Yes, OK, you can rent a desk here.'

Denny was a partially trained quantity surveyor and when things went well his moods uplifted us all. Some of the jobbing builders who got him to price up their estimates paid him if they got the job but avoided him and the office when they didn't. His day to day fortunes swung and he also dodged around avoiding his creditors in the same way, including paying the rent on his desk.

The all-encompassing love of Reverend McDonald was patchy to say the least when it came to Denny, who told us that he had been caught with his daughter in the rest room of the mission hall, apparently in an advanced state of undress and thrown out of the congregation in shame. 'Out you go and feel the disgrace!' the reverend had thundered. 'Think of your sins and repent.'

We curled up in laughter hearing this story and barely hid gleeful expressions whenever the reverend rushed in and cast Denny baleful glances then went on to preach forgiveness and love to us while he showed us pictures of his mission hut in Paradise and helped himself to paper clips and envelopes.

**

To our horror, a photo of the damaged house and graphic tale of the collapsed front wall made the local paper the following week. Some well-intentioned fool had supplied our name in connection with the reparation works and we had started to get enquiries about it. Chris took his completed sketches for the underpinning to Jeffrey Gold and contacted the Building Control section of the council. I had spent best part of the day fobbing off nosy parkers and several journalists. Just when I thought it had all died down I picked up again.

'Are you Chris Twice?' A gruff voice, not very friendly.

'Yes. How can we help you?'

'Just keep your noses out and your gobs shut or else.'

'What?'

17

'You know what I'm talking about. You don't know anything about that cellar. Butt out and forget about it. I'm warning you.'

I started to say I didn't actually know anything about it but the caller rang off. An excavation like that had to go through the council, there was no choice. I called Jonny Pearson.

'Hi, Sweetness. How's it swinging?' I didn't want to imagine that.

'Jonny, I just had a nasty phone call. An awful voice. Someone told me to butt out of the basement job or else! But the paperwork is at the checking engineer's. We can't get out now. Chris has to keep going over there. What's going on? They're your mates.'

'Ahh. Mmm. Try to keep calm. I'll talk to Jeff. Is Chris back?'

'No, and I have to collect the kids from school so I'm leaving now.'

'We'll talk later,' and he went. When Chris came back he was reasonably relaxed about it all so I stopped worrying and drove off in my scarlet Nissan Bluebird to pick up the children. I promised them Chinese takeaway from Mrs Chin if they did their homework and left me in peace to type out a homebuyer's report. Denny was back when we all bustled in. He immediately started hyping up the boys with his "high fives" etc. and Chris carried on with his figures as usual. He was our calm on a stormy sea really. While I squawked around getting plates warmed up and threatening God knows what if they didn't get their homework done and generally achieving nothing much, he plodded on regardless.

Later when books were put away and plates scraped clean we emptied the waste paper baskets and I did the washing up while Chris loaded everyone into the car. Denny was getting ready for a hot date and had been whispering into his mobile phone so he promised to lock up and we left for home. At least everyone was fed and I could shove a wash load on and have a welcome shower while the kids slept and Chris relaxed at last.

**

The next day was foggy and we crept slowly along the road with our lights on. Christmas songs were being played on the radio and niggling thoughts of shopping began to invade my concentration. I had to come up with a gift for the local old folks' home and present it at the weekend as the contribution from the infants' school, all part of the parent-teacher association I belonged to. Collecting the money from the parents should have been quite simple but it's surprising how difficult just gathering pittances together could be when purses got left at home with such regularity.

I bought a tin of biscuits and box of chocolates and various treats then displayed them as artistically as I could in a carved wooden bowl left over from Larry's treasures. Once I added a bottle of elderflower cordial and Earl Grey teabags I swathed it all in red glossy cellophane and it was ready to be presented. Their Christmas concert had been arranged and a few of the elders had formed a band, a small drum set and bazookas mainly and they sat to the side of the main audience waiting expectedly.

The children trooped in to start it off.

'Away in a manger, no room for his head,' they lisped and the rapt audience watched and listened patiently. They did their best at *Silent Night* in German and a version of *Frère Jacques* while they clapped along then finished with a short verse of *Auf Wiedersen* which had somehow been changed to "We'll feed again" when they were all given a lollipop and sat down to watch Santa who had arrived early as a special treat for the residents. He settled himself near the large tree, decorated with tinsel and bobbing glass baubles and placed the large black sack next to him on the floor. With a few "Ho Ho Hos" and lame jokes about Rudolf finding his way to Wanstead Flats which weren't flats at all but this lovely comfortable sanctuary and weren't they all lucky to be here and not outside on this dreadful December evening he delved into the bag and the first offering was raised aloft.

Matron took each gift from Santa substitute and passed it to one of our angelic choir singers who then handed it to the resident who held their hand up. All went reasonably well until a couple of the residents started to argue, a name was misread or misheard and our little messenger decided he wanted the present himself. Within seconds the situation degenerated. Half of the residents were standing and shouting at each other, a couple of the others sat banging the drums and hooting the bazookas. A tall red head vigorously shook a glass bottle with a spoon in it while laughing manically. I have never been easy around anyone whose behaviour was strange or alien in any way and once someone becomes unstable, deluded or deranged I have to fight down the urge to run, that is if I stick around long enough.

I watched with fascination as the scene deteriorated into complete chaos and came to my senses when some of the children started crying.

'Now sit down, Cherry love. Your present is coming. Yes, it sounded like Dulcie, I know. But calm down, Dulcie, please, everyone has a gift. I promise, no-one will be left out. Nurse! Nurse, could you help Cherry to put her hat on again and sit back down? I don't know, Alan dear, how she managed to put her leg up there. No, we don't want to talk about knickers. Oh, can someone get the present back from that child? The toffees have spilled all over the floor.'

Good Grief. We herded the children out to the waiting minibus taking coats and hats with us. Thank God some of the mums had turned up and took over settling them in. I went back inside, not knowing what I could do to help.

Old people are sometimes not nice, I thought. They have reverted back to spiteful children again. I tried to copy the firm voices of Matron and staff and joined them to soothe them back down.

'I think someone's been too generous with the sherry,' a soft voice murmured and it all struck me as funny. I have this awful habit of laughing when circumstances are bad or awkward and always inappropriate. The worse the situation becomes the louder I roar. I can't help it.

So, my new friend Denis, a helper and I went among frightened old ladies and militant grumpy ones and charming old men, old soldiers and lecherous old gits and gave them their presents and cups of cocoa. Then I downed far too much sherry and sloe gin and had to get a cab back home.

My own family were safely tucked up in bed and I related it all to Chris, who laughed like a drain. 'Serve you right for volunteering.' He grinned unsympathetically and poured me a large gin and tonic. 'There, get that down you, it's a busy day tomorrow. I have to go check on the basement and the factory down the road want to put in a mezzanine floor so you'll have the phones and some letters to do that I've drafted out this evening while you ministered to the demented kids of all ages. Oh, and Denny's in trouble again. You might have to sort him out.'

Getting up in the morning was a challenge; channelling our loitering children through the school gates complete with sports kits, bags and general paraphernalia was accomplished relatively smoothly for a change and I drove on autopilot to the office. Chris waved at me as he charged out immediately and I made some coffee for myself in order to swallow an aspirin or two to help me face the day's rich assortment of tasks, starting with a weepy Denny. 'Look Chris Two,' he waved a letter at me. I took it and noted his enormous eyes and tear stained cheeks. 'They're coming to take my stuff.' He made a sort of snorty sound and shuddered.

I read the crumpled letter. It was dated two weeks before and he had obviously carried it about in his pocket. The bailiffs were coming to take what they could unless he paid them ninety-six pounds. 'Denny, have you paid them anything? Have you tried to call them?'

'The last cheque I gave them bounced and the debt went up. It was eighty-nine before. I haven't got ninety-six pounds, Mrs Chris.'

'Drink your coffee, Denny. I will call them.'

I did. A rougher East London accent would be harder to find. They wanted cash. As their "client" had given them a rubber cheque I must understand their reluctance to be taken the Mickey out of again. He just deserved a smack. They would take a cheque from me if I paid the extra five pounds to have it sent specially. This was before the days of internet banking and transfers and I had insufficient time to get to the bank for the cash. 'I will meet you at Mr Black's house with five pounds and a cheque drawn on my company.'

I wondered when the two gorillas swaggered from their truck towards me outside poor Denny's house whether they would have "smacked" him.

So, Denny kept his furniture that day and his luck changed slightly as one of his creditors brought him in a cash payment and a bottle of wine and he received a cheque in the post, as well as the promise of a couple of estimates to do. When Chris returned from his basement visit he brought us in steaming pie and mash. Denny thought Christmas had already arrived and I had warning visions of my blouse buttons popping and skirt zip unravelling, although not so graphic as to stop me wolfing down the comfort food, until afterwards of course, when the tasty plateful morphed in my over imaginative mind to a gargantuan helping depicting such a sinful lack of discipline on my part that I wished I had eaten half of it instead. 'Salad tomorrow, boys,' I promised.

'Yeh, yeh,' they chorused.

Chris went off to measure the industrial unit, taking Denny with him to hold the tape which in a small way would repay us for settling the bailiffs' demand and I resigned myself to sort the filing tray, always the last job to tackle.

The term came to an end and the children began the countdown to Christmas. They came with us to the office and never seemed to be disruptive or bored. We had a small television in the end room and a huge box of Lego and as our client base built up there was a constant stream of visitors who included our offspring in conversations, often bringing little gifts and treats.

Now the weather was cold, icy even and playing in the small rear garden not attractive, but Chris often took at least one of them with him and they became adept at holding the tape steady and looking for hazards like drains and tree roots. We tried to teach them politeness, but also to be self-reliant and truthful. One Saturday morning when Chris had an appointment near to my mother's house, we stayed with her, helping to pickle beetroot and Chris took the youngest with him. The middle-aged home owner answered the door and, entranced by the angelic face of child No.3, reached out into the garden and plucked him a late rose. 'Here, little Mr Chris. Take this home for your mother.'

'Thank you,' replied No.3 sweetly and we followed Mr Ahmed into his home. 'Oh,' continued No.3 as we reached the end of the passage to the kitchen. 'It smells of bums and feet in here.'

'Stop it of course it doesn't. Sorry, Mr Ahmed, we've just been to the fishmongers.' Chris glared, daring him to continue and grabbed his arm, giving it a shake. Afterwards he explained that although he was right that the house had an extremely unpleasant smell, it was very rude to make remarks like that and to leave that sort of thing to Daddy, who would mention it if it was relevant to the job. In fact, it was relevant because Mr Ahmed had a nasty case of collapsed drains which had been damaged by thirsty tree roots and we fought a seven month battle, which was short for insurance claim procedures, to win him compensation and a new drainage scheme. He was so pleased with his new shower and WC room, not to forget the drainage out in the yard with its resplendent new metal cover, that he sent a colouring book and paints to child No 3 and we gained a new family of Mr Chris admirers.

Mrs Chin, herself the mother of four children, frequently sent a box of food, tasty sweet and sour chicken wings or prawn balls for the children to munch on and in turn we took Suki and Honey to play in the back room while she went to the cash and carry for supplies.

Chapter 3

Christmas came and went and our startlingly red bank balance sometimes flickered into black and we felt we had started to turn a corner. With two days left before the start of the school term we plotted an outing to celebrate but the inclement weather hindered our plans.

Denny was restless and paced around the office. The snow was thick on the ground and we felt thankful we had no appointments outside. Chris was busy with his basement underpinning drawings and I was tackling the dreaded book keeping. The children played marbles in the back room and kept looking longingly at the pristine white marshmallow garden. He offered to go to the corner shop for milk and brought back a box of Malteasers and an old sledge. 'Hey guys, look what Ali Baba sent down for you. We'll go over the flats and slide over the bumps.'

Amid screams of delight, hats, boots and gloves were found and they went off, Denny and No.1 child dragging the sledge and the others plodding behind, churning the snow into small furrows as their Wellingtons plunged through it. We hoped there would be no emergencies to disturb our short peaceful respite.

The local council in its wisdom had started altering the shape of the pond and adding all sorts of wild grasses and landscaping which had attracted a few more birds of all sorts. All was progressing enjoyably on the snowy outing apart from one short but severe panic when several of the Canada geese ran towards the creaking sledge, honking and flapping their huge wings in a threatening manner quite unlike their usual patient behaviour. Thankfully it was Denny guiding the vehicle with No.3 and he was able to steer it away from them skilfully before any of the creatures got that close but it was a strange thing to happen. I was glad it wasn't the children on their own in the rickety wooden sleigh, someone could have lost an eye or slewed the thing around onto the partially frozen pond.

One day soon after the kids' return to school we were building momentum with the appointments diary and Chris was out surveying a flat. I returned to my desk with a mug of tea and gave one to Denny, who was struggling to complete an estimate of works for quite a complicated refurbishment scheme. 'Can I help you at all, Den?' I asked him. I knew a little about it and was pleased when his shiny black face creased into his familiar smile.

'Oh, thanks, Mrs Chris. That will be welcome. If I call out figures to you could you jot them down here, like this?' His spidery writing undulated in waving columns on his pad which I had no intention of emulating but knew what he was attempting.

Together we continued and as he measured and plotted using his outdated second-hand Estimator's Price Book in conjunction with the well-thumbed BCIS costing book and charts he had compiled. I wrote it all down in a semblance of order and we cracked it. Denny usually farmed out his written estimates to several female acquaintances in the area and paid them miserable amounts when he could scrape the notes together. His life was quite hard, admittedly mostly self-induced, but he was irrepressible, cheerful and kind and we loved him. I was fairly up straight with my office chores and would be until Chris came back with his tape-recorded survey report so I offered to type it for him. 'Thanks, Mrs Chris, I owe you.'

Yeh.

A forbidding black Range Rover with darkened windows mounted the kerb and slowed down in front of the window. Two men dressed in black, one in leather and the other in a long woollen overcoat swept through the door. The leather clad thug stood by the door, his raised arm leaning on the frame. Without staring and trying to stop looking at a leather strap across his chest and an appendage which resembled as far as I could remember from gangster films I'd seen, a holster and gun. 'It's an umbrella, Chris, don't look,' I told myself. The one swathed in expensive wool approached the desk. His shoes must have cost three months of our mortgage. 'Hello.' I smiled. 'How can I help?' How hard it is to not look at a gun, keep smiling and not wet yourself. I saw Denny creep out the back door into the yard. 'Where's he gone?'

'Who?' Stupidly.

'Him, the black one.'

'To make tea, probably. Do you want a cup; won't you sit down?' Good God.

'Forget tea. Where's the engineer?'

'He's on a survey, only local, won't be long. What do you want?'

'Show me the basement stuff.'

'And you are? Not Mr Gold. I can't just show people other people's projects you know. There's privacy laws to think of. We could get sued.'

They looked like real law abiding people, carrying guns, wearing thousand pound coats and shoes and I boldly said it was against the law to show them our pencil sketches. Was there a God? A loaded silence and The Coat pulled up a chair. I tried not to swallow noisily.

He regarded me and nodded. Was that respect? Was he going to hit me? I hoped Chris would stay away, as I might be able to sort this. 'My name is Mr Smith.' Really? 'Del Smith.' He leaned from the chair and held out his hand to shake mine. 'Jeff's a good mate of mine and we help each other out.' His accent was not Cockney, not South East London but refined and utterly compelling. 'I wouldn't want to make you break the law, Dolly, but we need to get this basement project moving.' He pulled out a mobile phone straight off the designer's factory drawing board and tapped a few buttons then passed it to me. It was Mr Gold. 'Hello Del? Oh, hello Mrs Chris. Alright? Yes, show Del what you've got there, please, if you don't mind.' All the same if I do, I thought. 'See ya, mate,' and he hung up.

The drawings now were elaborate, one of Chris's works of art and I proudly showed The Coat the underpinning sequences and shaded drawings showing the arrangements of reinforcement, the beams and concrete casing. The pages of calculations proved the detailed engineering system and retaining concrete walls, all to be cast in situ using a portable mini mixer. A section of wall had been removed along with the adjacent floor to the side of the house and reached by the walkway. This formed a gaping hole in which a sliding ramp for wheelbarrows and access and a chute or complicated lift arrangement to remove the spoil and transfer it to the skips. I could tell he was impressed. I explained that the preliminary sketches and calculations were already deposited at the local authority. Mr Gold had provided the council fee and they had almost finished checking it all. These drawings were definitive to help the workmen excavate section by section and ensure the damp proof membranes were positioned correctly, plumbing had to be incorporated and wiring for sophisticated alarms and lighting. He nodded and I knew he was impressed. I think from that moment we had a mutual regard for each other; never friends but guarded acquaintance, like a cat and a canary. I was the canary.

Denny came in with a tea tray bearing a plate of biscuits and four steaming mugs. Nice one, Denny, I thought. Now it's all peaceful and the danger's past. Without meaning to I laughed, oh God, out loud and so, to my surprise, did The Coat. No flies on you, Mr Smith, I thought. We sipped our tea in awkward silence and stared in fascination at a convoy of funeral cars idling at the traffic lights, waiting to turn right towards the cemetery. 'Goodbye, Mr Smith. And my name is Chris, not Dolly.'

'Goodbye Mrs Christina Prentice, you're a doll.'

It was quite hard to pick up Denny's scrawls and think about formulating a suitable bill of quantities for builders to prepare their estimates after all that stealth and tension but I resolved to put our latest experience in the back of my mind and get on with the job. Chris would be back soon and I would have his tapes to type up. It was also lunchtime and I started to feel hungry

I left my desk in view of the window and the passing traffic and went to rake through the fridge for something to tempt me. My healthy resolve was a little dented after The Coat and his henchman's visit and I fancied a reassuring cuddle or comfort food at least. I still felt disconcerted when a funeral cortège passed by, which happened about five times a day; our office being opposite an undertaker's and within half a mile of the local crematorium. We became used to it eventually and able to discuss the turn out and the flowers, exclaiming at the beautiful and heart rending floral displays or wondering at sparse tributes with few mourners in following cars, or occasionally, none at all. It seemed incomprehensible for the passing of a life to mean so little, no sad family or neighbours and we often mulled over the worth of a life so isolated and probably lonely, which left no apparent mark on the continuing lives of the rest of us. But the world still turns and progresses, whether individuals make a tangible difference or not, people are good or not, and the flowers are modest or resemble a carnival float or simply do not exist. Denny made us laugh often with his Caribbean slant on life, calling a funeral of a black person like a film set or just acting utilising paid strangers. "It's Rent a Crowd," he explained, swearing that coach loads of people were brought in just to make a noise and act like mourners when sometimes they had few family members. The effect was everything it seemed. I remembered the scenes from an early James Bond film somewhere on a tropical island, when a funeral procession made up of black-clad followers, walked decorously. The brass band played dirge-like music and they chanted mournfully, then as they turned a corner it became instead a jazz musicians' performance of joy and celebration.

I turned away from the line-up outside and inspected a pack of washed salad leaves with little enthusiasm and blamed Mr Del Smith for my general change of mood.

Denny was always grateful for whatever I produced, be it soup, sandwich or in this case a limp salad, but by the time I added some sliced tomatoes and beetroot, cut up a chunk of blue cheese and scattered olives over, with pickled walnuts it all looked more palatable. I removed the foil cover from a few slices of cold roast beef I had brought from home and Denny volunteered to fetch some fresh seedy rolls from the bakers up the road. Excellent, all we needed now was for Chris to return and lunch would be served.

**

After lunch, we had a visit from Mr Comik. He was a highly entertaining local character who I would have preferred to converse with over the telephone. His clothes were rag-bag quality and shoes stuffed with cardboard; his hair was worn long and curly and greasy and he always toted a huge bag made of sacking. He didn't exactly smell but our affronted eyes imagined that he did and I hoped he wasn't leaving fleas in his wake. Occasionally I photocopied odds and ends for him and felt bad taking his pennies, so gave him tea and biscuits to make up. He entered, flourishing his bag and we watched with subdued horror as he allowed it to slither gently onto the floor and writhe at his feet. I admit my trepidation as the live occupant of the bag jabbed at the fabric covering and the whole thing shuddered. I knew he spent ages over the flats, a huge expanse of grassland, trees and lakes bordering Epping Forest, making friends with foxes and rescuing hedgehogs, badgers and such and wondered what on earth he had brought into our calm, well sometimes fairly calm little office, then squealed with delight when a tiny black kitten emerged. 'She's yours, my dear,' he gestured by waving his arms wide. 'You told me you'd lost your black one and this one here's had all her jabs. She needed a good home and I knew you'd welcome her. Take her for that little operation though, in a few weeks' time or she'll bring you more kittens,' he warned.

He sat back smiling hugely and I felt a dreadful hypocrite. Vets' bills were not cheap but he thought more of an animal's welfare than his own appearance, spending his money on a stray creature's well-being and neglecting himself. He looked like a tramp and wasn't averse to a drink or six when in the mood. He was probably on his way to The Rose on the next corner where the shameless landlord lined up the whiskies and took his pension pennies with careless greed. 'Mr Comik, let me repay you, please. She's beautiful. Does she have a name yet?' I knew any money I gave him would be liquefied by the end of the afternoon but didn't know how to reimburse him without offending him. Would you like a bath? Shall I dry-clean your clothes? 'No matter, my dear. It's a pleasure to see your face. Call her what you please.'

I had an idea and sent Denny out to put the kettle on. I was alone with Mr Comik for a minute and coughed a bit, finding it hard to speak diplomatically. 'Mr Comik, I know you live alone because you told me and I wondered if you could do me a favour?' He listened. I continued with more confidence. 'I don't know how you feel about this and I will understand if you say, "No", but I lost my darling granddad recently and I just can't bear to throw away all his things. He was about your size and such a caring man. You know he left school at twelve, but still remembered all he learned about geometry and algebra?' I knew I was rambling but stumbled on anyway. 'If you could take your pick of his clothes, I would be so grateful that they were going to you, yourself a caring, generous man.'

He looked down at his feet. He sat quietly for a few seconds, then stood up taking the sackcloth carrier from the floor and touching his forelock, began to open the door. I really stuffed that, didn't I? I thought. Poor old sod. What could I do?

Then he turned back and smiled. 'Mrs Chris. It would be an honour to oblige. I will come in tomorrow with a wheelbarrow.'

Whew. That was close. I regularly helped with the Scouts jumble sales and had been collecting house to house around our home district for days so our garage, I knew, would have a decent amount of clothing to pass on to Mr Comik. I would donate to Arkala enough money to cover the loss that a dozen or so decent cast-offs would perhaps raise on jumble sale day, so I selected the items with anticipation. A warm jacket with all buttons intact and some winter shirts of Clydella checked fabric and gentlemanly styled. I wasn't sure of his trouser size, but found some dark green cords with forgiving elastic sides and the length looked about right. A gorgeous lightweight wool suit was uncovered, which I secretly wished would fit Chris but that too looked suitable. I sorted out half a dozen pairs of socks (including some from Chris's drawer), some beautifully laundered underwear I found in a taped-down cardboard box which had been slung at the back and buried, then straightened myself up enthusiastically. Wow, this is looking good: all the same sort of style that he could believe had belonged to my granddad. A random tie joined the heap, a pullover, two sweaters and a scarf. It just left the shoes. I had to be careful here, my granddad couldn't have worn varying sizes so overlooking a plethora of pretty reasonable footwear of differing styles and shapes, I chose some brown Hush Puppies size nine and a half, some stretchy slippers in a nine and some black boots in a ten. I'll tell him they should be worn with thick socks, I excused.

Mr Comik didn't turn up at the office the next day, or the day after. I ruefully remembered the hours I spent sorting, sponging then pressing and folding the stuff to make it look cherished. I had heaped it carefully in my car boot and carried it bit by bit into the office back room. I thought it served me right. An old person had dignity and this one obviously didn't want hand-me-downs, or dead man's redundant gear as an afterthought. Then suddenly he appeared, with the promised wheelbarrow and came in.

He must have had a wash, I thought as I took him through to the end. 'I hope you can find a use, Mr Comik. I have sorted some things and the rest I was taking to a charity shop, but I have more at home if you have the room.'

Thinking of feet size I told him I had a few different sizes at home from other family members.

He didn't say much but I knew he was touched and off he went to goodness knows where to stow his acquisitions away.

Sometimes he walked past our windows, quite neat and tidy and waving cheerily and sometimes he came in. I had quelled my misgivings about fleas by this time and cheerfully made him tea and usually rustled up a bun then raced around with the hoover afterwards. One day he passed us on his way to The Rose peering in to spot us and I forgot about him as the afternoon stretched on. As I swivelled round to leap up and rush to school to collect the children I saw him staggering along the pavement, very much the worse for wear, and guided him inside instead. Chris as usual was out on site somewhere so Denny, bless him, went to pick up the kids for me. He sank down on the window seat and raised his head. I saw his poor face, red with smudged blood and dirt from the pavement and felt ashamed. I had thought him drunk. 'Who did this to you?'

He shrugged. 'Yobbos outside the pub.' His mouth dribbled and bent.

'Why? Did they rob you? Do you know where they come from? I'll call the police.'

He didn't answer and I knew he was all in. Twenty minutes later an ambulance arrived and I decided to go with him to Whipps Cross Hospital to be checked out. Luckily Denny arrived back with the children and I gave him money to get them all chips. I might be quite a while, I reasoned. It was past seven when I finally left the A & E department, having seen Mr Comik settled in bed for the night for observation. He had seen a couple of constables and given them rough descriptions. They had barely waited until he got outside the pub before they set about him, taking his watch and wallet and keys. They'll ransack his house now, I thought and one of the officers radioed to the station. Later that evening the thieving hooligans entered his home and were smartly apprehended. Being serial burglars earned them lengthy sentences in one of Her Majesty's places of dubious residence and Mr Comik was feted in the pub. The episode made the front page of our local newspaper and showed a nice little picture of our office, which couldn't be bad.

**

One morning we received a call from a local agent who urgently needed help. We had heard of Terry Jenkins and seen many copies of plans he had produced, which closely resembled ours in style and quality although our paths had not crossed before. I felt then that we had much in common. We each had three children and had to juggle our family life with our business. His wife was a tremendous support to him, she was active in negotiating with planners on occasions, wining and dining councillors and even cooked the books on more than one dodgy deal, I heard.

He came with his wife and brought with him bundles of files and papers and explained that they had decided to move to Norfolk and give up his drafting practice. Chris was surprised at this news but I had heard through the grapevine of the times their sailing took them into the wind rather than close to it, and the tales of occasional brushes with debt collectors.

We listened to their stories, me taking it all with a box of salt but Chris laughing heartily as they regaled us with tale after tale. We knew as any architect would, how seemingly stubborn and difficult some council town planners could be when feeling subjective and just downright awkward. We could all quote a practical and lucrative scheme which had been rejected on flimsy grounds then overturned on appeal, making the planning officer look stupid. With the weight of the council behind them the service was sometimes shoddy and their decisions irrational. We remembered a case we had where officers from an east London borough took a year to make a decision on whether to allow a struggling landlord to divide his shop into two. The place remained empty all this time but rates and insurances still demanded payment. A couple of people wanted to use the space but were stopped by enforcement proceedings and we, of course, had not been paid for our drawings and liaison. By the time the approval to the scheme had been argued and won, our client had lost his house and the shop building was repossessed, his family had left him and gone overseas and our client disappeared. Planning procedures now have been speeded up and the decisions arrived at more swiftly, but often the planners' logic and regulations used have no more sense.

**

We had now inherited a list of clients who happily transferred their projects to us. Chris, who spent part of each day driving from site to site, both speaking to existing clients and prospective ones, noticed little difference in his day and continued in beatific ignorance of the additional pressure the sudden expansion of our client base with all the phone calls to councils, contract letters and filing I had to contend with. We had gradually changed our bright red bank statements to multi-coloured and now a glistening black but neither of us felt confident enough to take on an employee.

It was then that I realised that children 1 and 2 had become quite useful. They could photocopy not only A4 sheets of calculations but the larger plans, using a dyeline printer, and fold the drawings professionally, enclosing my letters so that the address appeared in the envelope window ready for posting. As I mused I added that they were adept with a calculator and often checked my casting accurately just for practice, No.2 even used the electric typewriter with more skill than I had and they all filed with alphabetic precision. I decided to buy Chinese food from Mrs Chin and put my idea to them. I put plates into the oven to warm and left Denny in charge of the phones as I walked the few steps up the road to order our favourite dishes.

For years Mrs Chin served only fish and chips, which were tasty and popular with the locals and she progressed to special fried rice and pork, spare ribs and sweet and sour prawns and curries. As her business loan became paid up she decided to broaden her menus. We provided her with plans to extend the rear of her shop and helped her with the complicated forms to satisfy the Environmental Health Department with a suitable extraction system and grease trap within the drainage. Above the ground floor we added a family bathroom and loft conversion to accommodate her elder children, with a quiet study area and space. However, before she could make a start on her development, we had to explain a plethora of problems to her building which needed urgent attention.

The front wall was found to be weakened as the shop window beam had rotted and bowed downwards, causing the wall to bow outwards and fracture through the render. This then allowed rainwater ingress to seep beneath the surface and dampness to begin to damage the fabric and finishes. The outward movement of the wall had caused a widening gap between the top of the wall and the roof, allowing rainwater ingress at high level and exacerbating the damage. We tried to obtain some help from her premises insurance and, surprisingly, were partially successful. The building defects were classed as "wear and tear", which should have been maintained by the owner or occupier, therefore strengthening methods that we had recommended were struck from the claim, but they allowed a smaller claim to carry out repairs to the rotten timbers, including roof and floor joists and replacement Bressumer beam over the shop front window. This also covered patching up the ceilings and plaster work, which went a long way towards the essential refurbishments. The new bank loan secured the rest of the money she needed and a tribe of Yugoslavian workmen descended on the shabby, neglected building to create miracles. Their work was amazing. I popped out of our office periodically to check on their progress and took photos to show everyone later. It was strange to see huge white dust sheets spread over the stainless steel deep fat fryers. I noticed uneasily that potatoes had been peeled and cut into chips but obviously, due to the pending building work, would need to be thrown away unused. The disconcerting part was that they were being stored in cold water in the rear room in a bath. After buying her chips so regularly, I could hardly start to feel squeamish about them soaking in the bath but I hoped that no bodies used it too. A bit more sleuthing and I found the rear addition housed a ramshackle WC, wash hand basin and a shower, also to be refurbished. I reassured myself further by thinking of our drawings of the new works which clearly showed an upstairs family bathroom in the project.

Within the first day on site a large skip arrived at eight am and props installed at intervals across the ground to support the bedrooms over. Up on the first floor, further props held the ceiling joists of the loft space and roof over and when they were satisfied of complete safety and security, the whole front wall disappeared into the skip and was carted away, windows, ledges, rotten timbers and all. By six o'clock in the evening the new piers stood resplendent and new steel beam over the new shop front was supported on concrete padstones. It was a joy to watch the guys. As one spread red oxide paint over the beam another smoothed the cement mix at the ends. Within the shop, on workbenches, a new timber window frame was fashioned and as the skip lorry drove off the shared tarmac frontage the glazing delivery van turned up. Instantly several of them sprang to lift the large thick glass pane and together they eased it into the space. Smooth mastic filler was inserted around the edges of the glazing and frame on both sides and the new shop door fixed including locks. We had taken the opportunity to add another door at the front and a small lobby to provide a separate entrance for the family. This ensured the rooms over were self-contained and no-one from the shop waiting area could sneak upstairs while she was busy with her cooking. Security had been a constant worry for Mrs Chin, as her workshy husband had run away with a local young Chinese waitress from Forest Gate and had emptied out the bank account. Luckily the latest takings had not been paid in and she changed the details immediately. The bank manager was sympathetic to her situation and knowing full well which Chin was the hard-working one, extended her overdraft facilities to tide her over. She started divorce proceedings and the local court issued him with an order banning him from bothering her after he kept turning up at closing time demanding money. A few times she had been too slow at hiding the evening takings, or he came early but, partly due to the excellence of her food and generosity with those she considered as friends, the local constabulary took turns to line up for their supper and strangely, Mr Chin got the picture. Not long after the divorce was finalised he went back to China and she never saw him again as far as we knew. It had been an arranged marriage in Hong Kong, the money given by her family and they travelled to London to start their new life and she had used it to buy the premises and set up the business. From the start, he had big ideas and dreamed of owning a large successful restaurant and blamed her for the fact that the shop was small; he considered it second rate and run down and inadequate. As he became more resentful, he contributed less with the food preparation and cleaning, leaving her the day to day running as well as caring for their burgeoning family. On the days that he decided to help her he would often take off in the car after the lunchtime rush with the takings, saying he was going to the bank but instead he went missing and usually returned stinking of booze, appearance unkempt and in a vile temper. When she tried to stand up to him he hit her, even striking out at the older children when they tried to protect her. The children had been tired of his bullying and frightened of him due to the violence he showed when frustration overcame him and urged her to seek help. He eventually found himself penniless and unwanted by his family and luckless mistress, all due to gambling losses and alcohol abuse. They showed no sign of missing their father but revelled in their new shiny shop and loft rooms.

As a show of her gratitude, we accepted grateful discounts on the food we ordered and when she tried a new recipe we were guinea pigs. No.1 child even tried chicken feet with willingness but he was the only one. Thankfully they never found their way onto the general menu. These are often served as an appetizer among other titbits in China, I learned later.

We always enjoyed our Chinese food days and I knew everyone would be pleased, including Denny, with their meal. With all the help he had given us lately he deserved a treat.

Chris arrived back at the office with all three exuberant offspring and we discussed my idea as we ate. Chris was dubious, thinking I might fall foul of the tax man but the kids were enthusiastic and so we went ahead. I had worked in a bank when Chris first started his business, building it up at home then renting the tiny shop next door until the attempt to buy it went wrong, then finally to this office and the kids had all been used to having bank accounts since they could hold a pen. Not believing in child exploitation but wanting them to learn the value of money and develop a healthy work ethic, we decided to reward their helpful voluntary work by actually paying them a wage. So, I put them on the payroll. The amounts they earned were way in excess of the amount of useful work they contributed, especially little No.3, taking into consideration school days, travelling time, homework, lazing about and eating, but the scheme served two purposes and I did check it out for being lawful: the monthly salaries were tax efficient for our company and low enough to escape being taxed. They then were allowed their usual pocket money and the rest I shamefully saved towards their school fees.

Chapter 4

The Easter break approached and Chris surprised us all with booking a week away. Denny promised to take good care of the office and our current clients were informed. The work was due to start on the basement, lawfully, as we returned so it was a good opportunity. I had known his plans of course, a whole three days before we set off, but the children were totally in the dark. We packed warm casual clothing, trainers and huge bags of food. I heard them discussing the break and laughed at their predictions. 'I hope it's not camping,' said No.2.

'I hope it is,' retorted No.1.

'Yeah!' agreed little No.3. 'But I've not seen sleeping bags going in. So perhaps we've got a caravan or chalet.'

No.2 thought a bit. 'I saw towels in a bag but not bedding. And wellies and anoraks. So, it looks like an action thing.'

'Perhaps it's mountain climbing in Wales,' suggested No.3.

'Mum wouldn't like that,' said the others together, followed by, 'We would, though,' from the boys.

'No, it's not camping or mountain climbing, the food they've packed is too delicious and we'll need a cooker,' from the girl, our No.2.

'Yeh, I saw her wrap up a beef joint she cooked yesterday and it's now frozen. And there's a turkey and a massive meat pie all in the freezer waiting to be packed. So, it's not a hotel and we're not flying off somewhere because then we'd take cases.'

They thought a bit then an idea, 'The family on the corner hired a campervan at Christmas and went to Devon. It might be that; I saw Dad talking to them when they got back.'

I laughed to myself as I loaded a bag of tinned goods into the boot. I had a box of fruit and veg and some packets of biscuits with a ginger cake and sweets. Chris had stacked the deeply frozen meats alongside them, we checked we had driving licences, money, cheque books and cards, plasters and aspirins, a camera and Chris's newly acquired mobile phone, then announced we were ready to leave.

We headed off down the M25 and the M3, then followed the map until we reached Chertsey and an established boat hire company. We hired a beautiful cruiser to sleep six, which provided us with plenty of spare space and enough room to leave our belongings scattered without being fanatical about clearing up and being tidy. Ship-shape, we knew, was not us. This was the third time we had taken to the water, once on the Thames when No.3 was a baby and once on the Broads when we had a houseboat too. We had taken Bart, a school friend of No.1, with us on this occasion and I will never forget the expression on his face when he had first sight of the houseboat and day boat. His father had carpet shops in Essex and, I believe, earned a good living, which provided his family with a comfortable lifestyle. His mother worked in an office and exacted high standards of them all: they skied at Christmas, followed the sun at all the other breaks and generally she looked down her nose at rag tag gypsies like us, eating chips while we hurtled from job to job, doing the accounts and VAT at three in the morning, going off for a takeaway at ten thirty on Friday evenings and weekends and usually thoroughly enjoying ourselves.

Bart stared at the battered craft and gingerly walked along the gangway with cautious trepidation etched into every pore of his face and doubtful stance. When we got inside the tiny living space he looked up at Chris and asked, 'Are we all sleeping here?' We all nodded and he continued, 'All of us?'

Within ten minutes No.3 had fallen over on the edge of the water, completely soaking his jeans. By the end of the day, he had repeated this another three times. The tiny galley had all four pairs of his jeans drying in front of the struggling heater and we all went to the cheery pub later with him wearing pyjamas. We found bags of change for them to play the slot machines while we sat downing a few large glasses of red and watched them then strode the fifty yards back to the boat and settled them to sleep. I think it was the first complete freedom holiday that our guest had had: packed lunches, cooked breakfasts from the barbecue on the bank, easy going laughter and no arguments about spilling drinks on their best clothes. They foraged in the forest and climbed trees, and navigated the waterways of the Broads without adequate maps. Only once did we lose our bearings completely and finally reached our temporary home in darkness, using a small pen torch and a whole lot of luck to find our way back. A bit like our life really.

At the end of the week when we returned him to his parents he hugged us both and said after his initial shock at the size and appearance of the houseboat, he had had the best holiday of his whole life and would never forget it. I wonder if he will. I like to think that our attempts to live in harmony, striving for patience and tolerance tempered with a strong essence of respect for self and others, are forging strong characters of our children. We have rules, of course, but never pedantic fussy stuff for the sake of it. Their friends seem to like the easy ambiance which generally rules in our home so we must be doing something right.

So, this Easter on the Thames was the first water based break that we had taken for about four years and we knew they would love negotiating the locks and sometimes mooring up along the river, stopping anywhere we fancied to get supplies.

With five pairs of willing hands it didn't take long to carry all the soft bags of clothes on board, store the provisions in the galley, frozen goods in the handy freezer, shampoos and such in the shower cubicle: then Chris parked the car in the space allotted for the week and we were off, the powerful engine chugging rhythmically as we headed for our first stop through Cookham Lock and on the way to Marlowe. We all loved Henley on Thames with its strong nautical flavour, where we tucked into fish and chips for supper and the children enjoyed watching the tiny ducklings. We left the boat and disembarked at Reading and while strolling through town, we were entertained by a travelling group of dancers and acrobats dressed in bright clothing; then set off again, cruising slowly through Pangbourne and Goring, Wallingford and finally reaching the beautiful university town of Oxford. When we stopped along the bank to refill the water, empty the chemical toilet and stretch our legs it was all regarded as part of the adventure rather than a distasteful bore.

Chris smiled at me and swung the wheel. The kids all wore their life jackets and deep grins and lounged on the seats, looking over the side. I handed out apples and thought my cup ran over. Somewhere in my earlier life I must have done something really good to deserve all this. I reflected on our situation thinking ahead for the week after we returned. Always the working agenda was never far from our thoughts and had to be slotted in with the family and leisure.

Blossom was appearing suddenly on the trees and the grassy banks and fields of rural London into Oxfordshire. Spring was established and flashes of approaching summer could be seen everywhere.

I knew that Mr Gold was raring to go on his basement works on the following Wednesday after Easter and Chris was booked out every day to monitor the early works. In the preceding weeks, we had received only one threatening phone call, which immediately made my heart thump and my knees start to wobble. All had been quiet for several months and I had relaxed about it, thinking the thug, whoever he was, had backed off. I called Jonny Pearson who had kindly landed these clients onto us and he was noticeably shocked: also, Jeffrey Gold, our impetuous excavator himself, swore ignorance. I wondered how all this was tied up when the quietly menacing Del Smith visited us shortly afterwards and I mentioned it to him. I expressed my anger at being threatened in this way not letting him see that I was actually scared. He nodded and told me quietly to disregard it. So I did. One part of me wanted to know the hierarchy of his set up but the sensible fraction of my brain instilled caution. I don't suppose I could learn their secrets and live.

We were now fully accepted into the multi-cultural society of this little area. I would photocopy documents for neighbours and locals and enjoy a chat.

An elderly artist came weekly to have his black and white sketches copied. The drawings he brought were amazing and varied: A4 size and smaller showing buildings, bridges, landscapes and coastal regions presented in all weathers and seasons. He told me he ran a column in a magazine which printed his drawings and writings about the places chosen. He described the terrain, the buildings, the inhabitants, the shops, the pubs and hotels, even providing recommendations where deserved and tongue in cheek comments otherwise.

We had our share of religious people warmly inviting us to their gatherings. A beautiful lady of about forty came in for photocopies and she explained her spiritual beliefs. Being a Christian without being religious I listened to her, wondering and thinking it all sounded very nice, if only it were true. She always dressed in black, with black leather shoes and with her hair swept up in a bun and her high cheekbones with dark expressive eyes. I was fascinated by her. She looked like a ballerina with exotic ancestry. She said her name was Deborah. 'Please come to one of our meetings,' she asked. 'It's informal and friendly. I'll call for you at seven.'

So I went.

Chris was not pleased. He had to supervise homework, supper and get the children to bed, never easy when there was always a reason why one of them wanted to loiter downstairs which then disrupted the others. I promised to sort out their clothes for the morning when I got back and a few other private little promises.

Deborah tapped on the office door at five to seven and I locked up and went with her. We walked a short distance weaving along the back streets until we stopped by a bright green gate. The front door was ajar and I could see lit candles through the window. I wondered if I was nervous and realised I was hungry. I had taken advantage of a couple of hours quiet and worked on the VAT return, entirely forgetting to eat. I thought of the liver and bacon casserole I had left in the oven this morning and knew my family were satisfied at least. Lucky toads.

A grey haired lady greeted Deborah with a kiss on both cheeks and I was warmly welcomed. 'Come in and help yourself to sandwiches and tea,' she said. Her name was Lily, apparently.

Thank you, Lily, you read my mind, I thought gratefully and dug in. 'They are just cheese and tomato there and ham here, my dear. The others have fish paste but you aren't so keen on those, I know.' What? How does she know that? I greedily stuffed a ham one in my mouth and put a couple of each on a plate and followed Deborah into the front room. I then felt just a tiny bit nervous when I realised that Lily knew I was hungry and disliked fish paste.

The chairs were arranged around the edge of the room, tightly wedged next to each other with no other furniture. Lily closed the curtains.

My sandwiches were gone and tea virtually hoovered down so I settled down to observe the proceedings, my curiosity aroused.

The congregation, if that is the right word, numbered thirty-four and such an eclectic mix of folk jammed into that front room that I immediately wanted to laugh. An extremely tall thin man of about sixty said a prayer first and they mumbled a response to some of the lines. Then Lily enunciated slowly one that I remembered saying many years before in Sunday school and even remembered a few of the choruses. They obviously knew the prayers by heart because there were no books or papers to read from. Everybody shut their eyes except me. I didn't want to miss anything. I panned the room studying everyone and they all seemed to be completely relaxed. I was on edge, wishing that I could feel a similar peace but religion puzzled me. I have nothing against faith of any sort but had all my life believed that a person's own conscience should be their guide. The ten commandments were a pattern to follow, doing right by your neighbour, broadly meaning fellow human beings, leaving their animals and husbands and wives alone and not to covet anything that wasn't yours. I could hear Chris booming in my ear, and was glad that no-one else could, about throwing away the crutch and standing on your own two feet. He had no time for hypocritical do-gooders and God programmes. I couldn't get up and leave Deborah, it would be rude and she is such a sweet lady. I wondered what had happened in her life to bring her to worship in Lily's front room with such a motley crew. Then suddenly a portly ginger haired man with a densely freckled face asked us to take the hand of the person on each side of us and to wait quietly. I sneaked a look at my watch and was amazed to see it was nearly nine o'clock.

I held hands with the rest of them and waited. Only my eyes roved around and suddenly a woman gave a little cry. I jumped in surprise but no-one else seemed to, so perhaps she always did that. She stood up, her hands pulling away and the circle was broken. My heart was beating loudly as I watched her and I thought the others must hear it. To my amazement her arms started flapping up and down so violently that they became blurred. She started to squawk and chirp, while all the time her arms performed like whirring blades until someone spoke soothingly to her and another stood and wrapped a light blanket around her, cuddling and coaxing her down onto the seat.

I watched, a number of others did too, and offered explanations.

I had had no idea what the evening would consist of and listened to their conversations. This lady had apparently been visited by the spirit of a white bird, a cockatoo or similar which had quite a repertoire of speech. The sister of one of the congregation had recently died in a house fire which I gathered also killed the pet to which she had been devoted and they all took the manifestation to mean that they were together in peace. The woman was very tired after this and it was explained to me that when a spirit spoke through another live person, it was tiring. I knew Chris would be snorting derisively at all this but I was strangely affected. I wasn't scared or mocking but I was unquiet inside. Later I tried to flap my arms like wings but was totally unable to move them so fast that they blurred.

Off we started again with our hands held in a circle. It was quite dim in the room now as darkness had fallen outside and I watched all the faces in the flickering candlelight. For a while, random messages emanated from various members and this seemed to please others; of course, they all knew each other and their circumstances so I didn't know how relevant or comforting it all was. I half expected my own grandparents to make a visit or send a message but no-one from my departed loved ones seemed to know that I was there.

Finally, a last prayer was said and we were told to relax and imagine a scene in front of us. A few minutes later, someone turned on the light and blew the candle out. I have always loved the smell of candle wax wafting in the smoke, freshly extinguished and I was inhaling deeply when the thin man asked me what my scene had been. 'Sheep,' I blurted. 'Dozens of them, grazing quietly.' He smiled and patted my head, then pointed one by one around the circle. Weirdly several others also said sheep and I thought the whole affair quite creepy. I resolved not to go again. I couldn't be having flapping arms and screeching and was glad that Granny hadn't turned up or any of my dear departed ancestors. I wanted to go home and Deborah and I walked quite smartly back to the office and my car, saying little. 'Goodnight Chris, God bless.' She waved and I waved back.

"Get the gin out Chris, I'm on my way back," I texted and started the engine.

**

Half term arrived and during the break from school. No.1 went away on holiday with the carpet family to return the favour, as they put it. 'See what a bit of luxury is like,' she smirked patronisingly and I waved them off cynically, thinking what a cold, grasping bitch she was. Poor kids, no wonder her No.1 so loved our humdrum jollity. They must hate her where she works, I thought.

Off they went to the airport in their chauffeur driven car and winged off to one of the Canary Islands on a holiday company charter. I thought, that's nice but hardly luxurious. The completely catered three-star hotel had buffet meals at set times. Luxury it was not. There was a swimming pool and table tennis area and a short walk to the beach. Mrs Carpet Woman forbade the beach as she hated having sand everywhere. They stayed within the hotel complex all week, never venturing outside, not taking advantage of any coach trips or visits, saying they were just tourist attractions and not where you would meet worthwhile people. No.1 refused to accompany them anywhere after that, saying the lack of adventure and complete boring predictability day after day had "done him in". I wasn't keen on his English but understood his sentiments.

**

The circus and fair came to the flats and we displayed posters in our windows. Our No.3 was delighted but scared when a couple of clowns came in to get some papers copied. Clowns can be scary and many grownups have an aversion to them. We laugh at their antics but their faces are seldom jolly. Freddie was a cross between one of Enid Blyton's now banned golliwogs and a black and white minstrel, also banned. His jacket was red and white striped and his baggy trousers bright blue with patches on the knees and backside. He wore a black spiky wig and a tiny trilby hat which defied gravity by clinging to a bouncing lump of wool. His eyes were mainly hidden by oversized coloured glasses and his face was painted chocolate brown. His hands were the hands of a white man, however, and only revealed when he took off his monstrous gloves to hand me the papers and honk a device in his pocket which sounded like a barking seal. No.3 child shrank back behind his father's desk and pressed his back against the chair, trying to laugh at the antics but noiselessly begging him to go. Freddie gave him tickets for the circus and a tiny model of Bruno the bear which staggered across the desk when the little handle was wound round. 'Don't overwind it,' he told him, 'and he doesn't need feeding.'

'No,' our No 3 stammered. 'Thank you.'

'Good boy. When you come to the circus tomorrow you will have a free hot dog and ice cream.'

A real smile broke through the petrified mask and he asked if his brother and sister could come too and was reassured to be told that they would get the same treats.

We always printed their leaflets at a cut price, several hundreds of each at a time. They brought pictures of the animals for colouring and posters for handing round. They gave out A4 prints of Bruno or Jenny the elephant to all the children with a small box of crayons and told them the winning coloured picture would earn them a prize. Freddie or one of the other clowns would collect the pictures at the first break and the winner was announced before the end. The prize was usually more tickets to the circus and tokens for several rides. It was a fun time for our children and forced us to relax for a few hours.

Around the back of the caravans and lorries which were linked by huge cables there were a few Portaloos and listlessly lolling dogs. There were a few sideshows and sweets stalls and some animals had relative freedom of the flats as they were tethered outside during the day on long chains. It was interesting to see the camels and elephants swooshing water over their backs and greedily taking buns and fruits from outstretched hands.

The big cats had no such freedom, however, but at least extensions were added to their cages, which were outside and stationary so they could have a short run and observe the rolling green slopes and watch and hear the birds and other animals. I think they were as happy as possible in the circumstances and I never suspected any cruelty, unless you believe as I do that wild creatures should be left in the wild and not taught tricks for human amusement.

Chapter 5

We met occasionally with Terry and Marline Jenkins, who apparently loved living in Norfolk. Their children had attended the same school as ours but had changed to a local village one when they moved, saving them a small fortune in fees which doubtless helped them enormously to fund their project. They bought a Georgian mansion which was in dreadful condition and almost uninhabitable. They lived in a static caravan for nearly two years until the west wing was underpinned and the chronic dampness was eradicated. Much of the timber structure had to be replaced and dampness and wood boring beetle treatments carried out. All the while the timber work was going on the ceilings above had to be supported: the place was a maze of metal acrows and props. Much of the roof had to be replaced using clay tiles to match the original and many other materials sourced from reclaimed building materials throughout the county. He carried out most of the restoration work himself. calling in operatives for specialised things like electrics, installing a gas supply and boiler large enough for a small country and delicate glasswork and ornamental plasterwork. They showed us photos but we never knew the address.

Over cups of tea and a fresh packet of Hobnob biscuits he gave us a card bearing the name David Mozan and a telephone number. He apparently ran a hostel and owned the head lease on a warehouse building in Hackney. He needed help. We promised to do our best for this new prospective client, who had been so valued by Terry, and waited for him to contact us.

When a gleaming black Range Rover drew up onto our forecourt we knew immediately who the driver was. A tall thin Asian man stepped out and looked intently at our building then closed the car door and walked inside. He had a black shining mane of hair which would have done the Lion King proud and a thin drooping moustache. He raised his left hand and ran his fingers through his hair pushing it back from his face and stepped towards Chris, holding out his right hand in greeting. 'Good afternoon. Call me David.'

'Pleased to meet you, David, I am Chris and this is also Chris, my wife and assistant. She will endeavour to help you if I am out and about. Take a seat. How do you take your tea?'

Our children were in the office. No.1 was trying to draw up a lease plan copying an example from Chris. The middle one, our girl, was conjugating verbs in German and chanting into a tape recorder and No.3 was in his favourite position, lolling on the floor drawing a tank. Military vehicles and guns were a passion with him and I hoped he would outgrow it.

I was proud that both the older children rose to make the tea. No.3 stared at David relentlessly. To be fair, he was a sight. His black linen suit was impeccable, the shirt white and tie of grey silk. His dress brogues gleamed and I wondered where he had bought them. A huge gold pinkie ring had a smooth red stone which could have been anything. He looked like he had just stepped off a film set and his English accent was distinctly upper class. I felt a little humdrum. Chris was entirely unaffected by appearance, status or position of anyone or any circumstance, remaining calm as usual and looking acceptable and confident in his Marks and Sparks casuals and deck shoes. 'We're all the same, Chris,' he said. 'Never feel inferior; never let anyone treat you as such. You're as good as him, her and everyone.'

He told us he had been born with a silver spoon in his mouth. His family were very rich, he said, and still lived close to the Afghanistan border in Pakistan. His name was of course Mohammed but he liked to call himself David. He told us he had been expected to return to the village after university to learn and take over the family business, to settle down in an arranged marriage with a wife who had been chosen for him several decades before, raise children and to become even more successful. Instead, he had returned with his first class degree to the palatial home, learned of his family's rigid plan and rebelled. His father was intransigent, David was resolute and he left his birthplace, his family, home and glitteringly planned future the same year he had graduated. He withdrew all the funds from his own account, gathered up his personal possessions, packed a trunk and holdall and left to forge his own destiny. To date, he said he had never been back. He told us how beautiful the valley was in summer, how bright the flowers, how lush the greenery of the mountain passes and snow-capped mountains which dominate the skyline. But transport by camel, donkey and ass, unreliable communication systems and general refusal to learn or accept the wider information that he had experienced over the previous four years drove him crazy. He said everyone was embedded in age old customs which he could not adhere to. With their resolute refusal to make change he decided to leave. 'How can a man of twenty-five who has travelled the world and seen such wonders, learned so much of other cultures and ideals go back to a life where a father is absolutely obeyed,' he questioned. 'If I suggested a change I was called recalcitrant and if I tried to introduce western technology I was castigated. I was swamped, smothered, pruned to the point where ideas died before they found breath. I fled.'

I felt sad that he stood alone in our office, regal, wealthy, deadly handsome and torn apart from his family. We spent a long while listening as he regaled us with his tales of adventure and chance. No.3 was captivated and thought him a modern Aladdin or Theseus. 'David,' I said, 'That was fifteen years ago. Times have changed. They will have mobile phones and the internet. There are credit cards and bank transfers. The roads will be passable now. Is there no-one that you would like to contact? Your mother? A younger sibling? Have you had no word in all this time?'

He smiled slightly. 'I have had a little information. My father is a stubborn old man and my mother cries in private. I have three sisters and one lives in New York, we converse.' He shrugged. 'Now I have bored you too much.'

It was nearly six o'clock and the children needed feeding. I asked him if he had plans for dinner and whether he wanted to join us for fish and chips or Chinese takeaway. I thought it might be beneath him and never dreamed he would stay. Chris was sure he would be expected elsewhere but to our surprise, he agreed with enthusiasm and No.3 laid the table in the back room. We locked the door and settled down to eat. I envied the children briefly at that time as they had not learned to have inhibitions: their innocent faces as they offered the salt and vinegar to our guest showed no sign of inhibitions of his status or importance or standing. The class system exists of course and is more obvious to some than others but at that moment, as we all tucked with gusto into our fish and chips, the playing field was level and our innocent three knew no boundaries of the distinction of wealth or race or custom. The simple meal we shared, I believe, would have done more for world peace than many a false diplomacy.

We made arrangements for Chris to visit the premises in Hackney and carry out a dimensional survey of the hostel, then to produce his interpretation of David's ideas on to drafting paper ready for their next meeting.

At the weekend after the propitious meeting with David I called into our local takeaway and ordered Chris a lamb curry and a king prawn dansak for me and the assistant chatted away as usual. I asked him where he came from, as most curry restaurants are run by Bengalis and to my surprise he mentioned the same district that David had. He told me of the snowy passes through the Himalayas and the rich green scenery. I asked him if he missed it all and he did. I wanted to ask him if he knew David's family but thought better of it. I didn't want to cause trouble and we knew little about him.

**

I took a couple of weekends off halfway through the term to take the children on a few trips as Chris was so busy. We did the usual swimming and picnics. We visited the little museum in Walthamstow Village and I was astounded to see some exhibits that apparently had been manufactured by my relatives about three generations before. That set me off on a quest for further information of my ancestors but my mother was reluctant to discuss them. I resolved I would trace the family back and wondered why she steadfastly refused to tell me what she knew. I reckoned most of us had skeletons hiding away in cupboards just waiting for an opportunity to leap out, shaking their bones and rattling their teeth to shock away our naivety. Was Mother protecting those who had gone before, or preventing their shame from being laid bare to protect me? I never knew. I decided I would risk losing the innocence of ignorance and delve when I could find the time, which was becoming ever more precious in its scarcity.

The inevitable trips to the coast were always received enthusiastically and Harlow Town Park with its small farm of domestic animals was a convenient short trip, as well as Hainault Country Park with the lake and herd of geese, the tea hut where we could buy an ice cream, and long walk through the trees and eventual emergence at the pub, where we ravenously polished off a steak and jacket potato each before the long trek back to retrieve the car.

The summer holidays approached and Chris decided he could spare a day or so from the hectic cycle of surveying, drawing and site inspections, so he took a caravan in the New Forest for the last weekend. They seemed to have a riotous time doing things I would have barred. Some of the rides at a theme park must have been invented by a sadist high on hallucinatory drugs. Looking at photos later of my precious family miraculously remaining in their seats while the whole open topped carriage swung upside down and churned sideways in a wide arc which then swooped around at ever increasing speeds, I was glad I hadn't gone. The scenic railway which I had ventured on while young and stupid and thought thrilling and exciting had been replaced with something faster and sleeker, reaching new heights and plunging to surely deeper, gravity defying depths.

Chris said that what went on while on the break stayed on the break and they all resolutely kept their mouths zipped shut, even little No.3 who I could usually cajole with a small treat.

**

The holidays began and the plans for David Mozan's hostel were taking shape. The drawings were displayed on the large drawing board and Chris went off to measure the grounds of Reverend McDonald's mission. While he spent time measuring the distances from the boundaries and the perimeter of the main building, a prayer meeting was being held. It was the women of the congregation this morning. They sang and chanted and gave rapturous praise for the sunshine and the rain, the birds and the flowers, the fish in the sea and the animals in the fields. Their God this morning was well loved. Some of these women had lost sons and family in various African tribal uprisings, I had learned, but they managed to keep their spirits up by throwing themselves into these religious services. Strangely, the black Africans appeared to mix amicably with the Caribbean members. Chris was constantly plied with tea and biscuits and he almost waddled back to the office afterwards when he finally finished his survey. The "flock", as the reverend called the congregation, were collecting to pay for a covered area for his car to be parked off the road. This would save him twenty pounds a year for a resident's parking ticket, so Chris was preparing simple drawings for the planners to consider and approve. The application needed permission to construct a crossover from the road across the pavement and the stone wall to be altered to add two low timber gates. Devotion could not be calculated. His home was cleaned and polished by volunteers and his meals provided. His wife seemed to exist in an ephemeral sense. He frequently spoke about her but became quite reticent when we started to ask questions. We never saw her with him when he rushed in to see us and he always had an excuse for her absence whenever we asked. He said she went home to see her folks. This would probably be the island in the Caribbean that he himself jetted off to several times a year. He always changed the subject when we tried to find the name. We secretly wondered whether she had left him. If it hadn't been for Denny blotting his copybook with the parson's daughter we could have thought the mysterious wife didn't exist, but she must have done at some time to have produced a daughter. When Denny sat and thought about it he realised that he had never seen her either. The poor woman probably got fed up with all his carryings on and left him. The way some of the women in his congregation fawned over him and bickered to provide his comforts must have made her suspicious if not sick, we guessed, but the wily old boy never let on about her whereabouts or what had happened.

Deborah came in for some photocopying and I was pleased to see her wide smile. I hadn't seen her for a while and thought she may have been a bit offended because I never returned to the séance. I had often thought about it but Chris was so against the idea that I chickened out, but she had ventured in and accepted a cup of coffee, so we sat together for a chat.

'Don't fret about upsetting me, Chris,' she began. 'The spirit world isn't for everyone.'

I spluttered a bit. 'Truthfully, Deborah, I was quite intrigued when I calmed down and went over it.' Could I tell her Chris was completely dead against it? It wasn't fair to blame Chris because he never stopped me doing anything. I felt awkward about it because he rarely showed extreme feelings about ordinary things, reserving his passion against cruel sports and child neglect, so his repugnance for a bit of hand holding in the dark seemed over reaction.

'Not to worry, dear.' She bit into her biscuit. 'So, is everything going OK for you? It's coming up for a year now, isn't it?'

'Mm. Yes.' I chewed too. I was thinking about her spirits. Suddenly, I couldn't stop myself. I blurted out, 'I thought someone was going to tell my fortune.'

'Oh.' She stared at me. 'Sometimes that happens, Chris, but it's not a given. It's a prayer meeting predominantly, to thank the Lord and the spirits. Then sometimes someone comes through. Did you want to know anything specific or to contact anyone?' She looked earnestly at me. 'I will pray for you.'

Oh God! I felt like I was wading through treacle. 'Ah Deborah, please don't worry. I am fine, really. It's just a foolish attraction thing like reading your stars in the paper. We know it's not really true but it's a fascinating idea, having your fortune told, cards read, horoscopes, the future and all that, isn't it?' I was stuttering a bit but she just smiled beatifically again.

She drained her coffee cup and stood up. 'Take care, dear. Nothing awful is coming up for you.' She surprisingly hugged me then and swept through the door.

Denny saw her swishing out and stroked his face. 'How do you know her, Chris?'

'Oh, blimey, Denny. Why do you say it like that? She gets photocopies in here. She works in the herbal goods shop on the corner with the school and she believes in spirits.' I looked at him peevishly.

'My Church doesn't agree with what her lot say and do.' He frowned and went on, 'Don't get mixed up in it. I don't go to church often, especially since my little mishap, but there are reasons not to dabble, Chris, I've heard of people that got badly affected by things that happened to them and things they saw. No. Don't ask me about it because I'm not talking about it anymore.' He went to get himself a drink and obviously didn't want to go on. I wondered what he knew and Chris knew and what I obviously didn't know. I finished my coffee. I had to sort out some nice things to do with the children as the holidays progressed, they couldn't come here every day.

Chapter 6

Chris had been wondering why Building Control had suddenly stopped calling him with progress updates on the basement. He regularly drove over there and met Mr Evans and both agreed that it was progressing well. Excavating a basement beneath the entire house footprint is a huge task and progress was obviously slow. The underpinning around the perimeter of the exterior walls was being carried out in one metre sections, allowing the concrete to "go off" for several days before the area adjacent could be started. Huge beams had been installed beneath the floor of the living rooms and kitchen to hold the whole house up and this enabled the workmen now to excavate section by section. One time when Chris turned up unannounced, a lorry had just delivered carefully boxed goods which several of the men started to carry below. There were wash hand basins, a WC and cistern and boxes of tiles. Almost a fait accompli. We advised against the installation of a wet room in the basement as we knew that several converted cellars in the area had flooded during the last snow's melt and the appalling mess left to clear after the firemen had dredged them was undesirable and disgusting. Thankfully they listened to Chris and the gleaming white sanitary ware was despatched back to where it all came from.

Chris telephoned the council department and was told that Mr Evans had not shown up for work for a week. They had sent someone around to his flat and could see a small pile of post on his doormat so his absence was reported. The police had forced the door thinking he may be inside, sick or worse. He was a solitary person, primarily shy, we thought and his colleagues agreed that he was quiet and private, but Chris had built up a rapport with him after weeks of site inspections at the basement and didn't consider him an oddball as some had stated. His passport was found in a drawer; his bank account had not been used and it didn't appear that his home had been ransacked or burgled.

We had another threatening phone call to say nothing to no-one or we'd be sorry so finally Chris decided to tell the police. The missing Mr Evans changed the status of annoying calls into threatening ones. Jeff Gold was obviously nervous and we had not heard from Jonny Pearson. His secretary told us he had decided to visit relatives in Australia. Even Del Smith professed ignorance of our situation or the missing Mr Evans and we told him we had decided to bring the police in to try to monitor the telephone, as any of our children could take the calls. Then we had a visit from the boys in blue as a body had been found in a trunk and flung into the lake. The description fitted the missing surveyor. We had a nasty feeling that the poor man's death was connected to the basement and Jeff Gold was involved in some way, if only by association. He barked at his wife in front of us but seemed too timid a person generally to carry out the threats we had received and the abduction and murder of Mr Evans, who must have learned something detrimental during one of his site visits and been effectively silenced. Good God.

We went together to the council offices and were allowed to see the site notes recorded on his computer. Nothing leapt out at us until we saw a memo from his head of department, which gave information that needed to be noted and followed up.

The notes made uncomfortable reading. Mr Evans final visit found the men had started to dig out beneath the garden and had installed timber props and planks of wood. He warned them that digging a mine shaft in the grounds had not had the benefit of planning consent or his engineering section, so please could they fill it all in again. These notes had been scribbled down on an envelope and posted to the head of department instead of waiting for the end of the day, when he would normally write the day's notes up upon his return to the office. He must have felt threatened to do this and how right his suspicions.

Apparently the making good had been carried out, because when Chris carried out his site visit at the end of the week, he had not noticed the tunnel although he knew nothing of it at the time. He wondered if a panel of plaster board had been installed as a temporary fixture to hide the excavation. The authorities would investigate that now. I wondered if that knowledge was what killed him. He had not been seen since. The police stopped the building works at the basement site while they interviewed everyone. Luckily for us we knew nothing.

The school summer holidays started at this point and we decided to ship the kids off to comparative safety. My long-suffering mother was cajoled to take them to a holiday centre on the Isle of Wight. They all had a riotous time and it turned out to be an enjoyable break for them all, including Mum as she had little domestic stuff in the chalet to contend with and the activities laid on for everyone provided entertainment for all. They entered sporting event after yet another type of frenzied contest and actually did quite well. Even Mum won a glamorous granny contest and received a framed photo to keep. We spoke daily over the phone but we kept as much as possible away from her and them so they believed we had organised a holiday treat. It was quite an expensive safety precaution at a time when our financial state was still delicate, but worth it to have them out of harm's way.

**

Mr Comik paid us a visit and I was gratified to see him wearing one of the shirts I had given him and told him so. 'That shirt suits you, Mr Comik, Granddad would be pleased, he always liked that one.' How could I?

He smiled and excitedly told me that his son was visiting him. I hadn't known he had a son or indeed had even been married. This elusive son had not made an appearance when the attack happened.

I said I hoped the visit was a good one and told him if his son Benedict wanted to meet us he could and off he went, beaming widely and happy as a sand boy, into the pub on the corner. The staff in The Rose were more careful of him nowadays, watching the amount he washed down his neck and checking around outside for him when he decided to walk back home.

**

An elderly neighbour of mine had been helping me with the cleaning. It was a loose arrangement, originally to pad out her pension and hopefully as a help to me, the days and times to suit her, like if she was in the mood, health permitting, lack of a better invitation, no hangover, whatever, so I never knew until I walked in whether I would smell polish or disinfectant or indeed, if she had visited at all. The arrangement lately had been sparse, from four or five hours a week to nothing, so I went to check whether she was well or indeed still with us and found her with a few other ladies of similar age, having tea. I asked her if she found our arrangement onerous now and had decided to end it and she gave me a beatific smile and said she had solved the problem. What problem? I know our home can be a bit untidy: well, more like thoroughly ransacked sometimes, but I hadn't realised that it was a problem. 'Mmm?'

I think she read my mind. 'My problem, dear. Not yours, I have been so busy with my other commitments but I've got you someone else. Mrs Salter will ring you later. She cleans with her friend and they are such lovely ladies. Very religious, you know, and they love their hymns, but they'll sort you out.'

I just thanked her, said good afternoon to the greedy old ladies who were stuffing gingerbread and iced fancies into birdlike cavities like they were starving parrots, and went home. Not for the first time did I think that I didn't really like old people.

A bit later and Mrs Salter with her associate Mrs Barton arrived on my doorstep. I think they found smiling painful: in any case neither of them attempted it. I started showing them around, announcing the rooms but it was obvious that I was surplus to requirements, so I crept back downstairs and left them to it. 'This is a list of cleaning items that you need to get in order for us to clean your home.' I jumped. 'OK,' weakly.

Mrs Barton held out a sheet of paper. 'We will start on Wednesday at nine if you have the things. Have you a spare key?'

'Yes, of course.' I looked at the list. 'Well, I have some of this already. Do you want me to leave it all under the sink or in the hall cupboard?'

'That will be satisfactory. We will allow you two and a half hours weekly. Our time cannot be extended as we have other places to go. We want our money, in cash, left in the kitchen. We take no responsibility for what happens in your house.' What? No insurance then.

I thought they were a strange pair but obediently handed over a key and thought that any help was better than none and they can't be bad people if they go about singing hymns. Can they?

The children were still away and Chris and I were spending long hours at the office. I was worried that in a few days they would be back and although the nasty phone calls had ended, I didn't want them over there with us if something dreadful happened.

We had a site meeting at Jeffrey Gold's house as the police had been all over the place with their special equipment and chemicals and nothing apparently showed up as suspicious, no spilt blood or fragments of anything untoward, so he had been given permission to continue. The council had also agreed. We had been obliged to meet a few of Jeffrey Gold's family and friends before. I was a bit nervous in their company but their behaviour towards us was impeccable and polite to the point of being embarrassing, so we regarded it as part of the job. I remember remarking once that many of them were either jewellers or market traders and Chris trod quite hard on my toes.

We had a quick tour of the basement which was taking shape then I went up the site steps to the garden and walked round to the entrance door. Mrs Gold had made tea in one of those huge enamelled teapots and was pouring it out in a steady flow. I smiled at her, feeling quite sorry for the state of her home and conditions she was coping in: the constant flow of workmen, replacement skips and now the recent police interest. She was a little mouse of a thing. 'Getting on now,' I remarked inanely to her. She nodded and passed me a mug of strong tea, looking around for the others and moving the mugs into lines of sugared ones and non-sugared. 'They are coming,' I said.

'Jeff said the stairs are going in next. Then the back door can be shut.'

'Yes,' I agreed, then I asked her, 'Why did you want such a large space down there?'

Her eyes grew round as marbles and she sucked her breath in and spluttered, 'Shut up. Don't ask.' She turned back to her mugs just in time as the men all trooped in leaving muddy smears all over the floor. I was glad to see that Chris had removed his boots.

I knew then that this basement was not intended for normal use like a wine store or home gymnasium or masses of outgrown toys or even hobby collection. There were no light wells provided so the area could not be for living in or any other residential purpose, apart from storage. Storage of what? I wondered.

I couldn't help it. The tendency I have to burst out laughing when I'm scared also causes me to ask sensitive questions. Questions which had in the past got me into trouble could now get me strangled and thrown into a lake perhaps. 'Is the basement for your business, Jeff?'

'No, not really, Chris, just for bits and pieces that I've picked up over the years. Too public in the house. Risky, innit?'

'Do you collect things, then?'

'Here and there. Odds and ends.' He turned away. I knew he wasn't going to say any more. I persisted. 'Memorabilia, is it, or foreign valuables? You're all in the precious metals trade in one way or another, aren't you?'

Chris glared at me and said, 'That's how they met, at the wholesalers and gold exchange.' Turning to Jeffrey he asked, 'That's right isn't it. Your accountant, Miles, said you travel to Hong Kong several times a year? We went there once, loved the place. Who do you fly with?'

I felt cold inside. Something was definitely smelly here. Chris had diverted the focus away from me and turned the subject around. They continued to discuss the ferry and statues of Buddha, boat people at Aberdeen and all sorts of trivia. I felt quite miserable.

I could never be accused of snobbery. I didn't look down or look up at anyone, at least not without provocation; I try to make allowance for people but there was no way that this rag tag motley crew could be ordinary successful business people. I didn't believe it. Surely Chris wasn't taken in by them?

The rest of the visit was horrible for me. I felt I had put us both in danger just because I couldn't mind my own business or keep my trap shut. I looked at some catalogues and left Chris to talk to Jeffrey and the site foreman. They reckoned it would be a couple of weeks to complete the underpinning of the side walls then the floor completed, and surface could be finished by adding damp proof membranes and finally the top screed. Damp proof membranes had been laid beneath the edges and up the walls and plasterboard installed over it by a process called "dot and dab". Light switches and plug points were being positioned.

The electricity wiring was criss-crossing the ceiling and at intervals flapping down the walls and pipes laid probably for radiators. Perhaps they were going to add internal partition walls and doors afterwards. I wouldn't ask. I was sick of the project. Once the electricity had been connected and staircase installed the works could be signed off. I couldn't wait. It was our first job on the same day that we moved into the office, as our very own place of business became reality, where it all meant so much after a long time of struggle and it transposed into a nightmare. A client who seemed genuine at first glance, even though his actions had been stupid, who came with a pocket full of cash and a consortium of associates, hangers-on of dubious means or genuine villains always hovering on the edge of the project as it progressed, always turning up and glaring with suspicious faces at Chris or me. The guy I thought as Mr Big, Del Smith, seemed gentle after we had met a few of the others and we had no idea who had called us with vile phone messages or worse, who killed poor Mr Evans.

**

It was almost time for Mum and the children to return from the holiday camp. We weren't confident of safety until we were completely out of the basement project, then we had a lucky break. A long-time friend from school had a six-berth caravan on a site in West Sussex and she offered it to us for a fortnight. She usually rented it out to her children's church and it had been booked for the whole season. Sadly, the ones who had booked it couldn't take it after all but had insurance to retrieve their fees so nobody was out of pocket. My relief was paramount as we still had policemen wandering in and out of our office and we were not in a position to go on holiday.

I didn't have to cajole Mum very hard as the private beach was clean, the site itself well-kept and "select" as she described it, with a welcoming club house, restaurants and swimming pool. So I braced myself for a mountain of laundry to wash, dry and iron to be re-packed within 24 hours so the Prentice clan could again be away and safe from possible reprisals.

I took a trip to Sainsbury's and bought them a trunk load of tinned and boxed provisions and did my usual trick of cooking and freezing joints to help them manage through the first week. Chris and I resolved to go down ourselves on the middle weekend to give everyone a break. My friend, along with her husband and children, had suggested that we all meet up and I knew it would be a fun-filled weekend with plenty of action, good food and laughter.

Chapter 7

We had just begun to start the refurbishment works on the first-floor rooms over the office and had been wondering if we dared to borrow from our very obliging and patient bank again to speed up the process. Our finances had only recently started to straighten up, which eased the pressure slightly, so a further commitment could be a crazy thing to add and push our precarious financial position further up the panic scale, but we knew we could let out the space, once habitable, which hopefully would quickly finance it.

The condition was quite dreadful. How Larry had lived there was a constant puzzle. We had gradually cleared the old and broken storage and stripped out the kitchen and bathroom, ready for the new fittings when finances allowed. We had moved the staircase to the side of the office as a second street door was already there and made good the ceiling. This effectively closed our access to the first floor so our clearance and early demolition had stopped. We had no idea why this second door existed and the council had no record of it leading to a separate area, but had given us planning permission to convert the first floor to a residential unit and the existing doorway was useful. The new staircase needed to connect with the floor and this was our first task, as a gaping hole in the ceiling would be a bit unnerving for clients when they wandered in. We worked out a list of individual items which needed the input of tradesmen.

Top of the list was the staircase and floor connection, which was sorted out with a jobbing carpenter in return for preparing his own house plans for an extension. We had a plasterer who owed us a favour and he volunteered his Sunday morning to make good the ceiling over Denny's desk. This enabled us to remove the rest of the kitchen equipment and we spent a joyous evening, Chris and I, eating Mrs Chin's noodles, slurping a beer each straight from the bottle and bashing the old tiles off the walls with rubber hammers. Once these cracked and stained ceramic fragments were swept up into black bags and humped downstairs and rickety timber cupboards dumped in the skip outside, the whole space looked quite promising. So far so good and no financial outlay made to date: we were pleased. With the children away we had our evenings to ourselves and enjoyed a week of progress with our latest project. By the end of the week we had stripped the old layers of ghastly time-worn wallpapers, rubbed down the paintwork of the joinery which was good enough to retain and torn out the sections of damp and useless skirting boards, along with the rotten bathroom window frame and broken kitchen lino. The carpets, strangely, seemed reasonable in the living room and main bedroom but we would wait to pass judgement later and any case, they needed a deep clean. A mock Tudor fireplace with doubtful looking gas fire remained in the front living room hearth, which we decided had to go and use the room as the main bedroom instead. The outrigger part of the building housed a kitchen on the first floor which could then lead from the new living room at the rear and eliminate a dark passage. We believed that way back in the annals of time, the building had been two small units, as the kitchen on the right and bathroom on the left were housed in small rear additions to both floors. The internal walls of the upstairs were constructed of brick infill panels and lath and plaster sections. Luckily for us, the alterations we implemented did not involve structural installation such as beams but produced a more spacious two bedroomed flat, with a bathroom and kitchen leading from the living room. There now was a lot more plastering and making good to be done and the electrical and gas services were decidedly suspect. We made an evening visit to our local Wickes, armed with small measured diagrams of the rooms to see what their sales offered as well as the extent of goods required and costs involved. They had a good deal on flat packs of bedroom wardrobes, which seemed a good idea as we had salvaged a few reasonable chests of drawers and bedside tables from all the rubbish and rubble and we still had available funds on our credit cards. We unearthed a wrought iron bedstead out in the garden shed and decided to have it dipped to remove the chipped black lacquer and paint it cream for our own use. It would definitely enhance our own bed at home.

We ordered many boxes of plain white tiles, tubs of grout and an economy bathroom suite and to our delight, they even had a ready-made window of the size needed to replace the one we removed and bought obscured glazed panes to install. I remembered a small tube of putty and the window joinery, not forgetting screws.

Luckily the wardrobes fitted exactly either side of the chimney breast, which would need a ventilation brick to be installed and more making good of the wall. We intended to install a new boiler and radiators for economy.

My credit card was now maxed out and we dared not repeat the exercise with Chris's as we had the Brighton visit looming and at the back of my mind I knew there would be a huge list of new school uniform needed for the Autumn term ahead.

**

Saturday morning was sunny with a bright clear blue sky and we threw an armful of clothes into the car and left for the coast. John and Susie, our friends, were meeting us there with their brood and we were looking forward to a couple of days of family normality. The ages of the six children ranged from six to fourteen and we prayed for clemency from the older ones when the younger ones showed their age.

We had a clear drive down and we pulled into the camp site at coffee time. Mum scuttled around to gather cups and plates for a toasted bun and our little No.3 excitedly told us he could swim across the pool without arm bands and he played Bingo and won a box of colouring pencils. That's brilliant I laughed while thinking, "Pencils! Coals to Newcastle."

John's beautiful white Mercedes arrived at the parking strip and his horde swept down the grass, whooping greetings to ours. John strode over, waving a couple of bottles which from a distance resembled rather fine bubbly and we found a bucket of cold water to house them. Close up proved they were in fact rather fine bubbly, so I wondered what we were celebrating. They would help our dinner tonight taste even better, I thought. 'Forget the coffee, Mum,' I yelled and reached for a box of beers instead. We sat on the grass and caught up on latest tittle tattle, the children happy with their cartons of juice or milk shakes.

No driving for us until late tomorrow evening and we passed around the cans while toasting us all.

A game of cricket played by varying ages such as ours was expected to be tasking. Our older ones were learning to bowl and bat for England. The delivery speed was horrific and scared me. The little ones invariably missed the ball as, I confess, I did too, and then took such a long while fielding that the runs were mounting. In vain we coaxed, 'Gently now, he's tiny,' and the whole event descended into chaos, with rage and tantrums from the smallest to moans of boredom from the eldest. 'They're so useless. God it's like being in kindergarten.' It was gratifying for Chris and me that our three generally behaved with more patience and tolerance, so we gave up and went for lunch in the restaurant.

Pleasingly, the menu was quite varied. I snobbishly expected a chips with everything list but there were salads and Mediterranean dishes as well as English staples and all-day breakfasts.

The older ones pushed some tables together and the smaller ones found enough chairs, cutlery and condiments and we collected trays and lined up to sort out the food.

Chris and John chose homemade steak pie so our No.1 copied them, Mum had a ham and cheese omelette, Susie and I had lasagne and the other four kids had a mixture of fish fingers or sausages and the inevitable chips. We noted that they advertised a Sunday roast for the next day, which could be easier than searching for somewhere else.

No clearing up to do so we scraped our chairs back and headed for the beach after gathering up a selection of towels and costumes. Making them stand still to apply sun screen lotion was a challenge but finally achieved and at last they bolted like a small army for the gentle waves. The beach is pebbly at this part so we were glad they had jellies on and we took it in turns to watch them.

The site had nice communal showers and finally everyone emerged, fresh and clean and braying for dinner. Sensibly, we had brought a selection of foods for the barbecue so no need to brave the restaurant again. The children settled to watch an action film inside the van while we prepared a collection of new potatoes, side dishes and salads. Susie produced a wicked gateau for dessert and I washed strawberries and raspberries to go on top with a tub of crème fraiche and a can of evaporated milk which our No.3 had never tired of after being weaned. He smiled like a kitten with catmint when he was allowed to drink it undiluted as a treat. At home, sometimes I whisked this old fashioned tinned milk until it went thick and added a fruit jelly which miraculously produced a passable mousse when cool.

When all the delicious food had been eaten, plates and dishes washed and small ones put to bed, Chris got his guitar and we lolled around drinking the champagne, followed by port with dreadfully fattening blue cheeses until it was very late and we were stuffed like the Christmas goose.

I had thought that Chris and I would squeeze into the caravan, as it was only one night, and our friends would go home as they lived about a mile away, but as their children were now inside with ours, poor Mum had six to contend with and Susie triumphantly produced a key to the next caravan so we clambered joyfully inside. It was good to have moneyed friends and we could continue our conversation after sorting our beds and sleeping bags out.

Susie made silver jewellery in a workshop at their home and John was a jeweller. He had worked for a well-known chain of shops when they lived in London, then John's cousin asked them to move down to be near him. He was the manager of a small department store and they were carrying out a refit and general re-organisation. He wanted to increase the merchandise to include precious metals and gems rather than the costume jewellery it previously sold. Within a few weeks of the offer their home was on the market, new schools organised and off they went lock, stock and barrel. The move was a good one, the department store benefited from modern input and beautiful not to say expensive articles and appeared to go from strength to strength. Susie found herself with some free time now her smallest was at school and she enjoyed letting her imagination take over. Occasionally she produced a design that he put in the window of the store.

It was during this evening of drunken conversations that John remarked that there seemed to be a glut of gold entering the market. The source was unknown, he said, everyone in the trade was fogged. He explained that you can't add a chip to a lump of gold for identity and police had no ideas. I glanced quickly at Chris and noted he moved his head to give me a straight look in return. Make no comment, Chris! Then I knew. We would have to wait 'til we were back home, in private to broach my idea. From the slightest widening of his eyes in that split-second I knew he had thought the same.

**

On Monday, we decided to call our bank, to enquire with bated breath and screwed-up wincey eyes whether we could borrow a further sum of money. To be fair we had never been late with a payment, always set aside our VAT collected and our personal tax was saved in readiness. Our balance fluctuated by a fair degree and sometimes had to break the school fees into a few instalments which we knew the purser disapproved of. Happily, he appeared to like our children, which was an enormous bonus as others had been asked to leave over such minor issues. This was before the time of internet transfers and payment was given by cheque. Several times a year separate envelopes were handed into the office with a winning smile and swift exit by me, usually. 'Ahh Chris,' our manager exclaimed. 'Just the chap I wanted to speak to.'

Inward groan. 'I wondered if you could carry out a few staff valuations for us?' What? 'Actually, Mr Umm, sir, I'm not a chartered valuer, you know. Surveyor and engineer, but not valuations.'

'Nemmind, my boy! It doesn't matter about the valuation part. I just want to know whether they'll stand up you know. The stuck-up chaps we use are so long winded and expensive and everyone knows what they're worth anyway. You only have to check with the local estate agents for comparison. OK? We'll take it as agreed then. Pop into my office later, after 2.30 and we'll wrap it up.'

Our loan wasn't mentioned over the phone then but when Chris got back after his meeting he chortled with glee. 'Chris, it works out about two a week in a twenty mile radius. The fees are pre-set so I don't have to work it out and feel mean and I can add any notes I wish at the back, which basically means it's as good as a homebuyer's report for the staff members. We get a definite steady income paid straight into the account and it more than covers the new loan for the refurb.'

I wished we had one of John's bottles at that point but you can have too much of a good thing.

**

After work one evening later in the week, when we arrived home I was surprised to see the hoover in the middle of the hallway floor and dusters and polishes heaped on the bottom stair.

I found a note in the kitchen.

"Dear Madam, we run out of time and had to stop.

We need more Pledge.

The small duck got broke, Elaine Salter."

That infuriated me. The children had pooled their money and bought me two ducks one Christmas. I loved them. Now this stupid woman had broken one of them which I knew was not valuable but irreplaceable. I was filled with complete anger. She hadn't even said "Sorry." Or swept up the pieces, just left them lying in the bath. I gently gathered them together and wrapped them in a cloth. Maybe one day I could reconstruct it.

**

Irrepressible Reverend McDonald burst through the door in his usual dramatic manner and bestowed his beams all around, freezing slightly as he spied Denny and waved a couple of tickets at us. 'My dear children, how are you?' Peering past us at the back door he asked, 'Where are your children, Mr Chris? Are they well?'

'Away with friends, Reverend. Very well, thank you. Making the most of the summer break.'

He nodded vigorously. 'Quite right. I have invitations for you, my dears. The ladies are giving a small Thanksgiving treat in the garden to celebrate the completion of my car parking space. You arranged it for me so I would be honoured if you came to join us, tomorrow at 12.'

He swept out again after casting Denny a follow up glare,

Of course we would go. I thought it was about time Denny was allowed back into the fold and asked him if he wanted to join us. 'Oh, no, thanks, Mrs Chris. I'll wait a bit. The old codger still hasn't forgiven me, you saw the way he looked, but I wasn't the first with Avril and I won't be the last. You'll see, there will be a long list of the unforgiven before he realises I was the lamb to slaughter that night and not the other way round.'

Chris went out again to the first staff valuation job and I was pleased to recognise the name of the young lady. I had worked with her for a while a few years earlier and we had bought our kittens from her mother. We called them Sooty and Minstrel. Sooty was obviously completely black and Minstrel was black and white so he was named after the singing and dancing troupe we saw on the television some years earlier. They were young adults now but still wonderfully crazy, sweet and gentle animals. 'Write a good report for her, Chris,' I called to him. 'We're getting paid.' He gestured back.

**

We had a short time before drawn a conservatory for a friend of a friend about five times removed and received a picture in lieu of a fee. It was an artist's proof, whatever that means, and showed a view from an open glass doorway onto a balcony and looking over rooftops below. I had it framed but it still lurked behind a desk at home, as no-one had time to sort out a hanging position for it.

After this, news travelled around this arty bunch that Chris Prentice was a bit of a twit as he accepted presents and didn't seem to realise he was supposed to ask for a fee. He came home once with an enormous, hideous lump of furniture balanced on the back seats of the car. He and No.1 wrestled it out of the boot opening eventually and he stood beaming at me with a sort of simple pleasure. I didn't have the heart to bark at him, 'What the bloody hell is that?' Instead I smiled and waited. 'Chris, look at this.' I couldn't be off looking at it plonked in the middle of the front garden. 'It's a radiogram and it still works. You can play records on it. It has the most wonderful tone.'

Really. Why did they want to let it go then? I wondered. 'Where is it going?' Weakly.

'We'll find somewhere. Look at that beautiful wood, it's walnut, Chris.'

Wow. He was standing there stroking the thing. Ye Gods. No.I looked at me and shrugged, it was obviously beyond him too.

It was settled in the back lounge below the book shelves in the chimney breast nook. Chris listened to classical stuff in the mornings before anyone else stirred.

After the music thing came a succession of strange beer tankards, garden pots, demijohns for wine making, a tray full of frozen chickens and an introduction to a television chef. She was house hunting for a kitchen large enough to cook in with a television crew installed. The programme was booked to be shown in the autumn and she was desperate to find a suitable place and had been sent a brochure showing pictures of a lavish country house comprising twelve bedrooms, five bathrooms, several living rooms, dining rooms, a library, a drawing room, utility room, scullery and the smallest kitchen probably in the world.

Luckily, I took a call from this quite famous lady and managed to provide her with a fee quotation which she accepted, both for the survey and the drawings. I seriously feared Chris would have walked away with a signed cookery book or a frying pan.

Chris went off to meet her and, strangely, two partners. I am sure that one must have been a publisher or accountant or whatever but decided to learn from Chris and keep quiet. He rarely asked questions and accepted everything at face value. I, on the other hand was always vaguely suspicious and took around with me a pinch of salt.

He returned from the survey which took a whole day and he had to go back to inspect the drains and take photos ready to send to interior designers. He made me laugh at his description of the vendor, who sounded like a caricature of Kenneth Williams interspersed with Charles Hawtrey. Perhaps he liked Carry On films or just thought he was a class above everyone else. He may instead have been desperate to sell his pile. He hopped around following Chris from room to room becoming quite edgy when he lifted curtains, opened cupboard doors and moved rugs and feigned swoons when areas of torn lino were uncovered. 'If you want to lift floorboards I won't let you,' he waspishly squawked when a carpet corner was lifted to look at the floor surface beneath. 'I won't be doing that, sir,' said Chris. 'I'll leave that to the timber dampness and wood-boring beetle specialist.' A shocked look and hasty exit followed and Chris had relative peace for the next half an hour. All this time he was making notes and speaking into the tape-recorder which would be for me to translate into English.

It was a faded but beautiful house and promised to be fantastic once decorated. A row of garages, albeit in dire need of repair, a few outbuildings along with a wonderful garden completed the spread. 'By the way, sir,' asked Chris as he was now getting ready to leave, 'I wonder if your estate manager can tell me where the nearest coal mines are in the district?'

The scheme to convert one of the many family rooms into a new, state of the art kitchen for demonstrations and recordings was almost complete and to convert the existing matchbox kitchen into a wet room or saucepan store or whatever. There followed a couple more meetings and I was troubled to notice he was taking care to choose his shirt and ties and team them with velvet or linen jackets in the evenings when suddenly he had to go over there. He never minded what he pulled out of the cupboards usually and I asked him if the said lady was pretty. 'Yes, in a way. But I don't like her vegetarian food.' Good. I decided to be a bit more careful with the next steaks I cooked and upon reflection, eat fewer chips. 'Does she give you any tips on food?' What an inane question.

'God, no. We just talk about the kitchen and the positions of the equipment.'

I bet. 'Although,' he continued, 'I did ask her solicitor to check on the whereabouts of the ex-coal mines in the area.'

'Coal mines? Why?'

'Well, in the unscrupulous Victorian times they didn't check on boundaries and if they were following a seam, they would keep going. They went down huge distances and then turned off, following deposits so there could be tunnels beneath the grounds. I asked the vendor, Lord Torn Shirt, and he didn't know or didn't want to. No worry, it's out of our hands now.'

**

We arrived at the church garden, which was already full of people showing cheerful dispositions and Chris was immediately swamped with hugging, cheek kissing females thanking him for his help, bringing him tea, bestowing a glass of some sort of homemade lemonade and proffering sausages, strips of toast with something dubious on them and generally treating him like a minor celebrity.

I was about to wander off, feeling I was entirely surplus to requirements when the reverend himself, arms open wide and smile even wider, enveloped me in his generous aura and I found myself being shown round the church. As we climbed the timber steps to the balcony and changing rooms (why do they need changing rooms?) I had an overpowering urge to leap over the balustrade and run like mad and had to force myself to focus on reality. 'We don't need to go in there, Reverend,' I sang brightly. 'It's as nice as the other one.'

Thank God Chris came through the side door and looked up at the balcony, spotting us as if he knew where to look. 'There you are! Sorry darling, we have to leave. Thank you, Reverend McDonald, for a lovely do, I'm afraid we've been called away, there's an emergency in Walthamstow and Chris has to take notes.'

I can't remember how I got down those stairs but found myself gaily waving at him from the safety of the ground floor and grabbing Chris's arm with gratitude. Relief and pure love swamped me for a moment, until I remembered I hadn't had anything to eat or tasted the much praised lemonade and if he hadn't allowed himself to be completely affected by those effusive, simpering harpies I wouldn't almost have been the glib vicar's lunch. I wondered afterwards whether I was doing the chummy holy man a disservice and putting the whole thing out of perspective. I was a grown woman, perhaps a bit short and dumpy but Chris thought I was okay, or at least I thought he did so surely, I should have been a bit more assertive. Perhaps I misunderstood his intentions. I decided to water down the episode when I talked to Denny. 'So, where are we off to?'

'Southend. We'll treat ourselves to sea food in Old Leigh and go on to the front for a stroll along the pier. Denny's watching the office. I promised him a curry tomorrow.'

My hero.

**

The internal works in Mrs Chin's shop and rear rooms were finally completed. She had gone on to have the upstairs living quarters fully decorated and asked us about installing a small kitchen in order to fully utilise the whole floor into a separate dwelling. She had seen us unloading the flat packs for the kitchen and bedrooms on our first floor, which had set her thinking. Her roof space had already been converted to create a bedroom and study which her eldest two daughters had taken over. She was ready to fly.

A short time later she asked us to keep a look out for one of the small houses opposite if one came up for sale or rent, as she was ready to proceed and could rent out the flat above the shop to help fund it. I thought then what a foolish man her husband had been to behave as he had. Mrs Chin was achieving so much on her own. She looked after her family and ran the business, carried out most of the cooking, all the paperwork and was now ready to let out the upper level and buy a house.

This spurred us on and we contacted our electrician and arranged for the wiring to be carried out. We wanted a separate installation rather than linked in with the office supply, so the tenants would be responsible for their own power and bills. The carpenter was contacted next and the plasterer. The bank valuations had made enough difference to provide us with a little start-up cash and the small business loan was available to complete the job.

It was going to be a race between us and dear, brave Mrs Chin to see who could complete and rent out their first floors. We both contacted the local rental agency.

This also triggered another idea in my head, as if we needed another one: we still had our roof space left unused. I pushed that to the back of my whirring brain for another time.

**

While I opened a bottle of German Piesporter and put a few beers on ice Chris called the local takeaway and ordered our food. Denny loved a vindaloo and Chris a jalfrezi as he liked hot fragments of green chilli. I had a king prawn shaslik. This was a small acknowledgement of the thousands of calories that I would be saving to omit a sauce. The result of course was ruined as we tore into peshwari naan bread, oozing with sweet coconut.

Chapter 8

Denny popped into the corner shop for some more tea bags and succumbed to a box of jam tarts. We irreverently called the proprietor Ali Baba as he talked to the children about magic carpets and life in old Baghdad. Nobody knew much about him or his wife but their quiet, friendly manner earned them respect. I wondered if calling him Ali Baba, as we had heard others referring to him too, insulted him. He had a pronounced limp and rumour had it that he had fought with the British Army somewhere. We often bought odds and ends there but the goods were expensive compared to the larger supermarkets, so thinking we ought to support the small traders, as we were members ourselves, we did but sparingly.

Denny came back with his goods and reported that Mr Patel on the corner wanted to talk to Chris when he returned, so we now knew his real name. I had resolved to ask him next time I wanted last minute groceries and dived into the shop. We waited for Chris to return.

Chris arrived with a large box of chicken biryani which had been given to him. He had been walking past a small cluster of shops in Forest Gate and someone inside a takeaway had spotted him. He called him over and asked the proprietor to provide him with a takeaway dish. It was hot and delicious and enough for Denny too, so that was a generous thing to do. I asked him who the present was from and Chris said the cousin of someone who passed our name around. We felt warm and happy for the rest of the afternoon but I wished I knew who had sent it so I could thank him. I also ruefully realised I had eaten a marvellous hugely fattening meal again. Curry two days running. I thoughtfully put the kettle on for jasmine tea, a half-hearted attempt at weight watching.

Mr Patel wanted to convert his roof space into two bedrooms and a shower room and Chris got Denny to hold the end of the tape to speed up the dimensional survey. Apparently, his name was Ali and he loved to tell tall stories to children basing them on old films he had seen, *The Thief of Baghdad* being one and Sinbad adventures. He told Chris he had been born and lived in Africa but came to England to provide his children with a better education. We had seen two teenagers helping out in the shop and these were Mina and Ali Junior, twins, they were expecting to start at university the following term, Mina for pharmacology and Ali for dentistry.

He told Chris that the empty shop next door to the corner shop was also owned by him. He said when they first took the premises it had been used as a café and his wife worked in it while he ran the convenience store. At first it went quite well but loyal part-time staff in greasy spoons proved hard to get and keep. When someone failed to turn up for their shift and the café was not open the "regulars" went elsewhere. It was a constant worry as to which precedent they followed. Being unable to get reliable staff to help out regularly imposed enormous strain on them. Trying to operate both outlets with long and punishing hours, the children were often alone in the back of the shop and they kept wandering around to the front out of boredom. Mr and Mrs Patel then tried to use the café premises in conjunction with the corner shop, knocking a doorway through the party wall to combine them it but this wasn't profitable either as it created a small "black spot" area in the middle which was out of visibility and they noticed that their stock in this area was vanishing. Reluctantly realising that many people utilised this small un-overlooked area to stuff articles into spacious pockets or different bags, he closed it down again and filled in the doorway. They thought there was little point in leaving the place of their birth to start life in a new country for the sake of the children, only to work all hours of the day and night and leave the children more or less neglected in the kitchen. The shop had been boarded up for about eight years and they used the space for storage. There was no WC to either floor and no running water or electricity, but after chatting between themselves they were coming around to the idea of using it again. Probably they saw Mrs Chin and us carrying out works and that gave them the idea.

The permissions were gained for the end corner shop and thoughts turned again to the empty one. Chris was doubtful whether permission would be granted to use the area again for a café as the parade was close to the traffic lights, but Mr Patel thought as it had been used before it was feasible to use it again. They excitedly brought in local tradesmen to re-install a kitchen and an extractor fan to discharge high over the roof top in the rear garden and a customers' WC. He added a few little tables and chairs and advertised the place by putting a large notice in the window. A local man took it and his name was put over the door and the venture was a great success: we often bought his bacon sandwiches for belated breakfast, the smell was wonderful.

Our first-floor residential unit was taking shape. It was now possible to enter by the front door, proceed up the staircase and walk around safely with no risk of falling through the floor or out of the rotten windows. The lights worked. The new gas boiler performed beautifully and provided instant hot water, warming radiators and a usable cooker.

The new bathroom had been installed, bedrooms and kitchen fitted and we were gradually covering the walls with pale emulsion paint. Our children had wanted to join in the painting party before floor coverings had been chosen so we waited for their return to finish the living room, Chris painted the long awkward stretch down the staircase and landing walls from ceiling to floor by balancing on a series of timbers which to me looked as safe as a house of cards.

**

We were building up a small list of useful contacts and had been introduced to Peter Bates, who was a specialist in the treatment of dampness in walls and woodworm and dampness damaged timbers. Our area was an old one, with many properties having outward bowing walls due to WW2 bomb damage and cracked masonry with fractured brickwork. This was typical of London properties and some people were awarded financial help from the local council to carry out repairs if awarded a grant. This was a highly probing exercise. The applicant had an extensive questionnaire to fill in. They were required to supply wage slips, bank statements and passbooks, even their children's bankbooks if relevant. Many of the applicants had a family member who had mobility problems or invalidity issues and already had benefits. A local company heard of us and approached Chris. He had a team of builders and 'scouts' who tracked down these problem dwellings and needy owners and had been searching for a surveyor with structural knowledge to prepare the reports. We carried out a couple of trial surveys and the whole procedure went smoothly. We were paid for our survey as soon as we arrived at the house. I went with Chris and spoke into the tape recorder and this made it easy to type out the report when we returned to the office. The report was sent by post to the home owner and a copy to the local company. This grant survey work was enjoyable as the name and address was dropped around to the office and specific damage reported. In advance we were aware of the problem area to be inspected and reported on and we never had a doubt of being paid. As we walked through the doorway a cheque was handed to me and I scribbled out a receipt. There were a few times when the rebuilding of the flank wall or replacement rear addition uncovered a further problem and Chris was called out to pass judgement. Sometimes the drains were broken or new foundations interfered with the drainage run but all the problems seemed to be overcome. This nearly always involved the assistance of the grants officer at the council of a neighbouring borough, who invariably signed it off and approved the additional costs. Manholes were moved, new fences erected, even the odd conservatory appeared but we just carried out the work as it was requested. We were aware that no grant application could proceed without a damning report from Chris Twice or a similar surveyor but along with distorted walls and sloping windows the condition of each subject building was as we reported it honestly. There was no need to exaggerate as many of the dwellings were little more than slums, with outside toilets and a bath in the kitchen with a spare door laid over when not in use.

**

One day, while Chris was carrying out a survey for a bank staff member an attractive couple came into the office. They had a presence about them I was unable to describe, their clothes were very smart and she had the most beautiful red hair. I smiled and waited, beckoning for them to sit down on the chairs in front of my desk. He introduced himself as Graham

Snow and his wife as Lindsay. As I looked properly at their faces I gasped and so did she. We had worked together twenty-odd years earlier in a city branch of a well-known bank. Her appearance belied her character. A crazier lady would be hard to find in those days. I never would have realised this slim, elegant woman had evolved from the scatter-brained junior typist I had known then. If anyone lost her bag, missed the train, forgot the date, spilt her tea, dropped a box of paperclips, mislaid the manager's letters it would be Lindsay. The tape recorder became scrambled when she used it. The camera locked. The typewriter ribbon snapped. Her messages got twisted around and she confused her shorthand. I seriously wondered how she had got the job and how she kept it.

Out of work she was the same, a walking disaster. One shoe heel got stuck in the cracks of the pavement, another broke off on the escalator. The edge of her mac got trapped in the doors of a lift and she had to hurriedly pull it off before she was hurt. When the mac was finally retrieved, it was filthy and she had to throw it away. Now she looked like a film star.

After hugging and shouting, laughing and almost crying, we settled down and both of us turned to allow Graham to speak. Denny came in at that moment and he offered to make tea.

I had left the branch to go on a cashier's course and to join the East London Relief team, which meant I was sent wherever there was a staff shortage and virtually had to take over a variety of jobs at a few minutes' notice. Occasionally I went back to my first branch and kept in touch with a few people but I had never seen Lindsay again.

She had met Graham while still an office junior and left work soon after. A progression of half-hearted part-time jobs followed and then she married and started her family while still a teenager. Her two children were older than ours and were virtually off-hand so she had time to make herself beautiful and drape herself on Graham's arm when they ventured out together.

We drank our tea, reminisced a little, talked about other people that either she or I kept up with and finally they came to the reason of their visit.

Graham's father had died and he had inherited a few properties jointly with his two sisters. He bought them out as they were much older than him and wanted a lump sum to enhance their retirement savings. Luckily for him, they had no interest in property speculation or building development and this created an open pathway for him to change career course at the ripe old age of forty. He had gained a working garage about a hundred yards away which he thought needed tidying up to be sold. Three men still worked there, carrying out repairs and servicing and he intended to keep it operating. He had friends and associates in the motor trade so was confident he could shift it quickly but according to his description of the place it sounded quite dire, almost derelict at the rear where the office, small kitchen area & WC seriously needed upgrading. I reached for the diary to book the site visit for the garage and then he continued with the other properties.

This project again was a house with side garage and workshop in bad structural condition. He wanted to demolish the whole thing and start again. He asked what Chris thought could be achieved. I thought it sounded large enough for a pair of semi-detached houses or even a small block of four flats. Requirement criteria for London boroughs was to have garden or amenity space and enough area for parking, depending on the bedrooms planned, which often prevented suitable schemes from gaining permission. The site would have to be measured carefully.

At this point, Chris returned and I introduced them all. I went to get him a drink as he had barely time to catch his breath.

We arranged a date and time for the house replacement scheme meeting and he told us there were more things in the pipeline, which was nice to hear. I wasn't sure when they left our office whether she was still zany Lindsay or whether she had calmed down. Graham seemed very nice and I was confident that he and Chris would develop a sound business arrangement and perhaps we could add them to our burgeoning list of friends in due course. He was a gas plumber by trade and decided to keep some of his long-term contracts until he felt established enough to branch out as a fully-fledged developer.

**

At last the basement was finished. All the spoil had been carted away and Mr Gold's garden tidied up. The front wall had been the first thing to rebuild, which involved a section of the roof, complete with insulation in the loft space. Everybody seemed to be developing upwards, all wanting to create usable space from empty voids. I thought he would probably just convert the loft without the benefit of an architect, engineer or the council approvals or inspections. Good luck too, I thought. I want us to be left out of anything else that they might get involved in.

Just as I thought we could relax and welcome the children home tomorrow the phone on my desk trilled out. Chris had popped out to see a local client who worried about a badly fractured rear wall and was advising him how to claim on his insurance.

I picked up the phone and got a shock as the familiar voice croaked with menace down the line. 'Keep away or else I'll get the Mafia onto you.'

I don't know what came over me but I was suddenly full of rage. 'How dare you, moron! You don't know any Mafia. No self-respecting Family would listen to you! Shut up. Fuck off, idiot. I'll get the Mafia onto you. All this for a poxy little cellar!'

I realised the phone had gone dead and didn't know how much he had heard but to my embarrassment Deborah stood in the doorway staring at me. 'Sorry Deborah, you must think I'm awful. I've had enough of that horrible man, he has phoned so many times, threatening. I don't usually swear like that or lose my temper.' To my horror, a tear sneaked out and plopped on the desk.

She ran over and cuddled me close. 'Chris, Chris. Don't worry. I called to tell you I dreamed about you last night. You have some good fortune coming.'

Wow. Please don't come back, Chris or Denny. They took a dim view of horoscopes and fortune telling. I wasn't ready to share my experience yet. 'Thanks, Deborah. Do you fancy a sherry?'

**

We got up early on Saturday morning and headed off for West Sussex to reunite with our children and my lovely, helpful, long suffering mum.

The children seemed to have grown so much during these weeks, little No.3 looked like a charity case dressed in a shrunken frilly-edged tee shirt and very short shorts. His sneakers had worn through on the toes and his hair had sprouted inches over his ears and down his neck. The others looked better, but definitely their legs had outgrown their bodies. Our first shopping expedition would wear us down with bags and boxes, not only new school clothes but ordinary stuff too. The end of August meant, thank goodness, just a few days left of the holidays. The children were looking forward to meeting up with their friends again to swap holiday stories and compare suntans The year had gone quickly, must have been all the excitement.

**

We had a call from David Mozan, who wanted to arrange an outing for us. We invited him around to the office to admire our new flat above and the children were anxious to show him their painted areas. We contacted the rental agency as we were ready at last.

**

September means the beginning of the autumn school term and they all went off wearing shiny new black shoes, itchy new cardigans over starchy shirts and the correct underwear and ties. Kit bags carried the winter sports gear needed for the term, freshly marked trainers and running shoes, socks and paraphernalia. It wouldn't be long before No.2 had lost half of her tracksuit, No.3 had gained a plimsoll and No.1 had lost his crafts bag on the sports field. It was useless asking why his crafts bag was on the sports field as an evasive mumbled answer only served to annoy, no, enrage rather. How could anyone even as multi-talented as No.1 play football and sketch or paint at the same time, I thundered? Would you take football boots into the art room and use them there? Eventually, of course, he offered to confess. I gave one look at his sheepish face and started to reach for a gleaming bottle of red then thought better of it. Confess? Good God.

We went into the kitchen away from flapping ears and I gave him a can of Coke to help the flow.

His embarrassed face unnerved me and the vicious pulling of his jumper sleeve made it worse. 'Right then, Buster. Off you go.'

'OK. Look Mum, you know how you say that it's normal like to be curious? And you say it's normal to want to find out stuff and it's normal like to have feelings and sort of want to look at pictures and girls and that?'

Oh God. 'Mm, go on. We don't need so many "likes" and "sort ofs". How does this mean you took your crafts bag to the sports field?'

'It just, sort of happened. Sorry. It was so fast. I didn't mean for all that to happen.' Pleading face, desperate gulp of Coke.

I began to pluck my own jumper sleeve. 'What happened? Was anyone hurt?'

'Mm, well, I don't really know because I ran to get Coach to call an ambulance and he wouldn't let me go back. It was darned lucky he had a mobile phone though, Mum. They're pretty useful things. Can I have one? I could have called them myself, would of been quicker if I'd had one.'

'For God's sake tell me what bloody happened! Start at the beginning and carry on.' Patience, never a strong point with me, evaporated. 'It was at break when I went to get my kit that I looked through the telescope. I swung it round looking at the sports field, watching Jock inspecting the white lines, you know they've just been re-painted and then I just moved it a bit to the right, to the edge of those bushes that you like, by the little clearing and then I saw them. By the hawthorns and the crab apples and the rhododendrons, and the hollies,' he finished.

'Yes OK, OK. Who were they? What were they doing?' Why did I feel just a little uneasy?

'Dunno who they were. There were five of them with a lovely little vintage car so I focused on the car and, um, then I realised what they were doing.'

'What?' I started clawing along the work top and looked around weakly for the wine bottle which I had left in the dining room. My coffee was cold and didn't cut it anyway.

'One had a camera and the others were posing, and stuff, and so I just decided I was going to go and have a look.'

'On your own?'

'Yes, I wanted to tell John but he'd gone already so I changed and left. Then instead of going on the field I skirted around the bushes and hid behind the little fence thingy. And I started to watch. Well, I had a good position behind the broken oak branches and got out my sketch book.'

'Sketch book? You meant to draw what you could see?' Gulp. Stifle scream of wild laughter. 'Right, um, right then. So, what was the accident?'

'Well the one with the camera was telling the others what to do. I wished I'd had a camera there, Mum. See? A mobile phone could have captured it.'

'Go on!'

'Right, well I was sketching the first one, a really beautiful girl, Mum, with great big kn - boobs, I mean, and the bloke with the camera told the first guy where to position himself on the car and he climbed up then the other girl had to get on it as well, then the last guy. They were all twisted round with arms and legs all over the place. And did I tell you they were naked? Well, they were and I was just turning my pad around to get them all on the page, when I dropped my pens box and it made a little noise as it bounced on the stone and all the stuff inside fell out. Anyway, it meant that the photographer turned to look at what had caused the noise and saw me behind the ivy post, and he shouted out and somehow the four of them balancing on the bonnet all fell off. It would have been OK, I think, if they'd fallen towards him in the clearing but they didn't. They fell into the bushes. You know, the ones you like, um, the blackthorns and hollies. Well, they screamed, and couldn't get out and the photographer was trying to help. It was so loud that I just left my bag and ran to get Coach. And, well, then I don't know anything else.'

Good God.

'Wait.' I charged into the dining room and grabbed the wine from the table, opened it and glugged from the bottle. I went back into the kitchen, then reached for a glass and demurely poured a measure. No.1 glanced at the bottle and watched me pour. 'Have you heard from Coach at all, did he tell you what he saw?' Quieter now, but inside I was in hysterics. What a way to watch a porn film, in the flesh.

'No, he was angry because I'd bunked football so I've got detention on Friday. And I've lost my crafts bag because I couldn't go back and pick it all up.'

I made a quick call to Coach and I arranged to call into the lost property office. Coach had quickly summed up the situation and called 999, then gathered up the contents of the pencils box and the bag. An ambulance was summoned along with several police cars and four red-faced people wrapped in blankets were taken off to various destinations. 'Make sure you read next Friday's local paper,' he said, laughing.

Chapter 9

Our tenants moved in. They did not come from the agency we had booked but knew someone who worked there. This should have sounded warning bells but they had references and a bank reference which quoted in each case that "Miss whoever was unlikely to enter into a commitment that they felt they couldn't fulfil." This was a general response that banks churned out when they didn't really know much about a person but liked the look of them. One worked for Inland Revenue and the other for the army.

We received our first month's rent and two weeks' deposit. We were chuffed. All that hard work had apparently paid off. We paid our first payment on our business loan and thought we were entrepreneurs.

A few weeks later a bright green Austin car appeared in front of our window and stayed there. 'My auntie gave it to me.' The soldier said brightly.

What could I say? There was enough room in front of the office for that car and ours too with enough spare for a visiting client so it seemed petty and mean to complain. They did wobble off in it a few times and it was vivid enough to attract notice, so it was fun really.

We rarely saw the girls coming and going and were unprepared for their refusal to open the door or answer the telephone when I called them when rent payment day came and went. At last the soldier came in wearing civvies and gave me a cheque for half the amount. The remainder would be sorted as fast as possible, she explained, as the other girl had apparently lost her job. How on earth does a person lose their job from Inland Revenue? I wondered, I thought it was blue chip.

The rest of the month came and went and the soldier, when glimpsed rushing from the door and down the road, was without her uniform so it appeared that she was no longer working for the army.

I called their banks, who refused to discuss their clients or the bland references.

I contacted the DSS office, who refused to discuss the matter but when I got upset and asked why they were shielding liars and thieves and not helping honest hard-working folk who were just trying to earn a living and had children to look after and a bank loan to service, and ...

The crusty voiced operative, who must at that time have taken pity on me or just wanted to stop the onslaught of words that resembled ramblings interrupted my flow to say, 'Mrs Prentice, sorry but we have no files on these two persons. They cannot have registered for benefits or help with rent payments.'

Ahh, thanks.

I wrote to our tenants a letter giving notice to quit.

Nothing happened. They seemed to be settled upstairs and probably coming out when we had gone home, although Denny had seen several gentlemen callers arriving and leaving. How marvellous, I thought. We have a house of ill repute upstairs and impressionable children to watch and hopefully not learn downstairs.

Another month went by and we were more than anxious. We would have to spend more money going to court and then more money getting bailiffs to evict them, and it was our furniture and equipment up there so probably nothing to seize. Then we had a break.

A burly young builder had been coming in for engineering for a beam and he heard us complaining among ourselves. Denny knew him and filled him in on the woeful tale. The next day, we arrived at the office and found an envelope with the keys and a ragged cheque for a small part of the debt and an apology note saying they would pay us the arrears soon. There was no forwarding address.

Apparently, this burly saviour had seen them in the pub and threatened them. He spoke in a loud voice, so everyone knew where they were living and cheating us and as others among the drinkers knew and thankfully liked us, there soon developed a general roar of disapproval and boos. They downed their drinks and went home to pack, taking their belongings but leaving the car.

I contacted DVLA but they refused to let me know who had registered it. I contacted the police to report a dumped car on our forecourt and they told us it wasn't a hindrance or nuisance to the public, it wasn't dangerous so there was no interest. So, while Chris was out, Denny and I, with the help of the children pushed the car to the edge of the pavement, so it completely blocked the bus stop and one wheel was overhanging the kerb. We left it and slunk back inside. The next morning when we drove up to start a new day we noticed that someone, possibly the police, had towed the wretched thing away.

A quick call back to the rental agency started the whole thing again. They were sorry to learn of our experience and were unaware of their staff member acting behind all our backs and promised to find us suitable tenants. The helpful person had also left their job and we had no choice but to move on, lessons learned.

**

We were pleased to welcome Terry and Marlene Jenkins, who turned up out of the blue. They had been on holiday and their house was now halfway finished but they were still living in a caravan in the garden. They showed us some "before and after" photographs and I had to admire them for the skills and finishes. He had been a successful surveyor for years and now could turn his hand to building trades, only hiring help when he needed muscle to lift and dig, doing all the brick laying, plumbing, even stonework which could look horrible if not carried out properly. He confessed to using a specialist roofing company, however, and windows manufacturer. He had to use slate roof tiles and timber framed sash windows which had to be made to measure. The wiring for a new electricity system he had installed and was paying a suitably qualified electrician to check and sign off with a certificate. We were impressed. He had allegedly bought the dilapidated Georgian mansion for a song but could have made a serious mistake if the reparations cost more than he had allowed or budgeted for. They had been living up there for about six months or so and certainly looked well. They intended contacting David Mozan for a catch up before returning to Norfolk and I told them I had put in a call to him that very morning inviting him to join us for supper. Our No.3 silently adored him and would sit with his head resting on his arms, just looking at him. I asked him why the fascination and he shrugged. 'I like his long black hair, Mum and his hands. They're long and bony and his fingers are always moving.'

Terry and Marlene wanted to stay, too, so they went off on various errands and promised to see us at six in the evening. They passed me a crisp note which I accepted towards the food, which I knew would amount to a small fortune. Denny went to buy bottles of Coke and lemonade for the children and went to lay the table in the rear room, which would be a bit cramped but hopefully good fun.

**

Chris was on his way back from school. He had been to watch No.1 win a race and apparently set a new school record, which cheered him up immensely. The weather was beginning to lose temperature now and he had been standing around so the victory more than made up for the dampening chill. While there he searched out the other two and brought them back to the office. 'Homework to be done straight away, please!' I ordered. 'We have guests for dinner.'

The dinner had to be an early one as the children obviously had to get up for school and Chris sent out for a variety of dishes from Mrs Chin. We knew that Terry and Marlene had no dietary restrictions but did not wish to compromise David as he was a Muslim. He admitted to being lax and we had seen him drink a beer or glass of wine, but would never have served him pork, for example. Also we were not sure whether he ate shellfish. The boxes were kept separate and we allowed him to help himself as everyone else did, too.

The meeting was a huge success and Terry said we must meet up at theirs when their dining room was ready and we looked forward to it. We still had no idea of the address.

Looking at the glowing faces of our children we knew they benefited enormously from these social gatherings and were learning how to socialise with all sorts of people, religions and creeds were no obstacle.

At the door, David remembered he had an envelope for us. 'It's an invitation,' he explained.

'What for?' from Chris.

'The wedding of a son of a friend. I am the Best Man.' Did Muslim bridegrooms have a Best Man? I didn't ask. 'Bring the children too,' he added and off he roared in his beautiful car.

**

We had a call from the letting agency, who wanted to show a couple of young ladies our flat and when would be convenient? Could we allow them access tomorrow evening and if acceptable, could they move in at the weekend? I was so grateful I would have welcomed them at midnight. I assured them I would be here and if the paperwork had been completed they certainly could move in at the weekend.

Thank you, all sorts of guardian angels for watching over us, it all worked out well.

They were two school teachers who had just reportedly moved to London and changed schools and after searching for a suitable flat chose ours. Both coming from the Welsh valleys they had a delightful lilting accent which I have always liked. Both our boys appeared to feel the same and spent too much time keeping a watch on the buses and somehow needing to go out on the front pavement as the girls approached their door. One was blonde with blue eyes and the other was very dark with deep brown eyes and both extremely pretty. I believe that this was their first job but didn't ask. It was important for us that they kept the flat in good order and paid their bills on time.

No.3, being younger, had no teenage pre-puberty issues and shamelessly called them brightly to look at his latest picture or see the Lego model he was making. This enabled No.1 to sidle up casually, holding a calculus table or hideous geometrical diagram which he hoped they would be impressed by. They didn't seem to mind our young Lotharios bothering them, so I gave up in the end and hoped it was good for our relationship.

All seemed to go very well, but we had an anxious moment one evening when Denny called us to say he'd just been to get some chips before Mrs Chin closed and saw our blonde tenant carrying an armful of packs of fish and chips, all newspaper wrapped. 'You feeling hungry?' he joked. 'They're for my brother and his team mates. We've been in the pub now I've got supper. It's the Welsh Rugby team. They're playing the match against England tomorrow.'

'Ah, mate. They're not all staying up there, are they?' Lewdly wondering who she might pair off with, I've no doubt.

'No, No. there's a coach coming at eleven to pick them all up. Night.'

Denny thought this extremely funny as he related it all to us but we felt sick. The whole parade of buildings was old and if they had decided to have a party or twenty odd people did the knees-up, the whole timber floor stood a chance of caving in. We took deep breaths and waited and as the clock passed eleven felt lucky, as this surely meant the floor remained intact and there were no casualties. Chris thought he didn't want to scare them, but decided to warn them of the possible risk and hoped they wouldn't think he was censoring them.

**

We had the go-ahead to proceed as agents in the insurance claim of the badly fractured house Chris had reported on. The mid terraced house had a rear addition creating an "L" shape, which was attached on one side to the house next door, leaving a paved area to the side of the kitchen and in front of the dining room: the adjacent house on this side had an identical area leading to their kitchen door. The flank wall of the rear addition was badly distorted, curving outwards from the ground level to its widest part midway, being at ceiling level of the floor above and bowing inwards from that part towards the eaves. There were horizontal fractures between the window sills of the bedroom and bathroom and more at the window heads of the kitchen windows and doorway. The brickwork had vertical fractures from the ground leading upwards and the corner brickwork had de-bonded at the rear corner, leaving great gaps of 25mm between brick courses. The end wall of the kitchen rear addition was similarly affected, the whole leaning downwards towards the corner. Chris had dictated a graphic description into the tape recorder and I typed it. The client's insurance company had contacted us immediately and asked us to proceed with any tests that needed doing and prepare a scheme to repair the building. In cases of movement it was usual to carry out tests by excavating trial pits close to the damaged wall and continue digging until the footings were exposed. This usually showed about a metre of brickwork which corbelled out towards the bottom or founded on a strip of concrete. The idea was to then look at the exposed footings to see if there were any fractures which had continued below ground. A sample of the soil would also be extracted and sent for analysis and drains close by would be examined and a CCTV survey carried out. Often there would be roots found in the sub soil and tests would prove that they had gradually removed all the moisture in the soil in this area and caused the building footings to sink, known as subsidence. It was usual to fasten glass "tell tales" over chosen fractures and carry out a monthly inspection to monitor any movement for a year to cover the growing seasons of the trees. At the end of this time underpinning would be installed. This comprises about a metre deep of concrete being installed beneath a section of the wall, a metre wide at a time. Several days would be allowed for this to set or "go off" before the section next would be treated. Fractures in the walls would be repaired by installing metal rods and fixing with an epoxy resin then completing the repair by re-pointing the external brickwork and re-plastering internally to make good. The offending trees would have been pruned back at the beginning of the monitoring time, as fewer branches need less moisture and roots less likely to seek so thirstily.

In this case, with differing movement evident in one small property, there was no time to spare. By lifting the manhole cover it could be seen that roots had invaded the space and fractured the walls of the chamber and pipes and Chris did this on his first visit.

The apple tree next door and leylandii within this garden had between them unwittingly destroyed the drainage structure by blocking several pipes with their roots and drying the surrounding soil so badly it caused the rear wall to subside, which then continued to pull away the brickwork, leaving jagged edges. The flank wall had borne the brunt of a World War II bomb which had fallen in an adjacent garden, destroying their rear addition completely and several garden sheds. At least the insurers could not wriggle out of making a payment as the damage could not be passed off as wear and tear. There was no waiting period this time. Instantly the trees were severely pollarded and the manhole re-built. Around the edges of the brick built chamber a degradable boarding was laid to prevent further roots encroaching.

Inside the house the first-floor joists had separated from the wall where it had pulled out. There was a gap between the wall and skirting boards and a gap beneath where the kitchen below could be seen through the void. Wisely, they had pulled the bed away from the edge of the room.

The end wall could be underpinned and saved but the flank wall was too badly distorted and had to be demolished and re-built. The family moved out and stayed with relatives locally, so the children continued at school and they could keep an eye on their home.

The builders installed scaffolding and boards to support the roof and the ceiling over the kitchen.

Within a couple of days, the dangerous wall had been removed, a new cavity brick and block wall constructed, carefully toothing into the corner, the windows and door which had been stored was re-used, fascias and gutters replaced and the garden restored.

Internally the plastering had been made good, all the floor joists now spanned into the wall again and floors were re-laid with new skirting boards, primed and painted. The bedroom carpet had been stored and re-laid and the happy couple treated their daughter to new curtains.

We were particularly thrilled with this job and the swift way the insurers had responded, and by allowing us to act as the agents liaising with the loss adjusters and running the whole show, we were entitled to ten per cent of the total costs. Back in the office with no onlookers we high fived, as this fee alone had paid for three months' school fees.

The second bonus was a letter from the insurers asking if our name could be included in their contacts as they had been impressed by our workmanship and professionalism and wished to recommend us to similar clients. Of course, we agreed.

Deborah came into the office smiling and not minding Chris standing there pulling his quizzical unbeliever's expression and thanked us profusely for our help with that project. 'She's my sister, you see.' We hadn't known there was a link. I hadn't noticed any crucifixes or holy pictures on the walls. No statues of Mary holding an infant, nothing. They must have been staying with Deborah and we hadn't known.

She asked for a few copies to be made of a poem she had and I gave them to her "on the house".

When she left, I reminded Chris that our work came from many and more and more recommendations from people we barely knew, so he was not to show how scornful he was of another person's beliefs as you never knew when they could be useful. 'Righto, oh shallow one.' Bowing. 'Suitably chastised I am.' He nodded and irreverently did the sign of the cross. I threw a rubber at him which glanced nicely off his temple.

**

The day of the wedding dawned and we got everyone dressed reasonably tidily and made our way over to a large community hall in Upton Park. This was our first wedding reception for an Asian couple and we were intrigued. We knew that the actual wedding had taken place elsewhere, probably the local Mosque and possibly the register office too and this was the celebratory gathering for the wider family and friends. There was no sign of the happy couple or their parents. Oddly, there was a bar within the hall which was unexpected but welcome and we accepted a small glass of wine. I wondered if obtaining an alcoholic drink at this reception showed disrespect, but Chris said David wouldn't have invited us or installed a bar if it was supposed to be taboo for everybody. David was forward thinking, I believe, for a Muslim at the time, as he said just because it's there doesn't mean everyone has to drink it. He had ordered the bar with alcohol for those that would welcome it but did not expect trouble. I thought that many devout Muslims would not want to be in a place that had alcohol.

There was some dancing by the men but I thought a bit half-hearted and I wondered if the Westerners present embarrassed them.

The women clustered at one end of the hall, separate from the men.

Suddenly a mild commotion occurred and a small group entered. The bride, heavily veiled, decorated and wearing red and the groom came in, surrounded by attendants and went into a corner, whereupon the women encompassed her and he left them and walked into the crowd of men. This was clearly not the sort of reception that we had experienced. 'Why is the bride in there?' queried No.3 of David as he approached our table.

'The ladies are talking to her, giving their support and answering her questions,' answered David and smiling, he went to greet some late guests.

'Reading her the *Kama Sutra*,' muttered Chris at me quietly but I ignored him as I was thinking along similar lines. I felt sorry for her.

David returned to our table and said he had a few people he wished to introduce us to after the food had arrived, so I satisfied my curiosity.

I asked him if the marriage was arranged and if she had met him before, he affirmed it was arranged but she gave her consent to the marriage. I still didn't know whether he was a total stranger to her but it seemed that she had had a say in it, she had been shown some photos and trusted her parents' judgement. The bridegroom was not imported from elsewhere apparently and it was not forced. 'Why does the bride wear a veil?' asked No.3. 'Why can't we go to see her. She won't know who we are.'

He bit back a smile, I think his curious outspoken ways amused him. 'She isn't allowed to take off the veil until later. Her new husband is the first to see her face. She can see through it though and I'm sure she knows who you are. I will make sure they know what present came from you.'

Our little one nodded.

David was happily chatting to us and the children when I noticed that the numbers present had increased. An Englishman unknown to us approached and reminded David it was time for his first welcoming speech so he loped off across the hall.

The speech was not spoken in English but in Punjabi, with odd passages in Arabic, I believe, and he finished with a couple of sentences directed at us and the other Europeans present. There were apparently a mix of Irish, Swedish and Germans there, all looking as bemused as us.

I was just about to nudge Chris and suggest it was time we left as we were all getting hungry and sitting around in the hall, knowing so few, was a bit uncomfortable just as the food, arrived heralded by a commotion at the rear double doors where trolleys clanked in, bearing enormous pots of food. Trestle tables sprang up and the pots were spread along evenly. Somebody came and served the bridal couple and smells wafting over to us were amazing. We looked at the heaps of spring rolls and pakoras and other appetizers unknown to us which were being laid on plates and handed round the tables. 'Ladies and gentlemen, please come to the servery and receive your refreshments.'

We joined the already forming queue and the caterers, wearing huge white aprons, spooned mounds of white basmati rice and lamb curry onto cardboard plates. Another added strips of naan bread and chapattis and handed them to us. We took our plates gleefully and helped ourselves to an assortment of pickles and chutneys, paper napkins, a plastic spoon and fork and sat back down to greedily devour our fragrant, tasty food.

Afterwards they had sweets and Asian desserts, wonderful fruit salads and tarts and cheesecakes. Crystal bowls of sweet flavoured rice had coloured grains and almonds and raisins; cubes of a sort of fudge were decorated with silver and gold leaf and laid on trays. Many of the desserts were made with evaporated milk or dried skimmed milk powder and the children were impressed. I was glad we didn't leave when I first suggested it.

We had spoken to a few people and been introduced to more and would in due course meet them again.

'The food was marvellous, David,' Chris said. 'Please thank the happy couple for their hospitality. We will leave soon if you don't mind as it's getting late for No.3 to be out.'

I had to shake the little one's arm a little at this point, as he had started to shout that he wasn't tired and didn't want to go home. 'And,' he shouted, 'I haven't said "congratulations" to the bride. I still can't see her!'

I glared at him and David squatted down to talk to him. 'Our weddings are different to western ones. The bride has to have her face hidden from everyone else until her new husband has seen her. She isn't allowed to speak to men, so you cannot go to give her your good wishes, but you have given them a card and a gift and one day I expect you can meet her.'

'OK.' And he was quiet. I secretly wondered whether David could come to live with us. 'Thanks David, for this experience. It's been very enjoyable.'

'Chris,' he called, touching his arm, 'I wanted to invite you out for dinner to discuss my warehouse.' He looked down at No.3's questioning face and finished, 'It will be late, dear, so this one is just for your parents. Is Thursday evening OK? Come to my house, about eight?'

Then he promised, specially for the children, a trip to the factory to watch the glass being made, rolled into sheets then cut and go to the timber factory upstairs to see the pictures being framed.

**

The week started for Chris with a new local valuation in the morning and dimensional survey for an extension immediately afterwards.

I was making a drink in the kitchen when a couple of the police officers that we had known called in for a routine chat. They wanted to know if we had learned any more about the people or situation concerned with the basement. I told them I had had another threatening call but since I had yelled back at him we hadn't been bothered again. I went over the names of the thugs that I knew but I think there was nothing new. As far as we were concerned the project was over and the council had signed it off. One asked if we had been back and I said it was probably the last place I ever would go willingly. They left.

**

I had made sandwiches for us three and placed them on separate plates, which I was carrying in from the kitchen just as the two Yugoslavian builders came in to see Chris. They decided to wait for him so I offered the first plate for Mochan, known as Mickie, to help himself. Instead of taking one as expected, he seized the plate from my hand. I couldn't stop laughing when this happened as I was about to give it to Denny and the shocked look on his face was so funny. I had to go back to make another heap as his worker had now taken hold of mine and only Chris's was left intact. The salad had now gone and the replacements consisted of cheese and tomato. Denny was so cross that his second plate had no salad. I found him a little chocolate bar and slid it on his saucer but he sulked and fumed all the afternoon.

**

We received the document for planning consent to partially re-build Graham's workshop and garage. This had not been an easy achievement because many of the councillors had wanted to demolish it and install housing there. It was an eyesore but knowing the standard of Graham's work I was confident he would transform it and luckily the planners had seen the wisdom of our words on the application, that the jobs of four people and a couple of juniors would be safeguarded

I called Graham to tell him the good news and he was delighted. 'That's brilliant Chris, I'll call in later to give you some money.'

Wow. Result.

We had recently formed quite a good working relationship with our local planners and they had begun to allow us to call in with rough schemes, which a few of them would spend time assessing for appearance and impact and pass on their verbal advice as to suitability. Of course, this was just verbal and also at officer level only and could not be regarded as set in stone, but it enabled us to reiterate to our occasional pushy client the parameters involved. This was also useful as far as the officers and we were concerned and it meant a mutual trust had grown. I think it was initially because we refused to prepare exorbitant schemes which we knew had no chance of success.

The greed of some smaller developers was apparent in some of the schemes submitted. A rather annoying sequence of events had evolved whereby an unsuitable scheme for too many flats was submitted. Of course, it would be refused as everybody expected but the refusal notice would list the points which had caused the refusal.

A new scheme would be devised, trimming the scheme and suggesting a donation for the local park. This second scheme as it was considered a repeat application would not attract a second fee. During the following couple of months, a series of unfortunate happenings would occur on the site: the police would be contacted to report tramps or drunkards or drug takers or dealing. Rats would be reported to the environment health department and people would panic and tell of their terrified dog, children, rabbits and an engineered hysteria develop. A fire would break out in parts and reports of arsonists and dangerous thugs. Sometimes a ringleader would go door to door collecting signatures either in favour of the proposal or against it. All this nuisance propaganda would filter through to the planners, who were then pressurised to allow the site to be demolished and a desirable housing scheme to be erected as the people in the area were frightened and sick of the state. It was a brave group of planners able to withstand this type of onslaught and stick to their guns about the viability of a scheme and throw out yet another monstrosity until finally a suitable set of drawings showing decent landscaping and amenity space was submitted and approved, sometimes.

It was infuriating for Chris, who always endeavoured to produce attractive schemes and work within the guidelines only to see a housing association walk off with a substantially larger idea but providing smaller gardens, fewer parking places and sometimes inadequate room sizes. I never knew whether bribes were being passed over or how the blatant overlooking of stated rules could be ignored on these occasional developments. When we queried our findings, there was a deal of huffing and puffing and the explanation of such crippling lack of housing, it was necessary to form units for the growing waiting list of people in need. Our small private developers who were building and selling to the private market, however, received no such allowances. Planners were not taught to be practical and mostly had never worked in private practice and the concept of costings never emerged.

I couldn't wait for Chris to return but he would be in later. He had gone to school to collect the children and they all stayed to watch No.2 play in a netball match. He arrived with the entourage just after five o'clock, at the same time as Graham, so I sent No.1 to choose their suppers from Mrs Chin and he returned with paper-wrapped parcels containing pies and chips. I hoped there was a rudiment of nourishment in the pies. It didn't do to worry too much when these occasional late evenings happened that they were being malnourished as they had decent breakfasts and well balanced lunches. We were so busy and anyway I had a hearty hotpot slowly perfecting in the oven for tomorrow.

While the three speedily demolished their greasy spoon food in the back room and homework was tackled, Chris sat and discussed with Graham the scheme he had prepared for his site.

The shape of the land was a triangle, having the long side at the front and pointy corners at each end. The small left hand side corner was shown to contain the dustbin store, having sides and a roof. The dustbin collectors were allowed to walk a certain distance according to union rules so thought had to be given for this. A bicycle store was positioned behind it to encourage people to ride bikes and forget the car. Luckily bus stops were virtually outside. This was helpful as a more flexible parking scheme could sometimes be accepted and the planners during pre-application talks had indicated so. We had produced two two-bedroom units, two one-bedroom units and a split-level penthouse comprising three bedrooms and a small private garden on the flat roof. We showed Astroturf, a small paved area and various pots of unspecified plants. The scheme was modern with steel and glass and tiny balconies to the front and sides. Ingeniously the balconies' calculated floor space when added to the amenity space on the ground floor just scraped past the target criterion. Storage cupboards had been shown to the side but we changed them to show a garage to the penthouse and a small timber hut to house the mower and general gardening equipment. I was so proud of Chris for this innovative design and Graham was thrilled. 'Submit it, mate,' he said. 'We'll take our chance.'

I calculated the council application fee and ordered the Ordnance Survey extract maps which were needed to accompany the application. Bizarrely, we were allowed to purchase the map extracts from this East End council themselves, as they held a licence to print them instead of ordering directly from Ordnance Survey and I always thought it a paradox that the same department that provided them also requested them for the application packages. Coals to Newcastle or similar, but they obviously found the fees useful, I grudgingly thought they supplied the tea and biscuits fund or financed the staff Christmas party.

Graham promised that Lindsay would call in the next day with the relevant cheques for submission and a second stage payment for ourselves. I had been working on the quarterly VAT return and was quietly pleased that I had put enough away for Her Majesty's dues again this month, as well as saving for our tax bills and children's salaries.

I reasoned that our hard work was showing dividends: there were no red figures on our statements and our savings were slowly growing again. Our lovely tenants were nicely covering our small business loan payments and I figured if we could stand the pace for another year the flat loan would be repaid and Chris could change his car.

Chapter 10

To our surprise and relieved delight, we had a call from the missing and believed murdered Mr Evans. He had been in hospital apparently. He told us he had scribbled his notes on a large envelope, addressed it to his department for noting and filing and pushed it through a Royal Mail post-box, as he believed he was being followed and felt ill. 'But why did you not call someone? I've been out of my mind worrying about Chris being involved in it and we've had so many horrible calls.'

'I can only apologise,' he said, 'but I'm back now and will transfer to another Council. The bloody basement got finished and passed, didn't it?'

'Yes, but the police found your car abandoned and they found a body which they thought was you. Any ideas?' I was still angry with him, even if he had been ill. Perhaps he had overreacted. I knew I would never choose those clients as best friends or buddies, but this man's disappearance had terrified me into believing they were all deadly thugs. I thought of the hastily arranged holidays to get the children to safety and all those sleepless nights wondering if we could go into witness protection and how the children would react, worried about my mum being left on her own and how we would earn a living. 'I have informed my department and been to the police so hopefully it will be OK, but I just wanted to let Chris know all was well.'

What a fool, I thought. He could have asked a nurse to call someone. It couldn't have been pleasant for the Gold family to be chief suspects in a murder that clearly, they had not been involved in as Chief Mouse Evans had reappeared, large as life and daft as a brush. I wondered what had really happened to spook him so severely. I also wondered who the dead person was. I resolved to call the police to try for an update. Obviously, their enquiries had been prematurely ended and they would be back at square one, sifting through missing persons. How infuriatingly time wasting it was, like our situation when we got knocked back at the planning stage from time to time. Well, not so serious but a bit like it.

Chris had a valuation to carry out a few miles away and on the way to school so I went with him so I could tell him all about the resurrected council officer and make myself feel better by having a rant. He was suitably furious but in his usual good natured, forgiving way suggested he may have had a nervous breakdown. So, that makes it all OK then, I muttered.

We arrived at the terraced house to carry out an inspection and Chris promptly measured the site to arrive at a gross floor size in order to calculate a re-building cost in case of need. This was for insurance purposes. The house was shabby and garishly painted, unless you liked red or black ceilings and net stuff draped over some of the corners, like a spider's web, I shuddered.

Chris jumped all over the rooms. This strange habit of his, apart from being noisy, told him a lot about the state of the floors: if they were uneven, if they were suspended timber, if they deflected.

Suddenly he found a loose floorboard and prised it up. 'God, Chris, don't,' I pleaded and he laughed, pulling a box out. Having only begun to recover from our basement scare I didn't fancy someone walking in and seeing Chris on his knees, holding aloft a small security box which had been deliberately hidden in the floor joists.

With one of his Leatherman gadgets he picked the lock and the lid sprang open. 'Don't be a goose, Chris. The door locks have been changed, the house has been re-possessed. Look, there's a tape recorder and some old pre-decimal coins, the kids will be interested in those.'

'I'll tell the bank, don't worry, you know I wouldn't steal.'

We listened to the recorded messages. They appeared to be recorded bits of evidence as to why an unknown woman wanted a divorce: nothing really juicy, just a long whining account of day to day moans and vague threats. Chris knew nothing about the previous residents but clearly interest had gone out of the relationship and the mortgage unpaid, as the house had been empty for over a year and was being sold at a bargain price. Let's hope the negative vibes would be eradicated with the removal of the machine and Halloween style décor changed with a lick of paint.

When we collected our children, we went straight home, as we had arranged to visit David Mozan's home for dinner. I had left a mild chicken curry in the oven set on a timer switch and the house smelled wonderful as we entered the hall. I thought if I gave the children curry they would complain less about being left with a baby sitter, knowing we likely would be given curry by David. I set about making some pilau rice in the microwave and dished it all up. We managed to get ourselves showered and changed in record time and leaving our phone numbers with our minder, hurried off with glee. Free for a couple of hours.

David's flat was superb. It was clean and almost clinically arranged, painted throughout in white emulsion with pale carpeting, immaculate blinds and minimalistic furnishings. The wide hallway swept to the left into an open-plan lounge leading off to a dining area and kitchen with a utility room and WC room disguised as cupboards. Two other doors led from the hall to the right which I assumed to be bedrooms. 'Chris, twice,' David smiled, 'let me take your coats. Would you like to look around?'

Is the pope Catholic? 'Thank you, David, how lovely'

It was lovely. Two utterly masculine bedrooms, both with an en-suite and sharing a dressing room looked like pages from a magazine. No sign of a woman anywhere. I couldn't help wondering.

A huge white china vase held pink and cream lilies, enhancing the general Homes & Gardens scene, but they have a smell which I hate with a passion. Thank goodness they were near the hall, I would have had trouble eating if they were in the dining area.

We accepted a cocktail he had made and I am not sure what was in it, but honestly could have drained the jug. 'That's delicious, David. Thank you.'

The food was simple, as I expected. No shellfish, no pork, no beef. We had chicken off the bone with almonds and a creamy sauce, a lamb curry with yellow basmati rice and various vegetables which I spooned copiously onto Chris's plate on his behalf. He couldn't object at the table, far too rude, but managed a small glare. Then the crowning glory as far as I was concerned, as restaurants rarely stock them now, preferring ice cream, a silver-plated bowl of steaming Glulab Jamun and a jug of cream. I believe I squealed with delight, loving these little oblong puddings swimming in sugary rosewater.

David was grinning at me widely. Chris must have told him how the children and I loved them. 'I have a box of them for the children. Don't let me forget to give them to you.'

The talk turned to business and his projects. We were progressing well. The warehouse scheme was on the point of submission and the twin building drawn up ready to prepare the proposals for the bed and breakfast hostel.

He told us a bit more about himself. He had been married once, he told us. To the daughter of a wealthy Englishman who owned a major West End department store. The parents were never openly racist against him and he mixed socially with many extremely rich people in their circle. In the end, I believe differing cultures prised them apart, he had wanted children and she resisted. The large detached house on the borders of Wanstead flats was sold and she took her Porsche and he kept the Rolls Royce.

The next revelation which stunned us was his confession of once being in prison. I wondered if this was the reason he did not contact his parents. A thought flickered briefly of his kindness to the children and I wondered with churning stomach muscles what his crime had been. 'I acted as an estate agent soon after I arrived,' he started to explain. 'Business was booming and with another guy, my partner at the time, who was a surveyor and property valuer, we were in demand. Unfortunately, I am a sucker for a sob story and hated to disappoint the young couples who wanted to buy the houses. My business partner carried out the valuations and I helped the prospective purchasers to fill out the application forms to send to the building societies. I regret to tell you that acting out of stupid benevolence, we doctored the figures, which enabled our clients to afford the payments and we sold the houses. All went well until someone let the cat out of the bag and we were forced to stop trading. My partner lost his licence and I was sent on remand to Pentonville. I was in there for two months waiting for the case to reach Court but I enjoyed the experience.'

We both murmured something a bit vague and he went on. 'I was never put in with violent prisoners and was considered a low risk, white collar criminal if you like and met some interesting people. In fact, I have some of the guys I met staying in the hostel, the bit that's already open. The ones who've never had a home and can't hold down a job have their room and breakfast and can eat from the canteen through the day. Unfortunately, they like a can or six and live their lives in a sort of boozy haze but it's all they want or need. I get paid by the local council so it helps everyone. I have cleaners there all the time that change the bed linen and even wash their clothes, so in my way I am repaying my debt to society. Occasionally some of them have to let off intoxicated steam and the odd incident occurs but so far, it has never needed an ambulance or police intervention. We installed a small gym recently, which helps with the fitter ones. My secretary is brilliant and has managed to find jobs for some of the younger ones.

'Anyway, my case came up and the judge read through the charges and dismissed the case. He asked if anyone had been hurt. Obviously, no-one had. He asked who had been harmed by my Robin Hood antics and the answer was again negative, so he threw it out. He advised that I refrained from repeating the practice for anyone who looked worthy or needy and that I changed my job. So, I am no longer an estate agent. I had to pay court costs and my barrister of course, but I got a small sum awarded for the incarceration I suffered. Since then I have sold cars, imported foreign foods, and settled as a property developer and landlord. As I am now.'

He smiled. Wow. What a tale.

Obviously, we asked questions and he told us stories about some of his fellow detainees. He met a forger who produced replica masterpieces. Most people realised that a real painting would hardly be sold in a small art shop and the "originals" on show must be reproductions, especially when there were several identical copies of them, but there is no accounting for the stupidity and greed of some people and eventually a mean-minded moaner complained to Trading Standards and the artist was nicked. He had a fair judge, too. He said his time on remand would cancel out his three month sentence and he was therefore free to go. 'What is he doing now?' I asked.

'Exactly the same as he was,' replied David. 'He can't do anything else. Only now, he doesn't sign them as Rembrandt or whoever. He makes a few changes and signs them himself. Doing OK too. He does books and poster illustrations as well. I meet him from time to time.'

We told him of our recent experience with threats associated with the basement. He asked for the names of the people involved with the Gold family and their cohorts so we told him. He smiled a bit at the name of Del Smith and told us he believed they had been involved in the Brink's mat robbery as well as others, only partially solved. There was only one genuine shopkeeper selling jewellery among the group we had met and gold changed hands on the black market, was melted and re-fashioned and sold all over England and probably Europe. No wonder someone was nervous, but the warnings only served to make us suspicious. We were right to feel that the whole gang that we had met were charming and polite to us, but crooked, vile and dangerous and we were glad it had all ended. I could not get out of my mind that the unfortunate dead person was dressed in the same colours as Mr Evans and had similar thinning ginger hair. Mistaken identity perhaps: they may have thought they had silenced Mr Evans and when he realised what had happened, he was more resolved than ever to stay out of sight. He would be too scared now to tell what he knew, if anything, so the gang probably thought they were safe. I told my theories to David, who looked thoughtful.

We changed the subject and I told him about Ali in our local takeaway who, while chatting over our order one evening, told me all about his village in the Himalayas and his pictures reminded me of David's descriptions. It transpired, as I thought it might, that they came from the same place and he was keen to know more about Ali. I had not delved deeply into the matter as I hadn't wanted to bring David or his family into it, but I believe he was pleased rather than alarmed and said he might take a drive out to meet them at the restaurant.

We returned again to David's ideas for his warehouse and ever burgeoning doss-house and finally said our thank yous and goodbyes. It was a very pleasant evening but I couldn't help thinking that very deep still waters ran beneath David Mozan and what you saw was definitely not all you got.

The next few days were quiet which allowed Chris to complete drawings, make a few site visits and inspections while I caught up on our book-keeping.

Denny was exuberant as he burst through the door doing a tap dance and singing Satchmo's, *Wonderful World*. He swirled and chuckled: I waited. 'I'm in love, Mrs Chris, I'm in love.' Again, I thought.

'Great, Denny. Where d'you meet her? Is she a fashion model? A dancer? A barmaid? A hostess? A bunny girl?'

'She works in Marks & Sparks.'

What? Someone ordinary, steady, I couldn't wait. He would bring her in or invite us round and he would cook plantain and all sorts of delicious Caribbean food. He always wanted us to approve of the antics he got up to. I know he looked up to Chris and in a small way, we tried to be anchors. His father had melted away and his worn mother had her hands full with younger sons. We arranged a get together at the office for the following Saturday. It was hard to settle down after that interruption but irrepressible Denny could be such fun.

Graham and Lindsay had recently bought a small cottage in a village close to Walberswick and Chris had given it a brief inspection to ensure there were no major defects. I only slightly envied them the tasks of choosing carpets for the bedrooms and new furnishings throughout. The kitchen was new and in a country style, with an Aga cooker and boiler combined. The bathroom was lined with timber cladding and earthy tiles on the bath side walls and shower and a larger version on the floor. The ground floor rooms were paved as they had been originally and rugs were strewn over. The place was charming. It retained all the original 200-year-old features but with a spanking new kitchen and first floor bathroom and importantly as far as Lindsay was concerned, excellent heating installations, Graham's speciality.

There were two bedrooms only and access to the rear room was by walking through the first room, and the upstairs bathroom was at the end of that. Provided nobody ran about naked I supposed the lack of privacy didn't really matter.

I was still smiling about Denny when Lindsay called. 'Hi, Chris. Do you have a few hours free at the weekend? I wondered if you fancied a trip to the cottage as Graham wants to build a garage and we've got to get Planning permission.'

'Not in the week Lindsay, sorry and we have a sort of "do" on Saturday but we could come up on Sunday, the kids will be with us though.'

'Excellent. Come up early as you like.' That was the lie-in gone then. 'We'll have breakfast ready.'

Saturday afternoon was a success. Denny's latest flame was called Phoebe. She was small and dainty with strange mauvey coloured eyes, the loveliest coffee coloured skin, glossy tumbling curly hair and didn't seem the least bit outrageous. I took a few boring cheeses, crispbreads and salads and he provided the rest. He made a lovely dish of red snapper in sauce, a chicken thing with mangoes and avocados and a curry which he told the children was made of goat. Poor No.3 was dismayed. He stared at the Tupperware box and silently shook his head when it was offered, then huge beseeching eyes sought mine. We had recently been to a local petting zoo which had tiny fluffy kids and he had loved feeding and stroking them. I reflected on the fact that other meats obviously came from other animals: not being a tofu or Quorn loving family didn't seem to worry any of them unduly. I whispered that it wasn't goat, Denny was teasing him, it was mutton, meaning old sheep, and he regarded it quietly but steered clear. I actually felt jolted by the meat-eating thing again and although Chris's brother, being a butcher, eloquently explained all about the food chain I felt revolted. This was an occasional resolve of mine and we switched to chicken and fish and used copious herbs and flavouring to soups and pasta and, sadly, too many chips. The well-meaning regimes usually lasted about a fortnight, then we would go visiting or to a farmers' market or barbecue somewhere and the smell of cooking bacon and pork sausages would batter my resolve a bit, then, added to pressure from the family professing deprivation and my own lack of will power it would all collapse. I would suddenly think of lamb and mint sauce or beef with Yorkshires, roast potatoes and swamped in gravy. The intermittent longings would not subside until I cooked and served whatever the craving was and we would be back in the old habits again.

The next day was cold but bright in the morning and we all ate bananas and yoghurt and set off for Suffolk.

Graham had plans of the cottage, a semi-detached building and an Ordnance Survey print showing not only the extent of his land but also the few surrounding estates. Edging his boundaries in red, he highlighted the area he planned to build on.

The buildings had once belonged to the local church and over the ages, internal changes had been implemented. The dividing line of these cottages, being the party wall, had a strange shape on plan. The wall is usually constructed in a straight line from front to rear but the attached house had acquired a metre width of the front living room, from the chimney breast back to the partition wall with the dining room. The chimney and fireplace was flat against the inner party wall and the lost area of the recess had been taken and converted next door into a nook and library area. This was a loss to Graham's dwelling of nearly three square metres on the ground floor and slightly less upstairs and was known as a flying freehold. It was only while looking at the drawings that the stolen areas were noticed but obviously, this had been carried out too long ago to query. He had got what he'd paid for, a quaint and rambling cottage.

In the front garden, Graham and Chris chatted about the side land and distances to the fences and the next-door neighbour came out. He was anything but friendly and instantly enquired what our game was. Graham politely introduced himself and Lindsay as the new owners, as they had not met this person before, even when he carried out works to the bathroom and kitchen. It transpired that he was the vendor of the cottage and the sale had been reluctant. He was forced to market it due to impending death duties.

He frowned and muttered, 'I thought you were just a tradesman, not the owner.' Then looking at Chris with his measuring tapes, he barked that he would object to the building works. 'This is a village! We can't have every Tom, Dick and Harry newcomer blundering in here, adding bits and pieces. The house is big enough. I am a member of the parish council and a councillor at the planning offices.' Then, glaring at Chris, he finished 'You're wasting your money with him.'

'Thank you, we'll see.' Then Graham gestured towards us and continued, 'Lindsay, my wife, has also joined the parish council, in fact she is kindly helping them out at the office so she'll doubtless see you at the monthly meetings. Goo'day. Sorry, must get on,' smiled Graham.

Smooth I thought. Icily polite was a definite asset if executed well. I, myself, have never learned how.

I helped Lindsay dole out the pancakes and crispy bacon and piled the toast straight onto the scrubbed pine table. A huge glistening lump of local butter sat centrally with a bowl of scrambled eggs and pots of assorted jams. 'Did you make these?' I asked and she laughed.

'Me? Make jam? Good lord, no. One of the neighbours in the white cottages along the street makes it and sticks jars of it on a table outside the gate. Money goes in a box on a stick and apparently gets donated to the church. Lady is in her eighties and grows the fruit at the back and can't bear to waste it. Delicious. Do try it, that's gooseberry, that's blackcurrant and I'm not sure what that one is but it's moreish, whatever.'

Mmm, she was right.

After we had cleared the dishes away we all put our boots on and Graham put the leads on their dogs and we went for a walk. The wind was building up, but we thought a struggle through the sand dunes would blow away the cobwebs and work off a few calories. To the children's delight, we walked to the ferry and took a trip over to Southwold. Picking our way along the narrow pavements and enjoying the tiny shop fronts and pier, it wasn't long before the lure of locally brewed ale drew Graham and Chris magically off the green and through red painted doors to the well-polished bar. We decided to join them, as there was a small garden at the rear for the children and they settled down with lemonades and a board game. A bit of respite and we flexed ourselves for the walk back to the ferry and the march back along the sands to the village.

Chris, although stunned by the negative attitude of the neighbour, was confident that the proposals would be entirely within village curtilage rules and other planning guidelines and Graham was completely blasé about it. 'Little Englander. He's the sort who gives English people a bad name,' he stated.

I agreed, mentally adding drunken revellers on holiday in foreign countries, football hooligans, stag dos, hen dos and men who wear socks with sandals. 'Chris, you're welcome to borrow the place for a weekend or time in the school holidays you know.'

'Thanks, Graham, we'll take you up on that.'

I liked the fisherman's huts along the edge, and envisaged buying fresh fish. Lovely new bread and fruits and jams from the neighbours was tempting to me.

Back at the cottage Lindsay pulled a gigantic red enamelled casserole dish out of the larger Aga oven and set it on the table. We all had earthenware bowls and greedily shovelled beef and bacon hotpot into our mouths in almost total silence, punctuated by spoons stirring, dipping and scraping china, a few slurps and giggles mainly from our offspring and then satisfied mumbles from all of us. Sometimes I think stews can be plain and boring, but the addition of pearl parley and flavourings of goodness knows what, paired with a four mile walk, gave us all an appetite.

Our trip and time spent with Graham and Lindsay had infilled us with cheer and feelings of general wellbeing and next day, back at the office, we were greeted by a tearful Denny.

We wondered briefly what could have gone wrong as he seemed so happy on Saturday but he soon told us, 'My car's been re-possessed.'

His paperwork was entirely in order but he had missed two payments and failed to respond to the finance company's letter. I remembered the antics over his furniture and the bailiffs and felt sorry, but he was his own enemy. Chris sat with him and telephoned the local office. After a bit of Chris's logic and assurances which we hoped would be reliable, a faceless woman in the office went out on a limb and agreed to accept several small payments until he caught up. This was unusually kind of the manager and not at all expected. They worked out a new financial plan for Denny and we marked the dates and amounts in our own diary to ensure he kept them in mind. For the next year, he would have to party less and work more.

**

The property valuations, with structural comments attached for our bank staff members, was going really well and had spilled out to include a few of their customers. These jobs led to many people wanting to build extensions and convert their lofts and naturally, they turned to us.

Word seemed to be travelling around the local solicitors of our lease plans, which I was secretly proud of. These were site plans showing floor layouts, drawn by hand, having beautiful writings and shading. Common areas were depicted in a different colour and prepared on sheets of A4 thick tracing paper: these were printed and sent to land registry and copies used for rents, leases and legal documents. Our No.1 was learning to prepare these and went with Chris to carry out the dimensional surveys. He learned how to draw the site in the correct scale and to shade it in. The writing needed practice and he showed great promise but more importantly, he wanted to learn.

Our bank manager called unexpectedly on the off-chance that Chris was in so I got him a cup of tea while he waited. He walked around looking at our home from home and seemed to approve. I was glad I had cleared the kitchen after our toasted sandwiches and had stacked the dishwasher. We all need to eat and drink but somebody else's kitchen, even an office one, gives a bad impression if mucky crockery is left to lie. I showed him the photos of the flat above, which he had agreed to finance, and was starting to flag with conversation when Chris burst cheerfully in. 'Ahh afternoon Alan.' Alan? I thought he was Mr Jarvis. Once a bank clerk, always a bank clerk, I thought but Chris had no such parameters.

'Chris, my boy.' My boy? Good God. I crept across to stand with Denny and we played at elbowing each other.

There is no free lunch. This jovial old fashioned City type had been remarkably good to Chris and me, he must have seen Chris's potential and liked my figures in order to turn so many blind eyes to our wavering finances. We had skated on proverbially thin ice but always had faith in ourselves and I truly believe that confidence linked with honesty shone through. He wanted a porch. 'Only a little job.' He blustered even though he probably knew that it was anything but.

I let Chris explain that planners expected to see elevation plans of his home, front and sides which involved three separate drawings as well as the site plan and Ordnance Survey extracts. They also wanted a floor plan showing the layout as existing and then the proposal. The only little thing about it was the actual porch and, of course, our fee. We had to make allowance for the work he put our way so to expect to be paid more than expenses would be selfish. The appointment was made and he drove away happily.

We had started our married life together in a town house on the edges of Harlow New Town and rarely travelled there now, so it would be a sentimental journey, along with visiting my old branch and looking up staff members I knew then and I remember a certain Chinese restaurant opposite that we virtually lived in when I was expecting No.1 and had a penchant for their take-aways. The restaurant banked with us and paid in regularly. Almost as regularly a small group, some bouncily grinning and some dejectedly foot dragging wearing woebegone expressions would troop into the banking hall and ask for the securities section. These men were inveterate gamblers and on a Sunday night, when they closed early, would start their games. Losses would start small and grow to the ultimate and the premises and business would change hands again. At first the occasion was so awful that it was funny in a way, but this involved us in quite a lengthy operation. New mandates had to be completed and signed for us, new Articles and Memorandum of Association legal papers prepared and sent to Companies House on their behalf. Half of the characters could barely write and understood even less and the signatures were complicated or a "mark" that we had to identify and carefully record by using their passports. They always seemed to carry on the running of the restaurant without any obvious disasters so it seemed like a joint effort, with everyone pitching in and no debilitating tantrums as far as we knew, but before long the whole procedure would be turned around again and it would revert to the original three or four. I had forgotten their antics and smiled to myself when I remembered their stir fries, soft noodles and Szechuan prawns that my No.1 son ate while in the womb and craved Chinese flavours as soon as he was weaned to the present day.

While Chris went to Mr Jarvis's home and took the photos needed, I spent a happy hour in my old branch showing my photos to the remaining staff that I knew. The boys rarely stayed more than a few years and were moved on to higher positions in different branches once they passed their exams, but a few older steady men who were content in their senior roles would remain until retirement, being rich with experience and knowledge but devoid of those important banking examination passes to lift them off to better things, more lucrative status and, of course, pensions.

The girls there of course remembered No.1, the branch had collected and bought us a carry cot and stand and different ones sometimes visited us for a cuddle and play with him during their lunch break, so were delighted to see photos and learn of his progress. Chris had taken a new job in London when our baby was only four months old, so we moved to Chigwell and started making friends again. By the time we had gained No.2 our visits to Harlow were less and a few years later on, when No.3 arrived, we visited the town park and swimming pool but little else.

A well-known turf accountant, who had started out taking bets from the rear of his van and who could then barely read and write, was going from strength to strength. He had taken a shop premises and when that was successful he took several more. Never have I met a shrewder man, who knew the background of all the horses and greyhounds, their owners, their trainers and the odds for the races, who dealt with the finances of his company as a computer would, calculating figures at dizzying speed. His writing was rough and childlike but always correctly cast on his bank slips. He was a small man with the stature of a jockey but no obvious sign of small man arrogance. He was an inspiration, being from rough or humble background, polite in his dealings with all of us and growing his empire with acumen, lacking in so many financial workers that I had come across. At Christmas after a good year every member of staff would receive chocolates and wine, about forty of us, and specific cashiers or management would receive more. After a bad year, we still all had a gift, he just spent a little less.

The years had passed and his shops had increased. He had sons who joined him and helped to build the concern but I had left those years behind me and knew nothing of them all now.

Chris came to the branch to pick me up and I introduced him to some of the present staff and he remembered some others.

It was good to meet again the girl who took over my job when I left for maternity reasons. She was quite young for the position but we reckoned she was the best and brightest of the staff members and I think she made the job her own. I had tired of the whole thing by then and only wanted to go home and prepare for our baby and the subsequent house move. I remember just before I left, she arrived for work one Monday morning in a nervous state. She was out with some friends over the weekend and one had a slight accident so a few of them went to Princess Alexandra A&E department for treatment. While they waited, someone was brought in screaming and hysterical and tightly wrapped in a sheet. Once he had been registered he was swiftly transferred to the psychiatric department or mental health section.

He was high on a drug which had induced hallucinations apparently and was convinced he had become an orange. He was begging everyone not to peel him. To this day, I have never forgotten Jaq's shocked and upset self when she told me this story and wondered what became of the foolish boy who had taken the narcotics.

Chris had taken the dimensions he needed for the porch application and had called into the council offices to collect a set of the relevant forms. These had to be filled in four times just for the planning department use along with four sets of drawings, photos the Ordnance Survey map prints and of course the fee. An application also had to be sent to the parish council.

We drove around the roads for old time's sake and I remembered walking over Harlow Common, pushing the pram and meeting up with several other young mums I had met during the few years we lived there.

We were a bit early to collect the children, so we went to a pub by the riverside that we used to frequent and had celebrated our first anniversary there, when they had live music at the weekends and everybody ate steak and chips. It was still a pleasant place and had changed hands, so we had tea and fed bits of bread roll to the ducks. The visit had made both of us reflective and we swapped ideas and impressions for the last thirteen years.

We passed a picture postcard building that had been converted to a thatched roofed restaurant some years earlier. We had promised ourselves we would visit it if we became a bit flush. It was the place to go to see and be seen and used for special occasions unless you were wealthy, pretentious or pompous and wanted to show off. We moved away and the intention faded. It still was the most expensive place to eat in the area and obliged us to book in advance, so we swept by and forgot about it again.

Chapter 11

The café along the parade was doing a roaring trade. They opened at six in the morning and closed at two thirty. Many early risers went for breakfast and others bought their bacon sandwiches and took them away for later. We had warned Mr Patel that the original planning consent to run the premises as a café had expired years before for lack of use. A planning permission does not continue indefinitely if the usage is not kept up. The little shop was too close to the traffic lights and this, we thought, would likely be a reason to be prohibited, although vehicles stopping for food in fact was not a problem as most people crossed the lights and parked over at the start of the flats. Here ground was provided for walkers' parking and the ice cream van and café patrons walked back. We were lucky, being at the start of the parade and having space for about four cars. We had allowed Mr Pepper's patrons to use our space until nine am when we would usually arrive.

This morning we had barely scraped breakfast, flinging ourselves into the car and swigging from bottles of water and eating biscuits on the way. The school tuck shop was open so I gave the children some money and left them to choose themselves something, probably unsuitable but it was an unexpected treat for them. An occasional glut of chocolate was probably not so dreadful, I reasoned. They drink great bowls of milky chocolate in France for breakfast. In the great scheme of things our offspring usually had three meals a day with a few treats, plenty of milk and water and fruit and vegetables and they were growing at an alarming rate.

So, upon arrival at the office I slunk to the café to buy bacon and sausage sandwiches with brown sauce and met Jason Pepper, the proprietor. He said he had intended coming in to chat with Chris a bit later so I told him when Chris would be in and he nodded. It transpired that an eagle-eyed councillor had noticed the re-opened café with a plethora of bikes left outside and queried the use with planning. An enforcement notice had been sent to the premises for them to cease trade and a date that this had to take place. It was not satisfying to us to be correct about this use and the outcome but we were glad to have warned them all. 'So, what can we do, Chris?'

We contacted planning department and said we were submitting an application on his behalf. This would give him respite.

We wrote as factual a letter and lists as accurate as possible regarding numbers of customers who arrived by car: these actually were few, on foot or bike and included a petition of over three hundred names requesting that it could remain open. Sadly, after four months and heated arguments at an evening planning meeting of the councillors, the decision was made to refuse the application. He was then given another date by which time he had to cease trading, so we waited until the black day loomed and contacted the department again to advise that an appeal was being launched. This process could take up to a year and we applied to the government department in Wales for an application pack. This process was free. Three sets of documents had to be prepared; one to keep, one to the local authority and one to the appeals address. Eventually they responded with a reference and a name to contact. The council planning officer would have an amount of time to respond and was obliged to prepare their own sets of counter documents, which would include comments from Highways and any objections or comments they may have received and we would receive a set of these. We would then have an amount of time to respond. Meanwhile if our client could whip up a further list of comments or praises this was the time to do it. We did not hold out much hope. We had had a few zany decisions, in our opinion, which we had managed to reverse by lodging an appeal but in the main, a planner's decision is usually a fair one. This procedure took about eight months, which at the time was fairly swift as they were experiencing a huge amount of appeals. At this time the Inspectorate employed professional people whose work did not involve planning or council related jobs. It was more of a man in the street feeling and not biased.

Unfortunately, poor Mr Pepper lost his appeal and was obliged to remove his equipment and Mr Patel had his empty shop back. We, along with dozens of other people, lost our breakfast take-away. Well, occasionally.

Chris had become quite well known among builders who carried out the works associated with re-building and strengthening, financed mainly with the aid of housing grants and this part of our business was doing well. The builders came in all shapes and sizes, and were Irish, English Italian and a few were Asian. The clients, however, were mainly Asian. It was not usually easy to obtain a financial grant and we knew that extensive means testing was carried out. Even children's savings accounts had to be declared. We never took on a client or became involved in the form filling exercise as our role was simply to carry out the survey. Chris was scrupulously honest and had never reported that a wall was in imminent danger of collapse if it had slight outward bowing or needed restraint and his surveys were trusted. We created a set fee for this work: a small survey and report cost the same as a more extensive one, as this stopped haggling and everyone knew what would happen. We usually got a phone call from one of several people, either a trusted builder or a person we knew who carried out similar drawing work to Chris, but acted as an agent in these applications. A return visit was often made to the site after the works had started as a problem had been encountered. It could be a broken drain or damaged brickwork that had to be replaced, enlarging the contract. Chris would be obliged to agree to these requests and only rarely could he suggest a different solution. Properties situated in the periphery of London received the worst bombing of the war and damage was widespread. Reparations were carried out mainly for this reason.

We found out that these builders traipsed around the mosques and temples actively seeking houses requiring repair and drumming up trade. We were not involved in these practises and were busy enough with our own blossoming concern.

We learned a bit more when we were called by a person from a local council, requesting that Chris attended a meeting at a house that we had visited about a month previously, as he wished to discuss the conditions and recommended reparations. We both went to the house and met the person with his boss and Chris pointed out the precarious movement of an internal wall that needed urgent strengthening. He confirmed that no other work was required. The persons from the council thanked us and we all left.

We soon received a call from the homeowner asking us to hurry the proceedings up, so I called the grants officer and queried the progress. I was astounded to hear that as a result of this particular case, the entire grants procedure for the rest of the foreseeable future had been halted and he had informed the other local boroughs, who he believed would freeze their own grants applications pending investigation. He then went on to tell me in confidence that he had attended the house about a week earlier with his deputy and armed with our report, he inspected the area of concern. At that time, he agreed with the report and intended to approve the application, pending estimates. The would-be builder was there too. Apparently, the builder spoke quietly in his own tongue to the homeowner, promising him that the process was a done deal and he would also have a list of requests carried out in thanks for allowing him the contract. He was overheard by the deputy, who was from a different country but understood the language and reported the whole thing back to his boss. He went on to tell me what he had learned about the process which we had no idea about, that the "finder" of the site received a small cash sum as an incentive to seek more. The grants officer at one particular authority also received a decent chunk of cash for approving the application; the agent also was given a gratuity on top of his fee; the builder obviously was remunerated well and the homeowner got extra decorating and possibly cash back. Three estimates from different contractors were provided but they obviously took turns to "win" the contract. At this time the limit of a housing grant was extensive so applications were popular. It was also a closed shop for any other person who innocently tried to take on the role of agent. I was horrified that this official and his counterparts in adjacent councils could think that we were part of the ring, but he seemed to know that we were straight. It was the first housing grant survey we undertook for that council and the last for any others and it wasn't long before we heard, through the grapevine, that a few people in the first borough we had been involved with had lost their positions within the authority and had been shifted to different jobs. They were extremely lucky, I think, not to have been sacked. I think in hindsight the council tried to keep the whole sordid affair secret, it certainly did not reach the papers. Due to uncertainty of the builders and coming financial crisis, it was a long time before these grants were re introduced but we were never involved again. The main agent regarded us warily after that and we wondered whether he thought we had played a part in the collapse of the scam. Although he occasionally asked Chris to prepare him engineering calculations for a wall removal or similar, the previous amiability was strained and nobody ever brought the subject up.

It was at this time that we were introduced by Jonny Pearson to a trio of local estate agents. Their trading name was curious and the business seemed to be booming. Two gay friends had set up the business, including the lady who lived next door to them. Her husband had a shoe shop and being older than her, had decided to retire so the trio had taken over the premises but changed the use. They were successful and their distinctive sale boards were visible everywhere. The houses were all in the East End of London and usually of similar type and style, mid terrace dwellings within ribbon developments of C1920 build with front bay features, high roofs and decent gardens. The partners of the business soon created a spin-off from the agency and having the pick of the properties, bought some themselves. They used us to prepare plans for conversion of the houses into two flats, which were constructed then sold on. They bought at rock bottom prices, carried out the conversion works using competitively priced builders and sold again at top notch amounts but retained the freeholds. As this side of their business grew, so too did the list of freeholds that they retained, which each earned them two annual ground rents per dwelling house and insurance costs on top. They had the pick of properties that had been neglected or damaged and had the contacts to develop sought after homes and the means to sell the properties via their agency. Only builders or developers would be interested in obtaining these sad old buildings as costs to pay skilled operatives to underpin and strengthen, let alone remove entire rotten or worm riddled timber floors and install ground bearing concrete replacement, carry out re-wiring, new plumbing and a new roof were exorbitant. It was also impossible to obtain a mortgage for these damaged houses. We enjoyed meeting these characters, who always had an amusing tale to tell and seemed to know everyone who was anyone. If Chris was tied up somewhere it often fell to me to travel to a busy site to speak to the building inspector and liaise with the builders and I loved doing it.

Neither of them ever made an improper suggestion to Chris or our boys and I watched intently in the beginning, but of course plenty of innuendo studded the conversations which were hilarious. Our No.2, who adored her father and enjoyed traipsing about with us, as they all did, got to know everyone and although was quite young and ignorant, or so I believed, of the wicked ways of the world, told me in an extremely worried little voice that she was concerned at the way that the younger partner was watching Chris's hands as they swept over the drawings, indicating specifics and discussed the schemes. 'He's mesmerized by Dad's hands, Mum. He stares at them.'

I remember one day when she was at the office after school with a friend and they were supposedly doing English homework, that he came in to pick up some prints and was cheerfully chatting with them while he waited. Being young girls they were typically flattered at his attention and admiring of his fashionable stylish clothes and were flirting in an innocent and of course useless way. Her friend, being a little bolder, asked him the name of his aftershave as she believed it was the same as her dad's. He was delighted at this reference to his personal choice and agreed that it was Fahrenheit. No.2 used to answer the phone when at the office and took accurate messages. When these estate agents called, she would answer and invariably would be asked if either of her keepers were around. Both he and his partner were very personable and never camp in our company, but cheeky without crossing the line. I think our set-up intrigued them, as our children were so strongly a part of the concern, spending so much of their time with us in the office and learning to use an adding machine and office machinery, or being traipsed around sites where they helped to take dimensions. The female third member of the agency trio was older but adored them both and it was pleasant meeting up from time to time to discuss their current project. After that first introduction, we worked together many times sending ideas sketches by fax. Much of our work was now sent by facsimile, a machine I thought to be brilliant, feeding a drawing or written passage into one end and the person received it at the other end, while the document was retained. This was so much more efficient than copying and posting and the forerunner of scanning and emailing. Little No.3 always used to muse that one day a whole person could be sent down the wires like Captain Kirk of Star Trek when he ordered, "Beam me up, Scottie".

**

We received a call from school, advising that No.3 had broken a window and would be asked to pay to replace the glazing. I had just paid the deposit on a short break for the coming half term so was neither pleased about it or awash with spare cash. He had complained the day before that someone had taken his school case. This was a new one, bought during the holidays as a birthday present and expensive for a young schoolboy. A short craze had started where the boys wanted leather briefcases and each in the group clamoured to obtain one, therefore gloating little owners were goading the non-owners and largely behaving towards each other in a nasty way that we have never condoned. I told the form master about his missing case and by the time I got to the school it had been found. I think he had probably been lording the situation, displaying the wretched case over others still not owning one and several of the little horrors had hidden it beneath some coats to teach him a lesson. This only served to infuriate him, as he knew the perpetrators and generally lost his temper in the playground the next day when they laughed at him. He threw a tennis ball with all his might at one little scabby kneed, gap toothed tormenter and the missile went right through the window. Luckily it was very small and we agreed to fork out the money to have it fixed, but asked the teacher to watch the behaviour of the group because usually No.3 was relaxed and considerate and spiteful or aggravating behaviour was alien to him. We felt dreadful when the money for the repair was taken from his money box to pay for the glass and I swear something stabbed me in the heart when I saw his despondent little face as the coins and notes heap depleted to hardly anything. Mantras about teaching him a lesson and being responsible were superfluous as we felt such heels. It wasn't like him to be irresponsible and I think the breakage was the culmination of a possible bullying affair, nicely scotched by the house master, as it should have been. It did serve them all to see how losing one's temper rarely achieved a good result and quiet dignity was usually the advantageous option.

While reeling from this unpleasant episode, we had an invitation to the girls' school. No.2 had been awarded a prize for her charity work. What charity work?

We took time out from another busy afternoon to join the other parents in the school hall to watch the sanctimonious do-gooders, including our daughter, troop up to the stage to receive a certificate signed by headmaster and headmistress, saying she had raised quite a large sum of money for an old folks' residential care home. We had been unaware of this and it showed that she, too, had hidden depths. Wednesday afternoons were classed as "free time," not to be wasted or taken off but for a different pursuit from school activities. Some girls went riding. This had been queried with us at the time but I foresaw the need for a riding helmet, which then would stretch to jodhpurs and a jacket, let alone travelling to and from the stables and the cost of riding lessons. Being also that she was afraid of horses I couldn't see the advantage in that idea.

We had been through all the other money-swallowing pastimes that children try only to give up as soon as a new set of clothing has been bought, which is then redundant as your child no longer wishes to carry on. A buyer never materialises for the freshly purchased, still in the wrapping, outfits so the situation of hobbies for us rarely seems worthwhile. Over a few years, she had tried several activities including ballet, tap dancing, athletics, music lessons for the guitar and the piano and finally karate, which entailed me driving all over Essex and East London as her private taxi, as indeed most mothers do selflessly and willingly. I unfortunately undertook this grudgingly as there was always so much waiting for me to do and as Chris was always busy earning money, these important domestic duties fell to me as Hobson's choice. Little wonder then that sometimes things orientated in the background that I was unaware of and made me feel inadequate on occasions when forced to admit my ignorance.

However, knowing that few things on the list interested her, she had elected a programme of "good works" and spent time with a friend visiting care institutions in the area and generally chatting to elderly residents. She occasionally mentioned names and told us things, like, 'I saw old John sitting out the front today, he likes being in the sun.' Who's John? I wondered uneasily, seeing visions of a predator lurking in the shadows ready to prey on my child. He was apparently a war veteran with no legs, who gets pushed out to the pavement so that he can see the passers-by. She would visit the care home and take people like John for a walk, pushing the wheelchair. She started buying cake from the bakers in the High Road out of her pocket money so they could all have a slice when they got back. This escalated and she set up a trestle table every Wednesday by the pavement where local pedestrians were gently pressured into buying a slice, the proceeds to be used for the general good of the residents. She had no licence to trade, no food and hygiene certificates or whatever she should have had, no legal agreements or insurance and although we were so proud of her, we thought a more formal arrangement should be instigated. No reason to panic as a new term was dawning and Wednesday afternoons were now to be used for something else, so everyone wriggled out of that with high accolades and no calamities.

What a rich colourful cloth unfurling is our lives: one day we were concerned at small boys' problems and the next we swelled with pride at our girl's initiative and care.

I went with Chris to an empty house in Leytonstone and wound the tape back on my recorder to begin. I switched on the speak button to check it had all been rewound and felt my stomach lurch in fright as the voice spouting out of it sounded like me speaking backwards. Having seen too many horror films where actors are possessed by the devil, it sounded like I had become affected with evil spirits or whatever. I then laughed in relief as I realised it was No.2, chanting verbs in German on my tape recorder. Her voice over the telephone resembled mine as No.1's voice was sounding like Chris's.

The development for David Mozan's hostel was taking shape by a sort of design and build programme. The council, realising there was a desperate need for places for people such as these poor troubled souls, was allowing more than usually generous size extensions to contain them. A recent idea had been to excavate downwards as well as outwards at the rear, and upwards into the roof structure. The present size was far too small for the number of residents. It was a good thing that inspections were not frequent, as many rooms had up to three people crammed in. Sharing a room and generally being overcrowded, but with breakfast and heating throughout the building was preferable to sleeping rough in doorways, benches and under railway arches. Of course, there was lucrative profit as the number of benefit payments that arrived into David's bank account swelled monthly, the staff were all on minimum wage and not resentful, as they too came from disadvantaged backgrounds and the pitiful wages were increased in kind by food all day and being in the warm. A blind eye was turned to bags of laundry that found their way into the utility rooms in the morning and went out again hours later, clean, dry and ironed. We even saw some schoolchildren creeping in around four o'clock instead of going home to a cold, empty place and doubtless finding some pasta or pizza in the dining room that would save their parent paying out. 'It's a bit of a free for all, David, isn't it?' I asked one day and he grinned ruefully.

'I couldn't get the staff if I didn't throw in a few perks. And frankly, the electricity used and everything else is put against tax, so it's not ideal but then, what is?'

I secretly wondered how the youngsters felt. Some of the characters that were homed there were a tad unsavoury to my thinking. Smoking was not banned in the large room euphemistically called a lounge and neither, I noted, was drinking alcohol. Men of all description and colour with appearances of unkempt vagrants, some with wild hair and beards and tattooed to extremes used to come and go with a cigarette in one hand and a can of Tennants Extra in the other. I knew with utter conviction that I would never allow No.3 in there: perhaps Nos.1 and 2 when they were a bit older, as long as David or one of us were there too, as we believed in them knowing the plight of unfortunates or perhaps the possible consequences of flagrant over-indulgence, but were not exposed to danger or to be frightened. We were not rich or upper class but they still were privileged and one day, would be thrust into the harsh world to make their own decisions and fend for themselves. If sheltered all their lives, they would have no knowledge of deprivation or need of others and we both wanted them to be aware. Something too awful to be told had happened to some of these men and their mental state had never recovered. The smell too was offensive, odour of sweat and body grease hung over many of the rooms. I sometimes wondered if David ran the place to remind himself how low he could have become without his early advantages to help him climb out of a shameful situation, carrying with him now an aura of respectability, wealth and breeding.

We had become introduced to a community of Sikhs, they all have the name Singh included in their title. One family ran a couple of shops and the boys were branching out into property development. One, called PS, had a beautiful wife who had trained to be a nurse in Malaysia. We had gone to their wedding reception in a hotel in Docklands, this was lavish and modern. The actual service had been carried out in their temple or gurdwara, attended by their families. No hiding in corners in this wedding party. Everybody mixed and the parents circulated with the young bridal couple to personally welcome all the guests. After the sit-down, three course meal, the tables were cleared slightly and the entertainment began.

This was the first time that we had seen and heard Bhangra dancers and music. The music is produced using some western instruments, recordings and Asian drums. It is loud and joyful, originating in the UK during the 1970s. It combines the music of the Punjab and modern pop. The group consisted of five young energetic men who played and danced and everybody joined in. This reminded me of the beautifully choreographed dance routines in Bollywood films. After their stint of about an hour there was a disco playing western recordings and the party went on until the early hours. The food and alcohol was provided generously but we had to drive home, so could appreciate the fruit juices mainly. We thoroughly enjoyed ourselves and could see that the other guests did too.

This young couple owned a large house in Forest Gate and wanted us to apply for planning consent to convert it to a care home. Regulations were strict for any sort of multiple residential home: each room must reach the statutory size and there must be enough bathrooms, WCs and staff areas. There must be a quiet room and a sluice room, storage rooms and lifts. To achieve all necessary rooms and areas, not forgetting kitchens, laundry and dining room, there should be a residents' lounge large enough and suitable for visitors too. The parking area must be wide enough to cope with an ambulance or fire engines, allowing for loading and unloading and turning space and the grounds must be flat enough for wheelchair use, as well as all internal doorways must cater for wheelchairs and have the necessary fire precautions. Smoke alarms must be fitted throughout, wired to a different electricity circuit. Not only must every factor satisfy the planning system but also the Environmental Health Department and we all worked extremely hard to achieve this at the local authority. Then a severe blow was dealt to these aspirational couple as they were obliged to consult with their solicitor to remove the covenant attached to the land. At the time of purchase, they had been aware that the building was saddled with a covenant, but early enquiries indicated that the fee to have this removed or lifted would require a nominal sum to the local church. All legal costs for both sides would also be borne by our clients. When the awaited letter from the trustees arrived, we were staggered to learn that this well-known, established Church of England denominational body, known to have considerable moneys but dwindling congregations, could demand such an excessive amount. I telephoned the signatory at their office in an attempt to persuade them that the demand was excessive but he said the board were unanimous in their decision. The covenant stated that no manufacturing or car repairs, retail or business use could be carried out within the building and they considered that a nursing home was within the category of a business.

I replied that nursing was carried out in a hospital and that was not considered to be a business but a necessity and care for any aged or feeble person was surely a Christian objective, as well as humane, but he was adamant. I am afraid I lost my temper at this point and told him how mean minded, mean spirited and greedy he and his fellow trustees were, lodged in the past and full of avarice and no wonder people were drifting away from the church, any church and religion in general because there was no generosity of spirit, no care for humanity in their dealings and I was disgusted. I put the phone down at this point as I thought I would cry in frustrated fury. We had jumped through hoops for weeks and all our clients' research and planning was for nothing. There was the option of going to court to have the covenant lifted lawfully but they felt, and I suppose we did too, that the Establishment would be likely to side with the Establishment and they would be throwing more money down the drain.

Instead they moved out and the house was filled with students, immigrants, and a general mix of people and the gorgeous double fronted building became a house of multiple occupation which could not be stopped by the religious misers and the premises soon looked grimy and uncared for. The money they coined in from the local council for rent allowances and elsewhere far exceeded the profits that their care home would have brought them and we felt sad each time we passed the building which had once stood in gleaming hope.

We had a call from Jeff Gold and immediately my mind went to the dreaded basement and I waited for him to tell me what he wanted. Thankfully it was not for himself or a basement, but a loft conversion for his brother in south east London. This seemed benign in comparison so I reached for the diary and asked him for convenient dates and his brother's details. He apparently wanted us to bring the children and he had puppies to show them. We won't be buying any of them, I hastened to tell him as I could imagine No.3 would throw a tantrum if we said no on the day. 'Make sure you tell your brother to explain that none of the puppies are for sale, I can't insist enough,' I told him strongly. I also envisaged his idea that one of these wrinkled Chinese dogs which apparently commanded huge sums of money could be traded for loft drawings and all he would be liable for would be council costs.

So off we went, en famille, to the house. The strange man reportedly had a wife and family in one place and at least one "my other wife" in another. This worn out young woman had a new baby which stole the show as far as we were concerned and when he cheerfully suggested we all troop into the rear room to see his puppies, the attraction was reduced. The attraction vanished altogether when we entered the room and encountered the most dreadful smell emanating from the wrinkled Chinese dog mother and host of tiny, wrinkled Chinese pups. I could not see the attraction of these poor creatures. They all seemed to have too much flesh which clung in folds all over them, hiding their tiny eyes, which surely hampered their vision and this odd appearance, coupled with the stench was not in any way appealing. No.3 never mentioned once how he craved for a puppy, thank goodness, and we sat in the other room with a cup of tea which was not palatable, but this was probably due to the assault on our noses.

It was quite a cold day outside and we sat in our coats. Suddenly the client walked in with a glass of whisky and insisted we should all have a proper drink. Not advisable, Chris tried to say, when a house needs to be measured and one adult needs to drive home. 'It's cold in here,' he announced. 'Is that fire on?' the heater was a portable calor gas model plonked in the middle of the room and wasn't glowing. Before anyone could answer, he threw the contents of his glass at the fire, which belched out flames coupled with a small explosion and shocked us all with fright. 'That's Ok, then, it'll warm up in a minute,' he said and went outside again. He returned with a tray of glasses and a bottle of very good whisky. He had glasses even for the children, who were sitting now with deep grins and openly jabbing their elbows into each other. My weak little voice saying the alcohol was too strong for the children and the tea was OK, thank you, was swiftly drowned out by cries of 'Thank you' from the offspring so I gave up.

To my amazement, they all swallowed their tots without as much as a grimace or cough and Chris, who was standing in the doorway trying to get on with the job, shrugged his shoulders. 'No more, thank you.' I glared at No.3, who was overcome with a giggling fit, and dared him to reach for more. I had recently bought small hand-held games which operated by batteries. Mario Brothers games showed little characters on screen walking about and stacking boxes. The game, which could be operated by one or two people aimed to collect and stack the goods and to prevent the heaps collapsing. The other was Donkey Kong. Taking these from my bag and handing them to the children enabled me to help Chris and speed up the process and our faster departure.

Somehow the house dimensional survey was completed. Photographs were taken of the rear elevation, concentrating on the roof shape and we finally left. We had been given our fee and told that we would be called soon as his friend's shop needed work above to the living area.

With cries of '

'Bye,' 'Take Care,' and, 'Thanks,' we loaded the kids in the car and swept away in relief.

The following weekend we had been invited to a wedding. The groom was an Australian who had worked in the UK off and on for years, since his late teens. When the expiry of his visa loomed, he drove off on his motorbike and took a holiday in Europe. He had also worked for a while in Germany so was fluent in the language, had friends there and picked up work along the way. After a while he returned to the UK and resumed drafting jobs where he left off. During some of these stints he worked with Chris and often came home to the house for dinner and the occasional party.

About a year earlier, he met a pretty girl from Devon who knew some of his friends and she quickly moved in with him. We had grown to like her and in turn went to wherever they were living for reciprocal meals and parties. Inevitably his visa expiry was a few months off so he and his girl-friend went to Australia. '

'Bye, we'll be back,' they called at the airport where a huge crowd of friends, work-mates and her family congregated to see them off.

Then, six weeks ago, we received an invitation to their wedding. There was much excitement that they were back again and that he was settling down with D and we had been invited to the whole affair. We expected his family to have travelled to England to take part in the celebrations: we had met his brother and fiancée over time and all knew each other quite well. No.2 and I had gone shopping for their present and bought ourselves new outfits. The Army & Navy Stores in Ilford had a sale and we bought blue and matching pink bales of towels and felt we had done well.

The day loomed and we all got ready. I looked in the London Atlas and worked out our route. I had sent their card previously so we wrapped their present and loaded it in the boot and set off for the Blackwall Tunnel and road to Greenwich. We arrived at the church and were surprised to see no-one we recognised. Chris and No.1 went into the church and found no floral decorations for a wedding or order of service leaflets. There were a few people sitting in the front pews so he asked them if they were waiting for our friends, but there was apparently to be a christening at 3.30. We decided to drive to the house, address printed on the card, as obviously, something drastic had happened. There was no answer at the house and couldn't see his motorbike so feared our earlier thoughts were correct. Perhaps she had pulled out. Perhaps he had. He often said he didn't believe in marriage. We tried calling the number on the card and it rang unanswered so gave up. By now of course we were starving. We were all dressed up and nowhere to go. As we had believed that by now we would all be tucking into something tasty and festive, we had only had a late breakfast. I suggested going home and reheating the shepherd's pie I had made for tomorrow and got almost an unmentionable response. So we drove towards home and pulled into a nice hotel on the edge of Epping Forest and had a late Sunday lunch.

I wrote to the address in Sydney that we had for P and asked what had happened, not really expecting a reply, but thought maybe his brother or mother would let us know. To my amazement, he called us from Sydney, where they were still living. They had got married in Bexley, Sydney at a church of similar name but a Roman Catholic version and the reception had been along the same road. If we had added the correct telephone prefix number, we would have reached the house. Goodness knows who we actually had been calling and what they had done with the wedding card and I was glad I hadn't included a cash present at the time. He thought it screamingly funny that we had all traipsed over to a wedding which had actually taken place in his local suburb in New South Wales. We didn't feel it was such a hilarious occasion though because the children were very disappointed and had been looking forward to seeing them and taking part. I bought another wedding congratulations card and enclosed a bank draft drawn in Australian dollars so they could buy their own present and added the pretty pink and blue towels to my own collection.

A few days later I was sitting in the office alone. A young man ran down the street and pushed open our door. He looked about twenty-three and had shoulder length wavy hair. He told me his name was Mohammed and he apologised for the state of his shirt and jeans but he had been painting. He asked if we could help as he had bought a house in Walthamstow which had been split into two flats and he had been decorating it. I am not sure why the planners had issued him with a notice to convert the building back into a single dwelling house but it had frightened him and his young wife, as they had bought it believing it had the use and were planning on letting the first floor out. They could not afford to carry out the works and pay the loan without the help of the expected rent revenue.

We went to the house to carry out an inspection and prepare floor plans. The dimensions fitted the planning criteria by inches. In the cupboard under the stairs we found two electricity and gas meters and the cold water supply pipe appeared to split into two, one travelling upstairs. There were two boilers and associated plumbing. The kitchens were very old and shabby, with antiquated equipment remaining and the bathroom tiling from before the war.

I asked him if he could find out the names of the people who previously lived there but he wasn't able to do that. I contacted the relevant electricity and gas suppliers and they said they had records for the last four years only, so we asked for those. Then I contacted the planners and suggested the house had established use as the conversion works had been carried out more than four years previously and they said they needed proof of this by copies of the voters' (electoral) roll or rates records. They stated a date which was several decades earlier so I went to the library and looked at the records books. These books were huge and heavy as they contained every address in the borough with names of the occupiers, year by year. They were accurate and the names listed changed as the occupiers changed. The roads were in alphabetical order and I quickly saw that the house was listed as two dwellings, having more than two separate family names every year since 1952. It was paramount apparently in this case to prove established use by photocopying each page, truly an annoying task when the council had the same records and could clearly see the collection of two sets of rates for all these decades.

I called the council department and told the planner concerned that I had seen these listings in the library records going back to the 50s so would they agree to those for the last four years, as was usual, to establish the use required and a few from way back which indicated the on-going use? No, they insisted they needed a copy of all the pages to prove unbroken use and letters from the gas and electric services agreeing that two supplies had been in use since this time. This was finally achieved and the established use certificate issued. Mohammed and his young wife were overjoyed. We had met his brother, her sister and parents and their one year old daughter, who screamed every time her father walked away, she loved him so much. To find the criteria to prove established use of a property it was usual to obtain two different sources: the services which had been established, neighbours or previous tenants who were willing to swear affidavits and did indeed write letters in support of the two different tenants over the years, but in addition the officer insisted that this final and time intensive item was proved. I do not know to this day whether this case had been a one-off or had been a subjective matter at the time. Many onerous regulations have since been swept away by successive government law changes but replaced by others.

It was half term and I had booked a ferry to take our car and us from Harwich to The Hook of Holland. I belonged to a ferry club whereby a membership of six pounds gave me a guaranteed discount on ferry trips to France, Belgium, Ireland and other places. In the last booklet, they advertised a few breaks, including the ferry and holiday accommodation in several destinations. I booked a flat not far from the port, on the edge of waterways and countryside and convenient for village shops and roads for sightseeing trips. It was about 50 miles to Amsterdam and the accommodation was about halfway. The flat was spacious and very clean, with colourful furniture and rugs.

I had been to Amsterdam with a few friends when a teenager and was keen to show my family the interesting sights that I remembered. An interesting day at Alkmaar cheese market had been high on my list but the events only run in the summer on Friday mornings, we found out. The cheese merchants dress in national costume, white cotton trousers and tops and wear real wooden clogs. The porters haul sleigh type wooden trolleys with the large round cheeses to be weighed and have races. I was sorry to have missed the fun watching the porters and the bidding and the children would have loved it.

Instead we travelled by a small ferry boat to small islands called Volendam and Marken. Here many of the shop keepers still wore national costume, the ladies with their lace caps and wooden clogs. There are many different varieties of costume differing from region to region. Most have black trousers and the women wear dark skirts with coloured waistcoats or contrast fabrics on the skirts. Volendam is still a fishing village and nearby Marken is not now an island but an obvious tourist attraction. We saw from a distance the famous Zaanse Schans windmills just outside Amsterdam, which still operate. We ran out of time for a visit.

We had a short cruise on a canal and noted the narrow, terraced houses, avoiding Anne Frank's house so as not to upset the children, and visited a museum which we all enjoyed. We walked over the bridges, just looking at the different architecture and noted that the use of bicycles is still common. Cyclist lanes and their own traffic lights cater for this type of transport and highlight the shortcomings in the UK.

We spent an intensive few days, driving to various "must-sees" on their excellent roads, walking, eating and relaxing. We pulled in at a supermarket close to our flat for a few supplies. After a few minutes of all of us traipsing en famille along the aisles, picking up the items we fancied as well as staples, the children drifted off.

Our trolley was by now quite full and as we reached the end of the walkway and turned towards the checkouts we saw our three all sitting on the floor, quietly looking at magazines which had been strewn in a heap by the exit. I suppose they were out of date, we'll never know. They were looking intently at the coloured pictures and conferring together, pointing at different articles. How proud we felt that they were not running about noisily, like some children were behaving, not grabbing things at random or generally being nuisances, but sitting quietly reading. How completely stumped for words we felt when they all grinned up at us as we approached. 'These comics are great, Mum.'

'Are they? Oh, Chris, look at what they're looking at.'

'Can we buy some, please?'

'Um, I don't think they're for sale, darling, as they have all been thrown down. There are a few English DVDs here, let's choose one. We can watch a film while Dad picks up the fish and chips.'

Rarely have we seen pornographic magazines or more explicit pictures in the UK. We knew the laws in 80s Holland were more liberal than ours regarding sex education and printed matter, and I suppose turning a blind eye to foreign children avidly scanning these adult magazines did not matter to the shop staff.

I don't know to this day how much was actually taken in, understood or wondered at, or even if they realised what some of it meant, as they cheerfully sat there turning pages and comparing images for about fifteen minutes before we found them. How well our children were being looked after, I thought.

It was very soon time to get the ferry back. We had booked a night voyage and cabin. There were no cabins for five persons and we thought they were too young to split up, so we had four bunks only and No.3 climbed in with me. Very quickly into the journey the seas were rough and all plans of having a swim in the tiny seawater pool, followed by a sauna for No.2 and me were abandoned. Instead we had supper and went to bed.

Surprisingly, we did drift off for a while even though little No.3 became a mass of writhing arms and legs, tossing the duvet around as he became heated: a single bunk is really not suitable for two, but we were managing. Then suddenly while still far from shore, the ocean grew wild. We all woke with a start as the boat lunged downwards to hit the waves below with a thump. This was followed by it soaring upwards and crashing down again. As it veered towards the crest we all slid downwards in our bunks, our heads pressing against the end wall of the bathroom partition for No.1 in the top bunk, and me and little No.3 in the lower one, and Chris and No.2 found their feet jammed instead. When the movement followed the current of the waves and plunged downwards again, we all slid in the opposite direction. I was desperately gripping on to the side of the bunk and my youngest child to prevent him from being thrown into the cabin or against the opposite wall. Not a lot was said during this journey, which lasted for several more hours of pitching and rolling and finally calmed as we approached Harwich. Forcing ourselves to discard all desire of sleep just as we felt able to succumb, we splashed water on our faces, cleaned our teeth and clumsily dressed for the car journey home.

Disembarking was event free and we all had a semblance of breakfast in Harwich. I have often wondered since whether anyone has ever been thrown from their bunk during excessively rough seas and suffered actual bodily harm, because my arms ached with the effort of holding us down.

I expect the sailors and crew were used to all conditions, but we were shaken and now have a wary respect for the North Sea and the forces of nature.

On the Monday, the children went back to school with many stories to tell their friends and we went to the office to take on new challenges.

Our bank manager's application had been submitted and all seemed to be progressing well. The planning officer advised that she could foresee no problems to the scheme and would be signing it off, which was welcome news to come back to.

We had two small inspections booked and Mr Gold's crazy brother's application to complete.

We were delighted when Graham Snow called us to say that he had attended the parish council meeting in Suffolk and his property application had been discussed. In spite of his neighbour loudly condemning the scheme as out of place and unnecessary and confidently expecting the other committee members to follow his lead, they voted for the scheme to a man and he was left expostulating in vain. This indicated an approval from the planners, too.

Chapter 12

We were adding clients to our files at an alarming rate. We decided that the time had come to look for a draftsman. We placed an advert in the local paper and received a huge response from eager but useless people.

Our advert read for an experienced draftsman, competent with drawing building plans, conversant with current planning and building control laws. Able to drive. Suitable for part-time. Hours and pay flexible.

Consider: 'I was good at Art at school; I used to work at Fords and can draw engines; My husband has just lost his job so he can start right away. He's been a printer since he left school; I can't actually draw houses but I'm willing to learn; My son could do odd jobs until you show him the ropes.'

There were a couple who sounded more promising so we arranged interviews. They came to the office separately.

The first one was so nervous and his face gleamed with perspiration. The drawings he brought to show us were childlike and not to scale. 'Can you draw to scale?'

'What do you mean? In a box sort of thing?'

'No. Sorry, Mr L, but you aren't quite what we had in mind.'

The second arrived and his drawings were better and to scale, so we showed him a few of ours and asked him if he could emulate the style. He was confident that he could. We gave him a rough site survey and an old drawing to show how we wished it to look when drawn up and he said he would bring it in a couple of days. He did this and although the size was correct, he had omitted important details, like the drainage runs. The chimney was present on the front elevation but missing on the side views and Chris patiently showed him all the flaws.

He burst into tears and said the bus fares had cost him all the money he had in his pocket and please give him the job as he would improve and he needed the job because his mum was fed up of him hanging around the house.

God, what a nightmare.

'But, Mr R, we advertised for a driver, do you not drive?'

Pause, then he said in a small voice, 'I will be able to drive next year.'

'Was it drink drive, Mr R?'

A miserable nod, followed by Chris delving into his pocket and bringing out a handful of coins. 'Here, take this for your troubles and go to an evening class. And good luck.'

I felt like going for a drink at that point.

I put the kettle on. Denny came over to look at the offering and chortled in derision.

Every draftsperson, surveyor or architect develops their own style. They should all include the same information but hand drawn plans vary enormously just by the stroke of the pen. Thick and thin lines, sweeps and flourishes, with individual touches showing a person standing in a doorway or loft room, a car in a garage to indicate perspective. Trees can be artistic, and features such as fancy roof tiles, arches, windows and doors. The writing on the plans can slope backwards and forwards, be in lower case or capitals. Perfectly adequate plans showing all the information can look basic if there is no imagination and over the years, Chris's style had been firmly forged and often emulated.

The advert had been placed for three weeks at the price of two, so we braced ourselves for a deluge of sad cases again the following Wednesday.

**

The two girls from the flat above burst into the office just as we were about to go home. 'Oh, Chris, sorry to bother you but we have mice.'

Christ. 'Really? Where?'

'Come and look.' In the kitchen, they had taken everything out of the cupboard under the sink and there at the back was a little hole, just big enough to allow them through. 'They're bold as brass. They're not afraid of us and dance around the kitchen, then when I get the broom they run back under the cupboard.'

The other girl smiled and said they were really sweet but it wasn't hygienic, was it? Sadly, no.

I could now see a tiny gap between the cupboard front and the floor.

Marvellous. Only six months previously this had been a new kitchen. 'Sorry, girls. I will contact pest control in the morning and get it sorted out. These are old buildings and they obviously run backwards and forwards between the timbers and in the walls. The building work down at Mr Patel's shops has probably disturbed them so I think the whole terrace needs treatment. Don't leave any food out and put as much as possible in containers.'

I knew what my first job would be in the morning. I also knew I ought to go from door to door, letting them know that we had a problem which they too could be sharing.

How differently people react. Next door but one to us left lived the lovely artistic couple, he wrote music jingles for adverts and she restored ancient artefacts and had worked at Osborne House: they laughingly said they would join in the exercise. Next door on the right lived another lovely couple who had bought the flat over the little office that we had been attempting to buy. She worked in an office somewhere and he fashioned hand-made shoes. They agreed to join in very readily, so I suspected that they also were infested. The ground floor office had been rented as a second-hand shop. I don't think the proprietors had much money, they didn't seem to sell much but they agreed, too. Mrs Chin was furious and asked me if I was accusing her of being dirty after all the friendship we had shared. 'Goodness, Mrs Chin, it is nothing to do with dirty. Mice are tiny and they run everywhere. I know you are clean and you work hard. I was just telling you that we have them in the flat upstairs and the council said they ought to treat all of the places.'

'You have them?'

I said yes, we had them, which wasn't exactly correct but I thought it sounded better and we would have the traps and trays on both floors, so what the hell. We probably did.

Traps and trays were also put down in the empty café and Mr Patel's and the only one left was the black family next door to us on the left. At last I was able to catch her in and she welcomed me warmly into her house, waving her arms and beaming widely. She then ordered me out of the house, waving her arms about in quite a different manner and wearing a scowl. I persisted, standing awkwardly in the doorway, straddling the front step.

I quietly told her that the pest control officer had visited every other house and shop up to the corner and her neighbours on the other side and would also be visiting her. He wanted to treat everyone and there was no cost to her. I said that he would explain.

Over to you, Mr Pestman.

The kitchen above was cleared and the cupboards repaired. Everything seemed to die down and Mrs W from next door came in afterwards. I saw her approaching the glazed door and there was no time to hide. She was a wide lady, a noisy character with a changeable nature and she beamed at me again and related her news in a broad Caribbean accent. 'We got all dem meeces, Mrs Chris. Dey love da poison, dey gobbled it up, they walked real slow and got so fat. I'm sorry I was upset with you. When you'd gone, I went upstairs to the twins' room and I found da problem. I found all these crisp bags and biscuit wrappers that da boys just left under their beds and some old sandwiches too. Dey can't have food in their rooms now.'

'That's great, Mrs W. Thank goodness, it seems that it's worked everywhere.' Until the next time, I thought wryly. I thought it must have taken quite a lot for her to climb down like that.

I wondered how long the sandwiches had been there and how often she cleaned under the beds. I made a mental note to look under ours. Could stale food under little boys' beds attract mice to an entire terrace?

I was pleased to meet a young man who had been out to the house to see Chris in the past, when he was working at home while I went to work in the bank. He was destined to become very successful and confidence oozed from every gesture and word he spoke.

Chris had known him when he started his business by working out of his mum's back garden, selling ready-made concrete and delivering it to building sites in the area. He quickly made a name for himself, the standard of his product was dependable and his prices were reasonable. He had taken a building course somewhere and liked nothing better than to work with bricks, and carried out a fair deal of building work for his own burgeoning property portfolio.

The problem eventually highlighted was that the rear garden, although large, was classed as a residential garden and not allowed to be used for commercial or industrial use. Diverse workshops flourished in rear ramshackle garage buildings and sheds along the road owned by others and had been operating for decades. These gardens and yards of the whole road led into an access road running parallel with the main road in front, so it was easy for him, buzzing in and out of his little yard. The layout was mirrored, allowing another residential avenue to utilise the same access road, with some of their back yards culminating in small car workshops and spray booths. The numbers had grown over time, so that a type of mews development was forming. Planners issued their formal enforcement notice and Chris had made an application for him, knowing full well that it would be rejected but it bought him six months. When the fateful day loomed, he vacated the rear garden, moving all his sheds and equipment to the empty piece of land next door. The planners congratulated themselves, thinking they had stopped him but he merely started again, using the same telephone number but from the adjacent garden. Of course, the same enforcement notice procedure was started again but all these processes in those times took longer than nowadays. By the time the planning application was rejected for the second time, we lodged an appeal in the secretary of state's office in Wales and this dragged out for many more months. During all this time the council planners were powerless to stop him and they were resentful, but the processes were set down as government procedure.

Of course, the appeal was lost and a further letter issued, giving him a short time to vacate or else the bailiffs would seize his belongings and he would be evicted forcefully. The deliberate applications and appeal process were not costly and bought him the time he needed. His mother owned a parcel of land situated in an industrial estate a few miles away but within another inner London borough. In the meantime, Chris worked with him to prepare a planning application to run his business from this site. There were several buildings and enough turning, parking and storage space for his outfit to grow. This time his application was welcomed and passed with flying colours. His fleet of one mini mixer truck and a battered van gradually grew to more: larger concrete mixer delivery trucks, vans and Mercedes cars but he stayed the same ardent dedicated worker. He was on site by six in the morning and the last to leave at the end of the day. Helped by Chris, he adapted the existing buildings and built more. There were storage units for the sand, stones and cement and a complicated scheme of chutes and conveyor belts to batch up the mix. The trucks drove in and out, seldom waiting idly and delivery lorries drove in with supplies regularly to prevent hold-ups.

It was fascinating to see this little domain grow and he invited us to his home for Guy Fawkes evening. His two tiny sons looked like miniature versions and the evening started early as they were so young. We contrasted this November 5th with the previous year, when half the London underworld congregated together, including us, eating fish and chips on the common while an emergency scaffolding team battled with the winds to shore up a falling roof and partially missing front wall.

We arrived early as he wanted to discuss several ideas that he had for his house and the concrete batching site. Our children watched the toddlers playing. Wrapped in warm padded coats and boots against the damp fog of November they played at running a concrete site. They had several Tonka tipper trucks, cement mixers and tractors, all bright yellow. To everyone's amusement, we watched them fill the trucks with builder's sand until full and push them across the patio to the edge of the garden, where the whole lot was discharged onto another paved area. Then they pushed the trucks back to the heap of sand and repeated the process until it had all been shifted to the other side. Using little spades and buckets, sand was shovelled into mixers, cranked around by chubby little hands and despatched again and tractors pulled the trucks when strangely, one little boy announced, 'The starter motor's gone again.' He must have heard one of the workman say that and this was repeated several times with all the annoyance of a real problem. When the heap was all at the other side they proceeded to take it all back. I heard one say to the other, 'Shall we do another load?' One was two and the other three and I thought that I was watching magnates in the making.

Their mother said they played at building sites all day.

The firework display went off without a hitch, all the children enjoyed sparklers and watching the young dads running from fencepost to fencepost lighting Catherine wheels and pretty Roman candles and fountains. We all tucked into jacket potatoes, homemade soup and a trifle and afterwards the tiny "workers" refused to go to bed while people were still at the house. They had dummies at bedtime and because they were tired, they asked for them, but Mummy said they could have dummies when they went to bed but not when they were downstairs. While the other friends left and Chris wrapped up his renewed discussion with Lee, the babies compromised by changing into pyjamas and collapsing on the sofa. Our last view of them was of Daddy, carrying one on each arm upstairs to their rooms.

He wanted an extension to create a garage and utility room with another bedroom and bathroom over, so this job was added to our chalk board as a reminder.

**

The next applicants for our part time job were due to start their interviews and Denny rudely said he wouldn't miss it for the world. He had been quite busy lately and his financial panic seemed to abate, so he could watch the proceedings from across the room with amusement.

We had several school leavers hoping to start an apprenticeship, but although proficient in classroom technical drawing, we had to turn them away with regret. There would be larger companies, hopefully, who could take these youngsters on and see them through day-release college or sponsor them through university just as a London consulting engineers had taken and trained Chris. We, however, were still an embryonic company and just climbing out of severe financial restrictions and could only take someone on with established skills, who was able to work elsewhere as well as helping us, meaning part-time only.

Then, to our astonishment, a woman with a familiar face came into the office. We knew her but not her name. She also had been unaware that it was us that had placed the advert. After the grins and exclamations ceased the introductions were made. The latest applicant was actually a neighbour living at the end of the street. We had noticed each other as she walked her sons up to the main road to school each morning as we were scrambling about to load everyone into the car to leave for ours. Shortly, her sons switched schools and attended the same as ours did.

She brought some examples of her recent work and it was clear that she knew what she was doing. Not only that, but her style was so like Chris's without even trying to be, she was local and she wanted to work part-time. She was a small, shy lady who took her work seriously and enjoyed keeping up to date with ever-changing trends and building laws.

All we had to do was agree on terms and after that it was plain sailing.

Conveniently, she chose to work from home and seldom came over to us. Instead Chris rolled up the survey and site notes into a narrow tube, walked down the road to her home and pushed it through her letter box. When she had completed the drawing, she rolled it up as before and pushed it back through ours. Sometimes there was a list of questions inside, sometimes suggestions. At the end of the week an invoice was rolled up, as before, and despatched through our front door. Sometimes Chris drew the survey up to scale when he passed it over and sometimes it was roughly sketched out, with some photos and scribbled instructions, but she never seemed to mind and even more strange to me was that she always understood it. I believe the situation was of mutual benefit. She was a marvellous asset to Chris and took a deal of worry off his hands. If the jobs were few it wasn't a problem and when they swamped us, as happened quite often, she put herself out and worked for punishing hours: the dull thud of a drawing tube hitting the mat often happened at the witching hour. At least she rarely complained, although I think her husband felt a bit neglected sometimes.

**

The boys' prep school were putting on a show. No.3 had told us virtually nothing about it so we went in dubious anticipation.

When he started at the school a year earlier he had asked to have violin lessons and this was eventually arranged. I asked if we could hire the instrument from the school, at least until we all knew he intended carrying on with it. Neither Chris nor I can play anything, much to my regret as no-one would be tone deaf by choice, I reasoned. But after several surreptitious sit-ins watching and listening to No.2's piano lessons, whereby I ended up being just as useless as before, I accepted that musician I was not and never would be. No.3 could keep in tune, but learning the violin?

We took our seats in the beautiful school hall and studied the programme.

Year 5 violin recital. That would be him. Six tiny boys entered holding their instruments. They all sat down on the tiny chairs and tucked their violins under their chins and waited bow in hand, except our No.3. He alone had not graduated to using the bow and was still plucking the strings. Apparently, they taught them by plucking while learning the positions and reading the notes. I hadn't known that. He looked very fed up and, I think, self-conscious.

I was glad, sitting there, watching him and them painfully scraping a few notes of *London's Burning* that parents near us were unaware of his or our identities. 'Ahh, look at that dear little one on the end, he can't use a bow yet,' smiling idiotically. 'Hehe, he looks pissed off. I wonder who he is?' from behind a hand.

How dare you laugh at my son? I thought. He can't help it if his best falls a bit short. He's only seven.

I felt fiercely protective of his performance and pride that he was brave enough to carry this out in front of everyone. I also wondered why he hadn't given it up. I would doubtless find out.

A few other songs were sung and a couple of solo performances by budding choristers and instrumentalists, then a winter's story played out with the excellent narration of the English teacher and mainly mime from the children. When he got to the fairy dance we were intrigued to see our son's name on the programme, until the "fairies" danced in to the tune of the *Nutcracker* and saw that the first fairy in was No.3. The dance brought the house down. Wearing pale pink tutus and tights and pink feather head dresses rakishly skewed, they minced in, doing a cross-legged dance step which emphasised the size of their huge black boots. They had been borrowed from the combined cadet corps and stuffed with something to stop them falling off. Fairy Light, Fairy Cake and Fairy Dust earned huge applause and their cheeky grins showed how they had enjoyed doing it. I think his watery violin prowess was forgotten. He said afterwards he had found it hard to keep from talking about it as it was supposed to be a secret. Because he liked wearing the army boots he didn't mind the silly dress and tights, he explained and asked if he could join the corps. 'They use real guns.' Oh good.

When you're old enough, we promised. The violin lessons ceased, he apparently had already told the tutor he realised it wasn't for him and stayed for the performance to make the number up.

'*London's Burning* needed us all to play,' he explained. I thought it was decent of him.

**

We received a call from the neighbour of a lady who helped me with my accounts. She had kindly passed our details on.

The garage was set back from the main house and had developed severe cracks at the side and rear and across the concrete floor. As soon as we arrived we spotted the culprit. A huge oak tree behind the back of the garage would also have mighty roots and in their quest for water, would dry out the sub soil and affect buildings in proximity. We wrote a report for him to send to his insurers, citing differential settlement due to root encroachment. We also advised specialist pruning of some of the branches to reduce the incessant thirst. The tree was listed in the council's records and had a protected tree order placed on it, nobody was to touch it, but eventually the insurers' loss adjusters pulled rank and a few sturdy branches were removed.

A system of monitoring by glass tell tales was installed and readings taken monthly, we called around to visually check the situation. Once finally accepted as a claim, the insurers authorised the installation of a sophisticated system of electronic sensors over the cracks. They organised a test bore, 10m deep as a temporary bench mark for levelling purposes. A digital recording machine, mounted on a tripod in the garden, took the levels of the building throughout the seasons and a person came to take the results. This was a hugely expensive exercise, sprat to catch a mackerel Chris said. It went over my head and I tried to look knowledgeable. Nowadays the system has upgraded to send readings by computer straight to someone's desk. Our client worked nights at a newspaper printing works, so he was always at home by day, asleep in the mornings and walking around in a dressing gown all afternoon. The client had three or four Chihuahuas, a mixture of long and short haired tiny dogs and they ran wherever you tried to walk and yapped incessantly.

Each time we visited he wore the same red dressing gown. Occasionally his wife was home. One day, winking conspiratorially, he slipped a brown paper bag into Chris's case, which turned out to be pornography. He said his mates got the films from Ilford police station. He said you could get anything you wanted up there. We watched a couple of third rate romps which made us laugh, but refused some deeper, darker issues. I wondered what the use of the Vice Squad was, battling to rid the streets of distasteful material when colleagues merely sold them back to smutty dealers and sleazy householders at the back door. He probably thought we were prudes. Chris grinned and said, 'We don't need them.' I didn't know whether to look proud or embarrassed.

It was Chris's thoughts that the movement to the garage had gone too far. He believed a series of repairs to the superstructure and local foundation strengthening would not be sufficient. Insurance companies will not pay to improve a building. They will only cover repairs and making good. We advised that the garage be demolished and a new one built in its stead.

It would be a year later before a decision was made to carry out repairs. We registered our protests to deaf ears.

**

A developer had been using us for a while to draw his plans for conversion, houses into flats. He took a risk by loading his own house mortgage up in order to provide himself with a working capital. He was amusing, always with a story and always trying to get his estranged wife to move back home. He wore his hair in a halo of curls and bang up to fashion clothes. His was the first car I knew which had a private number plate. After a while he realised that we did not use the rear room much. It had a desk and couple of chairs and it was supposed to be a private room for conferences, it was used occasionally for the children to do their homework, but he asked if he could rent it. We thought for a bit, as this would also involve giving him a front door key but we didn't have valuables in the place and Denny didn't care, so we agreed. He moved a few items in and came and went as he wished. Our busy little hive just grew a little busier. I bought extra tea bags and sugar and the extra rent helped with the bills. For a change, he didn't wait for me to rattle the tin and always placed his cheque on the desk without any prompting. Denny, please heed.

His favourite builders came in to introduce themselves and I realised I had seen one of them in the last bank branch I worked in, his sister had her account there. It wasn't long before we drew plans for their use, too, and we recommended them to people seeking reliable builders.

We didn't know at the time, but we gave them a contact who accepted their quotation and it all went very well, which had saved them from dire straits. It isn't easy to build up a reliable contact list and these two had only worked together for a short while so had few recommendations. When a job cancelled at short notice they stood in risk of losing their homes and vehicles and our timely introduction had provided continuity, for which they were grateful. When they landed a larger project, they bought us dinner at a local Greek taverna and we met their wives.

**

To No.3's delight we had a visit from David Mozan and he taught him how to play chess. The little wretch actually understood the game afterwards and beat me every time. Chris hated playing me because I was so useless. He said you have to be analytical and to think ahead. I suppose

I already had a head full of forward plans, like typing reports and doing the invoices and working out shopping and always making sure they all had clean clothes: limited really.

David invited the children to visit the glassworks at the industrial unit next to the hostel and they all went off together, leaving me in comparative peace with Denny.

I helped him with a bill of quantities he was working at and we decided to treat ourselves to lunch, as we knew David would make sure my brood didn't go hungry and Chris was out somewhere in the heart of the East End, so he went off to Mrs Chin's with my ten pound note and I got plates and forks ready.

He brought in a small plastic bag containing cartons of Singapore noodles, beef in black bean sauce, some egg fried rice and sweet and sour pork balls. 'She told me to go back at five thirty as she would give us something to try.'

The food as usual was delicious and we wondered what she would give us. She had tried us with chicken's feet, which only No.1 sampled and pronounced as lovely. Even Chris baulked. Perhaps she had some more, beaks or minced feathers.

Our afternoon progressed peacefully and was shattered when Chris returned at the same time that David's sleek black Range Rover slid onto the forecourt. Denny went to put the kettle on and I listened to the excited chatter. 'Look, this is a sample of coloured leaded lights for windows.'

'This is toughened glass for walking on.'

'This is safety glazing for doors. Can I have a glass door, Mum?'

They had an enlightening afternoon. I had never been in the glass factory and had no idea what was produced there, apart from glass to put in front of pictures for framing and the framing procedure happened upstairs. They went into the industrial lift and were transported to the magical first floor, where they saw materials of all descriptions, all colours and fabrics being produced into frames and pictures made ready for sale and stacked into crates for distribution. These apparently were transported to art shops all over England.

I found out that the forger that David met in prison now used this company to market prints of his paintings. I never knew which name was scratched in the corner of the paintings to be shown on the copies.

The factory on the ground floor received huge sheets of plate glass in differing gauges and strengths for varying use. Machinery measured and cut it into sizes required and vehicles like golf buggies with side vents and fasteners were used to move the cut pieces of glass around the floor, into the various categories' areas. At the far end, they had gas operated kilns which melted smaller amounts of silica sand with washing soda and calcium oxide or aluminium and other chemicals to produce the various colours and these molten blobs were lifted by hooks and poles, apparently, to cool somewhere else, then fed through rollers like a pasta machine, which created sheets for cutting. The processes described to me sounded difficult, dangerous and involved but the children gleaned knowledge and had enjoyed their trip.

Chris had been to a scrap metal yard to meet two brothers to discuss moving their operation to a site in Essex and re-developing their present premises into housing. It was hard to see the boundaries of the yard as so much was stored there, but they had agreed terms and he was to buy the Ordnance Survey map and to enlarge it so they had a site plan to work from. The metals stored ranged from small boxes containing precious metals to steel girders, bits of railway track, iron bedsteads and copper pots and pans. I resolved to accompany him the next time he went there as it sounded fascinating, a trip into Aladdin's cave or Steptoe & Son's, but a change for me.

Chris and David both fancied a bowl of Mrs Chin's finest, which triggered the kids off too so I wandered the few doors to her take-away and ordered the same as Denny and I had wolfed down earlier and she gave me a separate carton of something new. They were called soft shell crabs and apparently expensive. 'These are a present, so share them.'

All forgiven over the mice incident then, I thought wryly, but it was her way of saying, "Sorry" for her outburst.

Back in our little kitchen I opened the top of the carton and peered inside. It could have been anything in the tin foil box, pale battered knobbly things so I showed them around. David declined but everyone else opted for a taste and I cut them up so we could all have a piece. The whole thing is edible, she told me, so trying not to imagine them in the raw I just dropped a piece each on their bowls and quickly shoved my bit in my mouth and chewed. Surprise, I wished I had more as it was utterly delicious. Listening to cries of 'This is great,'

'Result,' and 'Oh yes,' I resolved to buy more when a treat was needed.

**

Ray, our curly haired tenant in the back room had his offer accepted for a three-storey house in Wanstead. The spacious building was in good structural condition although neglected and filthy inside and from the lay-out, could be converted into three flats easily. There was sufficient off road parking space at the front for four cars and a generous garden. The property had a split level lay-out, enabling the middle flat to have its own staircase at the side, leading down to the garden so a section was marked out for this. The ground floor unit had internal stairs leading down to the rear kitchen and garden. The third flat on the second floor had no garden but a small area of the kitchen roof below could have the roof strengthened and allow him a terrace for sitting out.

Chris took No.1 with him to help with the dimensional survey and promised he could do the lease plans when they were needed, but advised he would need help with the common areas, especially as the ground levels differed from front to rear.

The two builders were delighted that they had this sizeable contract to look at for Ray and pored eagerly over the drawings when they were finished. They had been produced and submitted to the local authority as soon as possible after the deal had been struck, so that the planning consent would be ready without delay when his purchase had completed. We advised that a decent schedule of works be produced to enable them to work out an accurate estimate for the work, as we had seen more experienced contractors than these get into serious trouble for underestimating a job. We had witnessed both sides of the coin, seeing a building owner accept a quotation which was inaccurate. He paid readily in advance then ran out of money when the builders asked for more and after a bitter row, they stormed off site and left him in dire straits, roof incomplete, no heating or electrics. He had to arrange another loan just to seal the roof and complete the essentials, and the family had to live in this state for several years while he gradually sorted out his monies and raised more to finish the contract, using different contractors for each of the stages.

We always advise obtaining a schedule of works, a bill of quantities, obtain at least three estimates and when you have had discussions and are sure that you are all singing from the same hymn sheet or working from the same plans, to sign a contract.

An open-ended estimate, unless the builder is completely trustworthy, is an open invitation to expand the contract amount. All sorts of things can be introduced to raise the total, obviously not always deviously. Deeper footings can increase costs as each extra spadeful of earth extracted will require an extra spadeful of concrete to be installed; tree roots found in the excavated footings forces an increase in the depth of the foundations, or the need to change foundations to avoid drains can involve some nifty bridging details to be calculated.

A common fault discovered once areas become exposed during the works can be damp or rotten timbers, which then need treating or replacing due to leaking plumbing. Pipework is then found to be in need of replacing, which involves moving more joists; rotten or broken beams over bay windows or shop fronts often end up by needing replacement, not only of the beam but the window too, as well as re-plastering and making good. It takes an experienced developer, coupled with proficient tradesmen to produce excellence and accuracy. Not only that, you need a barrel load of money or a sympathetic bank manager because you never have enough. It is advisable to allow at least ten percent for unexpected extras as rarely will the project work out as anticipated.

**

Chris had been introduced to an Asian family, who ran a factory making and selling leather jackets. There were half a dozen workers known as "cutters" and about the same number, mainly men, sitting at sewing machines putting the pieces together. Chris wondered then, judging from the scared faces of some of the workers, if any of them were illegal immigrants but it was none of our business. At least they were getting paid and were in the warm doing their work and given their lunch. Somebody made huge pots of curry and rice and they all stopped to eat.

The jackets were superb. They were sold at several outlets known to him, locally and in Brick Lane. Chris worked out a flats conversion scheme for Ali which was accepted by the planners and he was delighted as even we thought it was borderline. Chris took Nos.1 and 2 with him after school one day to discuss various schemes and on-going work and Ali presented the children with a jacket each. The details to the jackets, I saw, were well designed. The sleeves finished with cuffs, fastened with studs and had a front zip as well as an overlapping section to conceal it and in the fashionable blouson style. They were black and gleamed. The children were so delighted. They looked like mini bikers when teamed with jeans and boots, it was a lovely present. They strutted and posed and imagined themselves as really grown up. Of course, this started No.3 off, as he too had been to the factory and been made a fuss of but they didn't make leather goods for young children, the ones presented to us were really the smallest sizes made, for slim young male adults. A couple of weeks later I was walking down Walthamstow High Street, down the market and passed an expensive children's wear boutique which had a sale. There in the shop window was a leather jacket, made in an elephant type colour, without the zips on the pockets or studs on flaps but the same blouson shape and it was reduced to half price. I went in and asked the saleslady who took it out of the window. She told me that people rarely bought expensive designer clothes for smaller children in that area and they had been forced to reduce it. Her husband had been annoyed apparently when she took it from the representative and then nobody bought it. At least I enabled her to get their money back. The size wasn't as generous as I would have chosen as there was little "growing room" but I knew he would be placated and I could pass it down to my sister's boy when finally outgrown. Also, the colour was softer, a black biker's jacket was hardly suitable for a seven year old but looking back now, it wasn't really suitable for eleven or thirteen year olds either. They didn't turn into thugs or fighting rockers and we saw no Elvis sneers so we laughed secretly when they tried to look cool. Their clothes were better than ours.

We had been invited to a christening and they all wore their jackets proudly, saying that, 'Ali gave them to us. Oh, not No.3's, Mum had to buy that. The factory owners are friends of Dad's.'

I wondered then if black leather jackets were considered acceptable for church, but Chris said we wouldn't be left out when the begging bowl was passed round so in his opinion everyone could wear what they liked. He had a way with words.

How impressed were their mates at school when they wore them out and I suppose most days they were rigidly cocooned in school uniforms, including hats and ties, so it was a relief to be casual and trendy too.

**

With the aid of our lovely drafts-lady, a scheme had been completed and submitted for our young concrete mogul in the making. It was good for us to witness him becoming more successful and we were pleased to have been instrumental with his achievements. As we drove about London and the immediate suburbs, we often saw his striking mixer trucks and felt pride for him. He had lost his father as a young boy and never had the paternal encouragement or congratulations when he strived and accomplished. We hoped that in a small way, our praise gave him a little comfort.

Chapter 13

Chris was making a return visit to the scrap metal dealers and I enlisted my help. I knew it was not a pleasant place to be, so I wore a pair of old boots and dark clothes. Denny was working in the office and would answer our phone if it rang. He knew to pass on Chris's mobile number if it was urgent and he liked to play King of the Castle sometimes. Besides, we promised to bring him lunch and that was always a bribe.

We slowly made our way towards Bethnal Green, passing several properties that we had been involved with along the way and Chris hooted when he spotted someone he recognised. I realised that our fame was spreading and a humble pride washed over me. The times when we had worked so hard we could hardly keep our eyes open and the times of sacrifice to make ends meet, or to find the mortgage or school fees, seemed to be worth it as the financial strain had definitely eased.

I had once felt diminished when I had telephoned the school to request a couple of weeks' grace for one of their termly fees, which were paid in advance, while waiting for a VAT rebate and the purser was so rude. He had once been attached to the RAF or Naval Paymaster General's office and spoke with an over ripe plum in his mouth, telling me I shouldn't take on financial responsibility if I couldn't fulfil it, that the school carried a status that was deserved, and more besides. I felt he had no right to speak to me in a demeaning manner and felt shocked and upset. It was the first time it had happened and hopefully not repeated.

I wondered then how other people coped or survived in different situations. If his situation had been different, coming from an ordinary working class family with no contacts as we had done, that if he had been brave enough to strike out on his own without a financial cushion from family or sponsor, if he had taken the overheads we had: property loans, car payments, staff wages and pensions and three children's school fees, if he could have managed as we had without a small blip occasionally. He had responsibility to gather in the school fees and obviously took it seriously but still no right I thought to treat me like a serial offender or guttersnipe. In those days, VAT had to be paid to HMRC whether we had been paid by our clients or not. If the fee turned into a refund or bad debt it was months later that this tax could be claimed back. A small company like ours could be financially damaged in the short term. Nowadays there are different methods of dealing with VAT.

I never told Chris the commander, as he wished to be called, had insulted me as I knew he might react rather strongly and pull them all out in protest. I decided to bide my time and would have a chance one day to report him. The time for negative daydreaming had ended as we reached our destination and pulled into the dingy courtyard. Chris introduced me and a lad went to make us tea which arrived in different sorts and styles of mug. I was allowed to wander while Chris showed them the enlarged site plan with things like drains and service pipes marked. Using the established crossovers in the pavement on each side of the yard, he had prepared a couple of rough schemes for their discussion.

We had developed a good working relationship with several of their planners, due mainly to the goodwill growing with the concrete works a few miles away, and were confident that eight flats could be built along with a small landscaped garden with seating and a couple of storage sheds for the gardener, a drying area for washing lines and enough off road parking for the minimum allowance.

The brothers had no desire to build the project, but would sell it with planning permission intact. It would be the purchasers who would further the scheme by gaining building control approval and go on to take soil samples and a bore hole, to establish the sub soil type and so decide the sort of foundations that would be needed. The distance was not far from the Thames or the Lea and the soil likely to have a high percentage of gravel, which would save the developers a huge amount of money. There also were not many trees in the immediate vicinity which could have an impact on the ground.

The brothers would recommend us to prepare the building control drawings and the engineering needed to enable the building works to be constructed but we had no guarantee of this. Experienced developers or housing associations usually had their own staff or companies who regularly dealt with their projects, so it was important to obtain a good fee first round.

I found a tiny Victorian cast iron fireplace lying behind a heap of railway sleepers and old steel beams and climbed over the ends to see if there was a price marked. I was reluctant to ask if it was for sale as we had been caught like that before. Sadly, we had become quite careful of showing interest in goods for sale or services that our clients carried out, as we always seemed to come out the loser in those types of exercises. I imagined a type of scenario where they came to an agreement regarding drawing and submission fees and then I asked how much they wanted for the fireplace and all of a sudden, the fireplace would find itself in our boot and our fee had halved. Perversely everybody else's goods and services seemed to be so much more valuable than ours. We referred between ourselves to this situation as "a bag of apples". Some years before a neighbour had asked for Chris's help but had not asked if there was to be a charge. We were torn between knowing that his advice was worth a consultant's fee but reluctant to present a bill, as we mixed a fair bit due to the children's ages and interests. Before we could actually make a decision, there was a knock on the door and there stood our neighbour's husband, also a neighbour of course but knowing him less, proudly proffering a carrier bag full of Worcester apples. 'For you. Thanks for your help.'

What could we do, other than call out, 'Thanks, Pat,' as he leapt down the stairs to the front garden and strolled the few doors along, waving gaily.

Another time, a person called and booked an appointment. Chris drew him an extension plan and the person suggested that to save tax and mucking about doing bills, he would do some plastering on our house in return: the cost was about the same. We agreed and posted the drawings to the house we had met in, measured and drawn up and never heard from him again. It wasn't his house and we never discovered who he had been acting for, but we got no plastering done in our home that year. We therefore took a jaundiced view of anyone who suggested a like for like scheme because for us it had never worked.

We had an unfortunate experience where Chris met a developer who also had a second-hand furniture shop in the High Road. He helped him measure up the small building close to his shop and he called into our office to pick up the drawings, leaving a cash deposit and promising the balance when he had submitted the package. Chris advised him that the house was too small to achieve planning permission to convert it into two flats but he just laughed and said, 'Don't worry, Chris. That's why I'm making the application. I'm a bad boy, I bend the tape and I know who to give it to. My guy won't check the measurements.' Quite an admission. We had never known or wanted to know the names of the people who played these games. No planner had ever hinted that he or she was up to this and we had never asked. A person's integrity surely becomes tainted when success like this is bought: like an athlete taking drugs.

We checked the planning progress reports monthly and ten weeks later, much to our surprise, we saw that this building had indeed received approval for two one bedroom flats. Our grateful client who had doctored the drawings to change the dimensions never brought the balance of our fee to us in spite of a couple of letters. I was so angry that he had used us in this deceitful manner that I wrote again, advising that I intended taking him to the Small Claims Court. Having threatened him with this I had to carry it out. It was a palaver, photocopying all the documents and sending him a set to his shop and another to the court and he never bothered to answer or provide any mitigating evidence, so when the day dawned I took myself off to Snaresbrook and filed into the courtroom when our names were called.

We were awarded judgement and costs. He glowered at me across the room and we all filed out. He had been ordered to pay us the money within seven days but we never saw a penny. We went off in separate directions and I never saw him again. He got back to Stratford and dropped down dead of a heart attack. Maybe he got divine judgement but we were left in slight shock. We could have made another claim to his heirs but the whole episode had left us with an aversion to the law. It is easy saying an action can be brought and someone can be sued but the ones who really benefit are solicitors and bailiffs. We would have had to spend more hard earned money to take the case further and the costs to us outweighed the fee that was owed in the first place.

More than thirty years later, the second-hand furniture shop in the High Road still exists. I had no idea who inherited it then and still no idea now.

The men finished their discussion and everyone looked satisfied. I could see that Chris was holding a couple of cheques and they would be for the council application fee, the Ordnance Survey map extracts and our services. Our brilliant draftswoman had helped to prepare the plans and it would be my job to fill in the forms, six sets of six forms, and when the drawings had been printed, to make the application. This would need one of our largest envelopes and a fair few stamps.

One of the brothers had noticed me looking at the fireplace surround and strode over to the heap of timber and soot-covered metals and dragged it out. It looked in good condition, had a raised design of tulips either side of the arch and a narrow mantelpiece. At the base it even had a cast iron insert which would be in front of the grate. I didn't want it to be a working fireplace, just an ornamental additional to the chimney breast in the bedroom, which must have had a similar installation once which was removed by an earlier resident. I envisioned putting a dried flower display in the grate so there was no need to examine the flue or make the chimney fireproof. I just stood there, as I hadn't said a word and I wondered why he had done this. I looked quizzically at Chris and walked towards him. He just did his funny little eyebrow movement and we both watched as the first brother brought it over to the car.

'There, my dear. That's for doing the forms for us.' And he waved us off, grinning.

'How did he know I wanted that?' I asked Chris and he laughed.

'I noticed it last time I came here and put in my order. That's just what you wanted in our bedroom, isn't it?' He grinned at me and I was quite overcome.

My Superman. And I thought he never listened.

**

We discussed what we fancied for lunch. We would buy something ready-made and take it back as I felt very scruffy and in need of a bath. A new Caribbean restaurant had opened a couple of weeks before at the beginning of the road, which Denny passed daily and kept hinting about. We decided to try it out. I rang him and told him to put some plates in to warm and get the kettle on. He lowered his voice and whispered conspiratorially, 'I've taken some messages down for you but we might have to wait a bit, Mrs Chris, there's a few people here to book appointments and the Yugoslavian builders want something drawn up at the Woodford house.'

'Lovely! Thanks, Denny, put it on low then. We'll shove the food in the oven, otherwise we'll be sharing it.'

I knew he would have remembered when his sandwiches got pinched and would want to preserve his surprise lunch.

'We have to ignore the hunger pangs for a few minutes and make do with tea and biscuits,' I continued.

He busied himself willingly with this as we drew up outside and I carried the bag through to the kitchen and put the foil food trays in the oven to keep warm. I hoped our choice of West Indian food would please him. It was a strange set-up that existed with Denny. He was not part of our businesses but we helped each other out. He enjoyed seeing the diverse people that wandered in and mostly they were friendly to him and included him in conversations. Likewise, we welcomed people that came in to see him and over time, met his brothers and friends.

I took the list that Denny had made and proceeded to call people back, making a few appointments for the following week A call to a planning department gave me some information to pass on to an anxious client and then I was free to join in the ensuing discussions. The three Serbs spoke English with varying accents and degrees of fluency. The sectarian troubles had not yet started, at least not reaching our press, and we knew they employed Muslim labourers too. Religion was never discussed and they seemed to get on well.

Mickie, the leader of the business, owned a large end of terrace house close to our home and he allowed his workers to stay there when they were working on a project. There were a couple of rooms which had mattresses on the floor and a heap of assorted bed linen and duvets for the workers to collapse on at the end of their stint. His wife fed them and, I presume, laundered their clothes, although having been close to a few of them on site this was obviously not a priority. He had installed a shower and WC for their own use and presumably paid them peanuts.

The other two lived locally to the office with their wives and children.

Chris had remarked the first time he went to the house that another dwelling could be constructed next to his own home. He would lose the huge garden, of course. Chris said if it was built he could move into it and sell the original, which would probably wipe out his mortgage. There would be no tax to pay as the sale would be part of his estate. He had spent about ten months ruminating about this but eventually decided it would be a good idea. 'Come out to the house on Sunday, Chris. Bring the family, I am having a pig roasting and we can measure up before it starts. You can taste our plum brandy. We make it at home, we smuggle it into the country in lemonade bottles. Better walk round or get a taxi.'

I was losing count of how many times people invited us to their home to join in a celebratory meal or a party, but Chris is obliged to measure up first, or take time out discussing a scheme, or expected to come up with a brainwave, all the time knowing that I was out there facing the throng of total strangers, trying to make small talk as well as watch that No.3 didn't fall in the pond or ride someone's bike or decide to try out an electric drill or try to climb up the ivy like Tarzan does. We all know a family where the children sit up straight on the sofa next to their parents and say nothing, for hours. They don't shout, scream, have a tantrum, wet themselves or run away. They appear to have no imagination and barely answer when spoken to. I don't think they are brain damaged. They are just unbelievably well mannered, well behaved, obedient robots. I wonder how their parents manage to instil this type of blind submission into little bundles of inquisitive energy on legs so that they appear like wooden zombies. Do they threaten them, or worse? Do these young paragons become bullies behind the scenes when they grow? Are these the youngsters who get drunk or take drugs the moment they leave the authoritarian oppression of home for university and utter freedom? Or are they the prigs that know it all? The office bore of the future? I try not to judge as I have yet to find out how our three will turn out. I know that for now they are polite, not usually rude without having a reason, considerate to a degree, lively, nice until niggled, confident and determined, strong-minded, stubborn, awkward, argumentative, noisy, probably normal, I ended.

At last the arrangements had been made and they left and I dived for the kitchen to salvage our food before it dried out. We had lamb curry and rice, long grain this time instead of the usual Basmati. I suspected it was Uncle Ben's; a chicken stew type dish with roti bread and sweet potatoes and peppers. Denny really enjoyed it and we thanked him for entertaining our clients.

I had saved some of the food for the children to try when they arrived later, confident they would love it. They always enjoyed treats that Denny brought in and all liked strong flavours.

Today was no different and I thought we could all have a slice or two of my mum's apple pie and custard when we got home and an early night. It promised to be a busy day tomorrow and Sunday would be a treat to remember.

The next day Friday was quite hectic. Ray decided to use his room for the day and kept coming out to talk to Denny and me. First, he wanted a drink, then his mobile had run out of battery so he used the office phone and talked and laughed loudly enough to put me off my report. It seemed that every time I got to a quiet bit on the tape that I had to concentrate on he would launch into a raucous guffaw that completely wiped it out. I kept rewinding it to replay but it was all proving to be a strain. Even Denny kept turning round and frowning. At last he put the receiver down and proceeded to tell us all about his conversation. After a couple of minutes I said, 'Sorry, Ray, I can't really talk this morning. This report is urgent and I'm having trouble understanding some of Chris's words. I have to highlight gaps so I can go back and fill them in when Chris gets back.'

Quite unabashed, he moved over towards Denny, peered at his drawing board and kept asking questions about the project. 'Where's this then? Who are you doing this for?' and Denny just quietly mumbled answers.

We didn't want to be rude to him but our hectic lives and stream of work was relatively constant, thank goodness, but his was busy in fits and starts. Once he had bought the property and the drawings were being considered at the council he could begin to obtain tentative quotations and discuss the scheme and finances with builders and his bank. Apart from sourcing kitchen fitments and bathrooms, tiling and finishes, his time was taken by site visits and liaising with suppliers for delivery dates, then making sure someone would be on site to accept the materials. Most of his days he cruised around showrooms and to the premises to annoy the builders and travelled back again. He was up with the latest fads and building fashions and sometimes I yearned for the opportunity to visit the exhibitions or attend an interior design course, but there was always shopping to get, cooking to do as well as the interminable laundry that five people generate, not forgetting when I doubled as the children's minicab driver to karate class, football, swimming or hurtling back to school after one of their clubs, so any spare time during the evenings was precious indeed.

I needed Chris to get back to fill in my blank spaces so the survey could be printed and posted off ready to begin the next one.

It was completed and sent, of course. Plans were printed, letters composed and typed and haphazard filing was done so I left at three thirty to post the letters, collect the children and take them straight home. Chris had a meeting at the office with the lovely gay estate agents to discuss their latest scheme and would follow later. It was Friday night so I sensed a take-away would be just the thing and rang our order to the local curry house for Chris to pick up on his way home.

Sunday arrived and we walked the mile or so to Mickie's house. We always had half an hour of entertainment when he and a couple of his guys turned up at the office and we always gave them a drink and biscuits, if there were any left. Mickie was amusing, his language was colourful, badly pronounced English because he spoke so fast, he gabbled and most sentences he finished by adding the word, "bloody" or "bastards", even when totally irrelevant. 'The traffic was bad, I got to the site late; bloody.'

'I forgot to buy my sandwiches, bastards.' He was harassed, panicky sometimes and always telling us he needed more money, but was generous and hard-working and we admired all of them for their bravery and efforts.

We had a large box of chocolates and fruit to give to his wife and looked forward to meeting the other wives. Mickie told us it was his son's birthday, we thought he would be fourteen so I got a card and put some money in it. 'What's his name?' I asked. Several times he repeated something which sounded like Zorkie or similar and I still wasn't sure. His accent was very thick and much of our conversation was guesswork, with plenty of arm waving. 'It's the same as Tarquin,' he said. I tried to remember where I had heard of Tarquin and thought he was an old Roman king or superhero, but that might have been Horatio defending the bridge. So I wrote, "Happy Birthday, Tarquin" on the card. He wrinkled his nose and gave us a very strange look, obviously thinking I was some sort of fool when I gave it to him. Mouthing, 'Thanks,' with a puzzled shrug and an Elvis sneer he walked off and as he passed his Mother he waved the card and said, 'Tarquin? Who's that?'

O well, can't be right all the time, I figured. He kept the money though.

A pit had been dug out and a mixture of charcoal and kindling placed in it and the fire lit at some God forsaken time that morning. A complicated construction of bits of metal, forming legs and a frame with rods and a handle, had been fashioned by Mickie and the unfortunate pig now turned slowly over the fire. It weighed about 30lbs apparently and had been marinating in salt water and herbs for a whole day in a plastic baby bath. The poor thing was trussed along its length to prevent it disintegrating and tasty bits falling off into the embers and the smell was utterly wonderful. Every now and again someone spooned a rich dark mixture over it, which was apparently olive oils and seasonings and flavourings which I couldn't translate. I resolved to take a closer look later.

I was glad we had taken some wine and fruit and put it on the trestle table with the other offerings. There were boxes of fruit jellies and nougats and fancy chocolates with foreign names. I had been looking forward to meeting the wives and families of these hard working guys and a glass and a half of a sparkling liquid later, I was seated with a few of them in a small circle in the garden. After we introduced each other, the conversation was flowing freely as if we had known each other for ages. I was full of admiration for these women. With their menfolk, they had uprooted and travelled hundreds of miles to begin life in a strange country where religion, language, customs were completely different. The men went to work for other Serbian countrymen and it was the women who built the home foundation for their children. They went shopping in strange shops and bought goods with strange money. They had to deal with gas and electric services, water companies and sort out bank accounts and insurances. Some had learned to drive and passed their tests. They had been to local schools and organised the children's places. One had a small daughter of only two and a half, who had been born over here. She said three years ago, when they first arrived she knew no English. I doubted that I would have achieved so much if it had been me that was uprooted to Croatia with the clothes I was wearing, two sons and a bump and very little else. Now they were buying a semi-detached house in Forest Gate, it was completely furnished and she had her own mini car and ran the household in a confident, assured manner. Her husband, Jovan, was Mickie's right hand man as his language was proficient and he had been a site foreman back home. He now drove lorries at night, travelling the length and breadth of Britain, arriving back home as dawn was breaking. He went to bed and was up again by eleven to join Mickie on the building projects. His wife confided that the extra money was useful and was paying for the house but she worried when he was so far from home. The only complete rest time for him was Sunday morning and then the children wanted his company and guidance. She told me that she had just started the little girl at play school but she wouldn't settle. She was at her wits' end, spending the entire morning in the church hall: whenever she tried to sneak out the little one noticed and screamed, forcing her to rush back.

I told her a ploy that I had used when my No.1 became clingy after No.2 arrived. I suggested that she gave little Maria her umbrella, or little purse or anything small and asked her if she would look after it for her while she popped to the shops. Little children believe that their mother will return for the object even if they fear being left themselves. It was gratifying a week or so later when Katya called me to say, 'Thanks.' She told me the little trick had worked perfectly. We both cried a little to think that a precious tiny child thought their mother would return to pick up a battered old brolly but regarded themselves as indispensable, to be dumped in a dusty hall.

Ilija was thin and wiry, with merry dark brown eyes and sun-tanned skin. His wife was English and worked as a machinist. They had two daughters. I was surprised to learn that they only spoke English. He said their lives were here and there would be no need for them to learn Serbo

Croatian. I thought it was sad that when they returned to visit grandparents or just see the land their father had left behind, they would be unable to recognise the towns or roads or join in any conversations.

Both Jovan and Katya's sons were bi-lingual, from being at school and the little girl would follow. I think if the mother is foreign, she will be more likely to take the trouble to speak to the children in her mother tongue and life in England with nurseries, schools and clubs ensure that children pick up the language quickly. Ilija and several others spoke English to their partners and had no time or inclination to teach their offspring their own language after a day's work on the site.

Soon excitement spread though the garden as we were called to collect a plate and fork and help ourselves to the jacket potatoes and salads, then join the line to be served with pieces of the roast meat. The crackling was crisp and perfect, the meat tender and moist as only pork from long, careful cooking can be. They apparently roasted lamb in the same way and this was reportedly equally delicious. I hoped we would be included at the next one if this was anything to go by.

Thankfully, Chris appeared in time to help himself to a gigantic plateful of food and a large glass of wine and for a short while there was a lapse in the conversation, while everybody concentrated on stuffing themselves. Even the children were manfully tucking in to lumps of fresh new buttered bread and this melting, flavoursome meat.

'Eat up,' yelled Mickie, 'Come back for seconds, it all has to be eaten, bloody.'

When we thought we had eaten everything we could, we were obliged to try some of the home-made desserts. Someone had brought a black forest gateau made with whipped cream and cherries, another offered a fresh fruit salad which is my dessert of choice when entertaining and another had concocted a wobbly Pavlova. I have never made a successful Pavlova and was impressed at the pure white texture and crisp peaks.

I asked Mickie if this was a celebration and he said it was a get together he did a couple of times a year to say, "thank you," to his men for working hard and just to meet up with everyone away from the building sites. He had hired an entertainer for an hour of magic for the children and we were delighted to see it was Alvin, who lived near us and who we too had hired for several of our own dos.

By now of course many of the wine bottles had been sampled and sunk, and little shots were being handed round of a clear colourless liquid which they called plum brandy. This fiery liquid tasted nothing remotely like plum, brandy or otherwise and scorched our throats as we sipped it. Households in the regions where these people had lived made their liqueurs from local fruits to secret recipes and presumably using homemade stills. The liquids were hidden in their luggage, among the bottles of water at the back of the car and smuggled into the country. We felt privileged to be treated as their countrymen and shamelessly quaffed the stuff as enthusiastically as they did.

Suddenly the music changed and a tape of vibrant local band music started. To my delight the men all joined together in a large circle and began to dance. It was like Greek music and dancing and got faster and faster as they swirled round, feet tapping and crossing. I saw No.3 copying them on the side, watching and concentrating on the little steps.

At last it was time to wander home, not too late as it was still term time and that day remains one of the best we have enjoyed.

We had at last received the official planning permission certificate for Graham and Lindsay's holiday home. They were spending more and more time there, while he was digging the foundations and laying the drainage pipes, ready to start the moment he had the paperwork. She toured around the shops of Southwold, searching for pictures and artefacts. She had a good eye for colour and style and it was looking wonderful. I couldn't help thinking if that had been us on site, I would have been wheeling the barrow to the tip at the end or fetching engineering bricks or bits of pipe for him, but then I was nowhere near as decorative as she was and you didn't keep nails like that by using your hands roughly, or using them at all! He didn't seem to care and he knew her better than anyone else did. When she wafted back, laden with carrier bags, he looked appreciative of the things she waved triumphantly at him as if she had acquired them by magic instead of spending his money. I know that if Chris had been standing in a trench nearly two metres deep that he had excavated and he felt dirty and sweaty from the exertion, he would think I was crazy if I ran towards him waving a wooden elephant and crying, 'Look Chris. How sweet this is.' He would probably say, 'Can you get me a drink please, sod the elephant.'

We introduced Graham to our fragrant estate agents and they had sold a couple of his units off plan. It was good for Graham, as his bank manager was more than eager to lend to him for the build when interest was this keen at this stage. It was also good for us when an introduction went well.

The partners had acquired a small strip of land in Stanstead, just on the edge of the village and at the end of a cul de sac. It was a side piece of ground and just large enough for a small house, they thought, and brought the Ordnance Survey map extract and various drawings which had been with the deeds round to the office. The land had a ditch at the extreme side, next to a field and we were a bit concerned that this could cause possible problems as the responsibility for the ditch was not known. We decided to take on the job and went through various styles of dwellings that we knew had gained good results and which we thought would suit the plot and the area. They had no intention of building the new house, however, and would sell the plot with planning consent for a three bedroom dwelling with double garage, for a handsome profit. At that time council planning departments did not always concern themselves about drainage and the various departments never worked with each other. Nowadays, when a planning application is made there are questions about existing trees and they want to know if there are intentions to remove any. Many applications are obliged to submit a tree survey as part of the package. Any existing drainage has to be indicated on the drawings and proposed drainage shown. Any new house now has many more questions to answer. What environmental impact will there be? The area has to be surveyed by a specialist for the existence of bats and great crested newts and if evidence is found, the entire building program can be halted or refused completely. Although there was not a pond on this land, we feared that evidence could show the newts using the ditch, as they lived partially on dry land and environmental issues had just started creeping onto the planning agenda. In addition to keeping up with the current building laws, there were also the ever-changing planning dictates to conquer. Sometimes these bye-laws to the planning rules were worded so confusingly, I thought it allowed the planning leaders to influence the outcome by interpreting these passages to suit themselves.

Although J and J chose not to concern themselves on the possible intricacy of the build or difficulty with fundamental issues, I knew it would be down to me to source a local wildlife enthusiast before things progressed far and possibly screeched to a deafening halt later. The partners could have sold the land but we would likely be still associated with it and I always tried to protect our integrity and reputation.

I researched Land Registry for information on the ditch, as the map was not clear enough to define the exact location of the boundary. When there is a fence the boundary of the land is clear and usually is shown on the documents. Unless the fence is moved surreptitiously over time, the ownership of the fence is defined by the side of the fence posts. When a hedge and a ditch edge the land on one side, the boundary is not always clear cut and I urged J and J to seek clarification from the vendor, who expressed ignorance and reduced the cost of the land. J & J whooped with delight and the deal was done. We felt that this was a bad omen and cheap land usually meant bad soil, contaminated maybe or prone to flooding. Maybe the reason for the ditch, which had probably been dug in centuries past, was to aid irrigation. I suggested that they contacted the farmer for definition, who then passed it to his estates manager who passed it on to their solicitor.

Eventually confirmation was obtained that the boundary of the land was in their favour for building plot purposes. It extended across the ditch and included the hedge, terminating just inside the field which on paper increased the plot considerably.

It was decided to put in a klargester to dispose of the foul drainage, as the main drainage of the next dwelling was a considerable distance away and this detail was added to the drawings. The cost of this huge balloon-like contraption buried beneath the ground seemed at first glance to be expensive but compared to excavating trenches for pipes, constructing manholes with covers, providing ventilation pipes, not forgetting the hoops to be jumped through to satisfy the relevant water & sewage company and the council, it seemed reasonable. Obviously, a new water supply pipe would be needed and gas and electric services and telephone, but these details would be for the eventual developer to deal with. Our job was to draw something which looked nice, attractive enough to sell and in our book, that meant legally able to be built.

We had been waiting for several decisions to arrive. The family from the leather factory needed more space, to accommodate two new brides who were arriving from abroad. At least there were two of them travelling together, one for each of the older brothers and who knew each other, I understood, so moving from the other side of the world to live with strange people may have felt less daunting. The look on my face must have been transparent as they hastened to explain that these were not the sort of arranged marriages that the bad press exposed to their readers. These were with the girls' consent and they had known the families for years, everyone was in agreement. What could we do? Chris gave me an almost imperceptible glare. I knew he agreed with me but he was able to succinctly put a different point of view forward where nobody took offence but I was too direct. Subtle as a flying brick, is how he described me.

So, the large double fronted, six-bedroom house was measured for loft conversions. The house was beautiful and had a wide double staircase separating at the top and dividing off to form a separate landing each side. Chris told me it was a modest version of an Imperial staircase seen in grand houses of Europe. The loft rooms would be formed in the whole of the roof space and provide two suites, comprising large rooms with en-suite showers, dressing rooms and plenty of storage. Luckily there were no parking restrictions along the road and ample parking space in the front garden, albeit utilising a section of the lawn. At that time, inner London boroughs allowed one parking space per bedroom in an attempt to control overcrowding. This criterion was often overcome by labelling the bedrooms as study, nursery or library or even adding a partition wall after the building inspector had left site, to create two rooms instead of one. In this case the yardsticks measured up and the Ali's got their planning consent. We hoped they would all live together happily. Although that is the aim for all of us, I suppose.

The other family to celebrate was Graham's, who had achieved the permission for a garage and rear extension at the holiday home but had returned to seek consent for a large summer house with conservatory, like a glorified log cabin, at the end of the garden. I thought the conservatory addition would be a step too far but hadn't reckoned on Lindsey's persuasiveness at the parish council meeting. The planning section of this Suffolk area paid attention to the parish council comments and were a bit tired of the aged reverend with his endless complaints, so the objection was overruled and Graham had more work to do.

It was approaching No.1's birthday and we decided to make a visit to Theatreland.

I knew he disliked musicals and most shows. He couldn't understand why someone would suddenly burst into song when a few words would say what they meant. He liked to listen to the radio and could belt out with enthusiasm the refrains of the latest songs in the hit parade and keep surprisingly to a reasonable pitch when in his own room. Singing songs is not proper conversation, he maintained. Chris told him about opera, which we had not taken him to see. He thought that was even more stupid. There followed a few days where he would fling out his arm and break into song to ask a question. We indulged him and sang back, 'Are we having lunch at school today?'

'Nay, lad nay. It's Saturday.' Needless to say, the craze didn't last long.

I had bought tickets for Agatha Christie's *The Mousetrap*. It was even then the longest running play on stage and at St Martin's theatre since 1974. I learned later that by 1957 it became the longest running play and Noel Coward sent a congratulatory telegram to Agatha Christie. Chris decided to drive to town and park somewhere and we picked Mum up on the way. We squashed up in the car: it was before having seat belts became law.

We parked somewhere near Leicester Square and walked to the theatre for the matinee. The younger two children were very excited. I had recently started to take our No.2 to the ballet. A school-friend also with a daughter often met me and the girls had become hooked. No.3, since his own performance in the triumphant school show, liked anything theatrical but I wondered whether the plot of a mystery play which twisted and turned as Christie writings do, would be too difficult for him and he would get restless. I remembered one year, I booked a small box for the children and me at Sadler's Wells to see a children's ballet called *La Belle Fille Mal Gardee*, loosely translated as *The Badly Looked After Girl*. It has a clog dance performed by the principal Dame, who by tradition is performed by a male dancer. Both boys were hideously bored and fidgeted and moaned after the first act. Sweets got spilled, shoes got lost, the program was dropped over the handrail and an annoyed person down below gave me a dreadful look and the outing turned out to be a mistake. At least Chris and Mum were with us today, so it wouldn't just be me that would battle to control them and we would go for a Chinese dinner afterwards.

I don't know if any of us guessed "whodunit" but we all enjoyed ourselves. We were asked politely to keep the identity of the murderer a secret so as not to spoil the show for others.

We walked afterwards to Shaftesbury Avenue to a restaurant we had discovered several years before. They did the usual A La Carte menu but we found that a set meal for four was sufficient, as No.3 didn't eat much. Of course, Mum was with us, so we would choose something else. She had been with us that first time when the meal turned into a hilarious riot.

No.3 loved special fried rice in those days and apart from some chicken or pork which we made him eat, would be happy with a bowl of that. We realised that we needed more Singapore noodles and raised a hand to order more. No.3 asked for rice, except the waiter couldn't understand him. There followed a conversation where No.3 politely asked 'Please could I have a bowl of rice?'

'What?'

'Just a bowl of rice for me, please.'

'Bolla lice? What?'

'Not bollalice. Bowl of rice.'

'Bolla lice, bolla lice. What?' He stood still next to the table, looking at us, looking at the serving staff in their white chef's hats, shrugging and silently mouthing "Bolla lice" over and over.

No.3 was almost apoplectic with anger and my Mum was in hysterics. I stood up and went over to the serving area and pointed to a basin of special fried rice. I think I tried to smile but was holding back from exploding into laughs like Mum, as I didn't want him to get offended. After that incident, we often saw the waiter when we visited again and apart from a slightly guarded expression the first couple of times, all seemed to be forgotten. They remembered, however, that No.3 loved special fried rice and gave him his own bowl to start us off.

The restaurant had been closed for several weeks and we were surprised to see it had had a makeover, with a completely new shop front and name over the window. The familiar old timber frontage we knew had gone and a new glass, black and steel framed façade gleamed enticingly instead. Gone were the odd cloths on the rickety tables surrounded by mismatched chairs, instead equal sized tables adorned with crisp white

173

linen and shiny cutlery stood, with smart seating and benches. The value for money menus had also disappeared and posh new lists showed posh new prices. We changed our minds after doing a quick mental calculation and walked back towards Leicester Square to where a fairly new restaurant called Poons had opened, where we could eat duck and pancakes and stuff ourselves with special fried rice to bursting for reasonable costs. This was a fast moving place with no formal seating areas and we sat down where we could. No.1 said he thoroughly enjoyed his birthday family treat and that was the important thing.

The next day, on Sunday, the school held a special service in the chapel and we felt obliged to go as although No.3 had given up the violin, No.2 had started to sing with the choir. Chris's mum was in hospital so we took Chris's dad with us. After we took him for a tour of the beautiful old buildings and the service ended, we filed out and went into the Great Hall where they supplied light refreshments. We admired the buildings as some of them were historic and thought he would enjoy seeing where some of his grandchildren attended school, but Chris's dad said he felt out of place there and wanted to go home. I expect he was missing his wife and we hoped he would relax a bit after we had eaten dinner and we had taken him to visit her, then delivered him safely home.

**

The young concrete mogul had introduced a few of his faithful clients to us. One was Joe and his partner, who seemed to be accident prone. They had known Chris for a while and had travelled out to our house when Chris worked in the tiny bedroom and I worked at the bank, so I had not met them before, just heard snippets of their antics on site. Joe had inherited a few large houses, previously owned and run by his parents. They were Dutch Jews and had apparently arrived just before the war, with the clothes upon their backs, having fled from the Nazis and certain death. They rented a few rooms from a house owner who had left London for the comparative safety of the countryside and she took in washing. He of course went to work, I believe down on the docks. Soon she had a lodger or two and fed them as well as taking in washing. Before long she had the whole house which she filled with immigrants, fed them all and kept up the washing, which obviously must have been worthwhile, if not extremely hard work, even when her children started to arrive. He meanwhile still went to work doing something on the docks. The house owner decided that life in the country suited him during the war years and sold his house to Joe's parents at a knock-down price and their path was now set on the acquisitions side of life. From that house, they moved to another, the laundry part of her business ceased I believe at that time, but she kept taking in lodgers and these people were the ones that paid the housing loans. I understand that after a while, money permitting, they repeated the exercise. I do not know how many properties the family owned at the time of their eldest son meeting Chris, but a planning officer I was talking to one day while discussing a planning decision remarked that they owned a huge slice of Forest Gate. The buildings that we had become aware of were not well maintained internally. Each room contained a resident or two. I don't know if they went to work or claimed benefits, but the rooms were sparse. The sticks of furniture were cheap and shabby, belongings were few. A sink was placed in each room but there was only one bathroom per floor. Some of the rooms stunk of body grease and odour and the solitary kitchen on the ground floor was filthy.

It was a shock to me to see bare mattresses with no sheets, pillows with no cases and discoloured duvets crumpled up with no sign of a cover. It was hard for me to keep up a friendly relationship with seemingly nice people when it was known that these homes of multiple occupation owned and operated by them were so grim. David Mozan's heap of shelter for the dispossessed seemed like luxury by comparison, but his place was actually run by his team, who cleaned the rooms and all common areas and treated it more like a hotel. Even hostels I figured showed an element of cleanliness and care. Chris said you can do so much for people but the rest is up to them. They pay rent for their room and what they do in their room or how they look after their room was not Joe's decision. Likewise, Joe can tell them to clean the cooker and the kitchen but was unable to enforce this and if some of the residents objected it was up to them to do something about it. Students worked out rotas so it should not have been beyond these people to affect a similar idea. A couple of trips around these types of buildings soon lost their appeal for me and I no longer jumped at the chance to get out on site, asking cagily where it was first. I preferred to help to transform a blank plot into a stunning family home and my favourite projects were loft conversions. Besides, I had most of the admin of the office to do as well as our book keeping and spent an anxious couple of days quarterly, when the VAT return had to be completed and the dues paid to HMRC. I often sat up until around 3am completing these forms and on the first of the month, had to drive to Stratford to deliver them and our cheque directly at the office.

This time Joe needed a plan drawn showing the whole building including the front common entrance, the rear garden and side way. It was for the fire brigade to upgrade their records. Once they received several copies of the layouts they studied it and returned one copy duly stamped as approved. This in turn was needed for their insurance company and for the council.

The last time we saw Joe and his partner Joe strolled in smiling and his partner struggled in on crutches. One foot was bandaged like a character's in a cartoon, a balloon shape of swaddling and a large plaster on his nose which did not conceal his black eyes. 'Good God,' from Chris, 'whatever happened?'

Gasps from Denny and me. 'I was wearing socks at home the other weekend and trod on a rake and the prongs went in my foot, then the handle swung up and bashed me in the face.'

'So, he can't work, again!' from an exasperated Joe. His mother swore he did these things on purpose so that he could lounge on the sofa and watch TV.

A previous car incident, shelf falling on him, tripping over slates preceded this latest accident. He was always pursuing an insurance claim of some kind so perhaps Joe's mother was wise.

**

We submitted a scheme to the local council planners for an attached house for Mickie and had received the department acknowledgement, which meant that posters had been attached to the lamp post in the road, advising that a scheme had been applied for and under consideration. The poster advised that any person having adverse thoughts about the idea could contact the department to discuss or register an objection. There was a time allowance for these comments of about three weeks, but immediately an irate neighbour contacted them to report that there were many illegal immigrants living in the house and this was lowering the tone of the street.

Mickie had a letter the next day, telling him that the following day a site visit would be carried out to inspect the inside of his house. He panicked and his fast gabbling escalated to a pidgin mix of Serbian and English swear words, so Chris drove round there to inspect the staff quarters.

Two rooms had mattresses laid on the floor, apparently covered with bed linen, Chris told me soothingly, knowing my revulsion for dirt and deprivation, that there were clean quilts and crocheted blankets, stands of towels and toothbrush holders, with shampoos and shower gels in the shower cubicle. I had not seen this when we went for the hog roast. Chris told him not to worry. Just three men were working with him and living with him in this way and would return home when the contract finished. If and when he needed a specialist plasterer or stone mason, he would again bring in the skilled workers and put them up until the work was finished.

He was not breaking the law, he was not housing illegal people, he was not charging rent or using his home as a hotel, therefore there was nothing that the council could do and they went away.

I have no doubt that there were times when the singing perhaps became loud, and people are naturally afraid of strangers from countries that they are ignorant about and become suspicious of their own way of life being eroded by interlopers.

He was told that he would receive a letter telling him that the present set-up was acceptable, but to keep their movements in and out of the house and garages to a minimum as too many trips could cause a traffic problem and Highways could intervene. How, I thought? A Range Rover pulls out of the side way every morning, between 6.30am and 7.30am, containing four or five workers. At some time after dusk it returns again. Some days, Jovan calls round with another worker to discuss their work plans, but mostly they meet on the relevant site. Most days Mickie's wife drives her battered car out of the drive and returns with shopping bags. Most ordinary men go out to work in the mornings and most women go to the shops then ingeniously they return again later.

People and their ways will always fascinate me, mainly lacking in tolerance and full of blame.

Chapter 14

Reverent McDonald had not been by for a couple of months and he burst in one morning, with his flashing smile and huge teeth. 'Good morning, my dear child. Is your wonderful husband about today? I have a little job I would love him to do for me. It's only tiny and won't take him long.'

Mm. If they tell you enough that it's just a little job that won't take long, it's because they don't want to pay much. Truthfully, with a planning application the fact that the planned addition is small detracts little from the overall work or costs involved, as the whole floor needs to be measured and drawn up; the whole first floor, too, if a loft conversion is wanted; and all elevations have to be shown, regardless of the size of the extension.

I went through incidental charges that were nothing to do with us but which people believed went into our pockets too. The cost of the Ordnance Survey map extracts; the cost of prints and postage; the council application fees for planning consent and building control approval. Further application fees to Highways for kerb crossovers and maps for water supply pipes and sewage drainage pipes. I wrote them all down for him to take away and reflect on, being careful to tell him that our fees for measuring his house, his whole house from top to bottom and front to back, would be needed to be drawn up accurately, before his kitchen extension and bathroom en-suite on the floor above could be plotted and submitted. 'The council fees are the same, Reverend' I explained. 'Our fees are larger for larger houses and cheaper for little houses but in the main the fees are the same, as basically most houses are similar in size. A two-storey dwelling with a side attached garage is the same wherever it is situated.'

His loud jolliness was slightly abated but he nodded, so I told him that if he wanted us to prepare a quotation I would make an appointment for Chris to visit and he could then discuss it. I also told him that Denny could do this for him cheaper and without the VAT, but he just looked reproachfully at me and left, forgetting to scoop up his usual stationery bits and bobs.

No.1 had drawn up excellent plans of Ray's flats for lease purposes and Ray rewarded him with a few notes. We had to issue him with an invoice, however, in order that our company stamp was printed on the side and our professional indemnity cover was in place, but felt obliged to reduce it as our budding surveyor had received a separate payment and we were proud for him.

On Sundays, sometimes No.1 cleaned one or both of our cars. Obviously, we gave him pocket money for this, probably not as much as he deserved. One memorable Sunday proved a bonanza for him, as a neighbour saw him and asked if he would clean the doctor's car, which was her husband's. He obligingly agreed and she thankfully gave him some money for his efforts.

On the following Sunday, she came down and asked him if he would clean her son's, too, and her own and the following Sunday, her friend came for lunch and wanted hers done as well. I think the record became seven in a day, with a few spilling over to Saturday afternoons when he was around.

While at the bank, I often took bottles of wine into the branch for the members of staff to buy. A local insurance agent desperately wanting to be an entrepreneur rented a garage behind the launderette on the High Road and sold wines by the case on a Saturday. This was known as the Saturday wine warehouse. His prices were competitive, shaving pennies off the costs of the supermarkets' equivalents and was proving to be quite successful. Some of the girls I worked with wanted two or three bottles at a time and couldn't stretch to twelve, so I would pick up the boxes on Saturdays and they would pay me for their choices, which I would then drop around the following week. It became laughable when even the management, learning of cut price wines, clamoured for lists and tried to bait me down. I was awarded a discount for being a regular customer but I always passed it on to my colleagues. I explained that bringing wines to work was not a side-line of mine, it was a favour for friends and I personally made no money on it.

Just inside the doorway there were racks fixed, a few expensive wines stood on display and champagnes were lying on their side. I wondered who he thought might pay over a hundred pounds for a single bottle when a whole crate of Niersteiner cost about fifteen pounds, but then I know nothing about wines, grapes or regions. One day while he was busy and took his eye off the front section, somebody stole a bottle of something outrageously expensive and made off with it. He always had a suspicion of the thief's identity but nothing could be proved so he didn't try. He made sure the expensive display case was a bit more protected after that for when he was chatting or making up an order.

One day, while No.1 was sloshing around outside with his buckets and cloths, he drove past on his way to the front lock-up and stopped. He knew our children, of course, as they were almost an extension of us and he was impressed with his exertions. 'How do you fancy washing the van?' he asked him. The height of the van appeared daunting, but he said he had steps in the yard and a hose pipe and he would give him the same as three cars.

'Done,' agreed No.1 and their agreement started a monthly activity. I am sure this would have provoked Health and Safety nowadays or broken children's labour laws.

During this time of car washing, he raised enough money to buy his own music centre and CDs for his room and other technological things hankered after by the youngsters. Nowadays I feel guilty that he did this. Children and teenagers rarely have this prodigious work ethic and I wonder whether we should have allowed him to act like this, when all his friends generally lounged around but received the paraphernalia as gifts anyway. I wondered if he wanted the gear and felt he couldn't ask us, so worked extraordinarily hard in order to get them.

We wanted them to know that an effort has to be made in order to progress, like school homework, but perhaps we went too far in allowing it. At least it was never us that found him the cars or asked him to wash them, so I hope he never felt exploited.

His car cleaning round grew: most weekends a few people knocked and he happily set his own prices. Out of the money he bought car shampoo and wax cleaning materials and proudly showed us some real suede cloths he'd found for sale in Epping Market. One Saturday No.1 was riding up and down on his bike and Chris was home doing odd jobs and a young man who lived halfway along the road stopped to ask the price of a plain car clean. He agreed and he said he would want it washed monthly which, like the wine warehouse van, became a routine. After a few months, he went off as usual with his bucket and tools and a few minutes later he was back. He was clearly shaken up and asked Chris if he would go back to the house to collect his bucket, as he didn't want to do that car any more. Chris knew that something must have happened and gently asked him.

No.1 explained: he arrived at the agreed time and rang the bell of the front door, which was open. He pushed it gently and put one foot on the mat to call out that he had arrived and needed his bucket filled. To his horror, Mr R stood completely naked at the top of the stairs, apparently swaying to music and beckoning him. 'Come up,' he invited, but instead the bucket was dropped and No.1 ran to us.

'Stay there,' ordered Chris and he walked down the road, where Mr R now fully clothed stood on his front step, wincing and apologising.

'I didn't mean it. I am so sorry. It won't happen again. I was only joking.'

'No, it won't, Mr R. I will be watching you and if you want me to keep quiet about this you will make sure that you don't proposition any other youngsters. Ever! Am I making myself clear? I don't want to hear any gossip about you from anyone. Oh, and he won't be cleaning your car again.'

Nowadays, of course, we would have reported him to the police, I think we were all a bit more innocent and slow to accuse then. We saw him ever afterwards, scuttling up and down the road, often escorting his elderly mother who always looked grim and never smiled at anyone. To my knowledge, after she died he remained there, living alone.

**

181

Reverend McDonald returned to make his appointment. He had studied my list of costs and decided he wanted to proceed, so Chris drove out to see him at his home. 'Look for wifey things in the bathroom, Chris,' I instructed him and he laughingly agreed. There were feminine articles all over the house apparently, fresh air sprays, artificial flowers, china ornaments, fluffy slippers and much else besides so it looked like there was a Mrs somewhere and, of course, his daughter.

When a visit was made to a purely masculine home it was always apparent by the contents, the absence of a woman's touch: no women's magazines, knitting or sewing machine, no cosmetics or perfumes. A girl-only home will often have an unopened tool box in the cupboard under the sink. A broken home seemed to have an atmosphere of sadness, clearly lacking any fun, only half the wardrobes in use and no sentimental items on show.

The reverend agreed to our fees reluctantly, but we offered for him to pay us in stages, for which he appeared grateful. It would have been easier if he remembered to bring his instalments regularly, however, and not waited until he received my reminder every month. Stamps and stationery costs added to our expenditure and chipped away at my time.

We began to prepare drawings for a neighbour of ours that I had become friendly with when No.3 was in play school. This was before I started helping Chris. They ran a fish and chip shop and seemed to always be in a rush.

Their first takeaway venture was run jointly with another couple, but once children started arriving the women ducked out and left it to the men. They then got in a muddle with their finances, forgetting how much cash could be syphoned off by each partner each week and into pockets and the couples split up before getting seriously in trouble with the tax man.

Finances appeared to be on the line as they several times re-mortgaged in order to take out shop leases, so needless to say our costs and fees would be a closely bargained business.

Our deposit consisted of a surprise box of chickens.

One day his little red van turned up at our house and he rang the doorbell. I had no knowledge of the arrangement discussed between him and Chris and was a bit perplexed to receive several dozen small chickens, plucked and ready for the oven or to be quartered and deep fat fried, and I had to wrap them all in cling film and find room in the freezer.

Planning permission was sought and obtained and a proper fee was paid for the outstanding amount.

When the second stage of building control was ready for application we received more chickens, but I was prepared for those; and a free long weekend in one of their caravans somewhere in Clacton. They all turned up on the final evening and I made a curry, yes, chicken, for us all before we cleared up and journeyed home.

I was glad that they used builders of their own choice and not recommended by us, as they were dissatisfied with the workmanship and therefore not happy with their huge double extension when it was finally completed. Several things happened during these times and we stopped seeing them. We also never received the balance of our fee as one day, when I telephoned her to enquire about the outstanding amount she told me that they wouldn't pay us as she thought we were too expensive. What could I say after receiving dribs and drabs for about a year? You can't please everyone and we'd had a fair few chickens. Perhaps some fish would have been a good substitute.

**

Our neighbours across the road were getting married. We were not invited, as it was a small family event, but we were pleased for them.

When we first moved in, Alvin introduced himself as a magician and member of the elusive Magic Circle. His wife was quiet and reclusive: she always wore a headscarf and gabardine rain-coat and spoke to no-one, keeping her face lowered as she walked by. One day he told me that she had moved out and he was getting a divorce. We hadn't even realised she had gone. Sometime afterwards he introduced us to Mary, an outgoing, vivacious person with a never ending repertoire of amusing anecdotes and an infectious laugh. Mary very quickly moved in with him and gradually the house was decorated throughout and the furniture changed. We included them as occasional dinner guests and he performed at our children's parties as well as a dinner party for adults. Of course, they were guests too. The usual tricks of linking and unlinking metal rings and cutting lengths of string only to suddenly have them all in one length again; of pulling endless rows of scarves out of nowhere and hiding glass balls under completely flat card always fascinates youngsters and us. Try as I might, I was unable to fit those rings together or undo them once they were fixed. His adult tricks were fascinating. He had a shallow box lined with black velvet and various objects laid into the fabric, like a key, or cotton reel, a bottle opener, a thimble, and many more. He went around the room asking us, one by one, to silently pick an object from the box, memorise it and not to touch or remove it. He then returned and told us the item we had picked and was correct every time. I asked him if he was able to tell me how this was achieved, as it was forbidden to disclose tricks to outsiders of the Magic Circle and all he could say was there was a formula which, if you knew it, would explain it. Some days she worked in London for a small exclusive designer company for women's wear. She brought scraps of spare fabric back sometimes and gave them to me, which I used for clothes I made for No.2. Thanks to Mary, we had Liberty fine wool prints and cream silks from China. When that job folded, she took on dressmaking from her home and seemed to do very well.

One day she went to the doctor as she had found a lump in her breast. The doctor told her it was nothing. After a while she went back as she knew the lump had grown but again he told her it was nothing and she must stop being obsessed with it. Finally, she went again and got really upset because she knew it had increased and insisted on a second opinion. For his unknown reasons, he deeply resented this request and fulfilled it begrudgingly. On the day she went to hospital for a consultant to see her, Alvin went too. The specialist was appalled to diagnose a growth which he believed to be cancerous and she went in for tests which proved the case. Not only was the initial lump found to be cancer but it had spread through to her back and she had surgery to remove the affected area and radiotherapy treatments of the day, as well as medicines for life. He was unable to predict the life span she had left and warned her that it may have been too late to stop the further spread of the disease, but they tried to remain optimistic. She changed her doctor after that but I believe nothing ever came of their complaint regarding the dreadful negligence of the first one. After a while she had reconstructive surgery and was an inspiration to others. Soon afterwards, Alvin came home with a bunch of red roses and asked her to be his wife. His romanticism after the huge ordeal was touching.

Alvin's father was Jewish but he was brought up to recognise no faith. Mary was Jewish. She was not observant and had lived in Israel with a former husband for some years. She fascinated No.2 who loved to hear stories, loved to taste some of her Kosher food and decided she wanted to be Jewish. She asked for a Magen David or Star of David necklace for her birthday, a little gold emblem on a chain which she wore proudly, ignoring the inquisitive questions and remarks from other friends and some of the bewildered family comments. Many of her school friends were Jewish and she strangely felt an affinity with non-Christians for years. Mary felt attached to No.2 in the same sort of way and wished she could adopt her. Sometimes during busy times, when the child in question is behaving particularly badly, when the stress you find yourselves in seems insurmountable and a tantrum or throes of a shouting attack is under way, the idea of a willing foster carer just over the road was too good to be true. Mary never knew how many times she almost got No.2, complete with baggage and school fees invoice. The boys thought it would be wonderful to eject her from the house and often suggested we gave her to Mary. They insisted there would be no-one to argue with once she was gone and No.3 could have her bigger bedroom as she wouldn't be needing it. No.3 got quite voluble about it, not realising the whole thing was tongue in cheek, querulously asking why we didn't go ahead as it would be the best thing for everyone.

**

The foundations were being excavated at the leather factory in Walthamstow and the digging machine uncovered what they thought was an unexploded World War II bomb, just as everyone was on the verge of going home. With a minimum of panic, the factory and site workers were sent home to safety and the police were notified. An ambulance was sent for and someone from the army arrived, who confirmed it. The immediate neighbours on all sides of the building, across the road and beyond the gardens were evacuated from their homes and a cordon put around. Some of the people went to the shelter of family and the local school offered temporary accommodation in their hall for the night. The army bomb disposal team arrived and successfully dismantled it. It was a large security exercise carried out by our police officers and disposal squad and it went smoothly without incident so that they could move back in the early hours. Many stayed in the hall until the next day, either enjoying the atmosphere or in no hurry to rush back at that time. A few of the older residents said it was like being back in the war time days and the spirit of the Blitz helped them to chill out over the whole thing, singing a few songs and cracking jokes. Food was brought in by various concerns and I think they all had a passable evening, then settled down in sleeping bags to pass the night. The children at school the next day were full of the excitement of their adventure. Boys especially loved the war aspect, weapons and soldiers, without understanding the graveness of the situation.

Luckily, we had not been involved in this escapade and heard about it later.

**

No.2 saw an advert in the local paper for karate classes and asked if she could join. It was held in a church hall in Leyton and I drove her over there to join a beginner's class. She loved it and after a couple more classes, we ordered her the white cotton suit. Beginners had a white tie belt and immediately she was keen to attain ascending colours. The class was about ninety minutes, including a short break and I took knitting with me to pass the time when I wasn't fascinated with some of the displays. The Korean karate type was known as Tae Kwon Do and had been started in this district by an Oriental gentleman, the Sensei, who once he had a few incredibly enthusiastic young men suitably qualified and wanting to instruct, spread his organisation wider, hence the newspaper adverts. The incredible speed of the young black belts was awesome to watch. As their legs swept through the air in a combat move a real "swish" could be heard. I loved to watch the leaping and jumping of these agile young people.

The church hall, the Dojo for the night, obviously had to be paid for. I often wondered if our Wednesday evening instructor worried about collecting enough fees to pay the rent. It was operated in as business-like a way as possible, with a register of names and ticks when the weekly amount was paid, then once the dues had been removed and an amount creamed off for the Chief Sensei commission, like a franchise fee, there was often piteous amounts left for him. It took a dedicated person to carry on. Many people joined and left again before even taking their first grading. Some enthusiastic beginners had to leave due to circumstances like moving house, starting work or evening classes or family situations like losing their job or starting a family. Time is the precious factor here and missing a lesson often grew into finally leaving.

I usually sat with a few other 'mums' watching our offspring carry out the press-ups and lunges, and go through the warm-up drill while shouting something unintelligible in an Oriental language. Between us we made tea for everyone and cleared up afterwards. It was more than a class for our daughter; it was a congenial get together for many different people. All classes, creeds and nationalities trained together and there was never any hint of racialism or social mistrust. Wax-on and wax-off it was not and there was no resemblance to the Hollywood take on basic training, apart from the discipline of repetition and learning the moves and obviously defensive reasons for them.

The instructor of a different group was a close friend of our young Sensei. There were suggestions that he may go forward to compete nationally but he was also a keen footballer and trainee lawyer. I loved to watch these talented exhibitions and hear the air move. It was interesting to watch the newcomers become confident with the shouts and moves and very proud to watch a grading and see your child move up a grade and become the owner of a new belt. Gradings were carried out on Sundays and involved the other clubs in the area. Many friends and family members crammed into the hall and shrank as close to the walls as possible, to allow the floor space for the tests and feats. At last the white belt was thrown into the bottom of her wardrobe and she dressed with a yellow one instead. Yellow was changed to orange in due course and then to green and somewhere along the way, following others lining up ahead of her, she jumped and with one leg outstretched she broke a board and then a tile with her foot.

It was about this time that she asked if a Mezuzah could be fixed to the front door frame. This is a small rectangular box, apparently containing some scriptures and fixed at a diagonal stance, which is touched by those of the Jewish faith when they enter the home. We drew the line at that and said, 'No.' It was supposed to remind those that touched it of the Ten Commandments. We agreed that Moses's apparent tablets of commandments written in the wilderness was indeed the only list of rules that everyone on earth should follow and we would all be safer and possibly happier if everyone complied to the instructions therein as basically it covered all laws.

Another scrap of wisdom she learned was the carrying out of a Mitzvah. It means translated loosely to carry out God's will or through his love I think but a good deed to someone could be regarded as such. Without bringing God into it she carried these ideals in her head and performed small kindnesses to people and complete strangers when an opportunity arose and was pleased to have been helpful. I wasn't sure how many Mitzvahs led to sainthood but wondered how karate and Mother Teresa could have been linked.

**

We were travelling out to Stanstead to meet our lovely gay estate agents, who wanted to introduce us to their builder, Albert. He carried out the works to properties in the area, travelling as far as Harlow or Epping but not the East End of London, so they had other builders involved for those. They lived in a village which had the sort of community which is often shown on television programmes. They had fêtes, and fairs, cricket on the green and everybody knew everybody else, and their business. The permission for the new house on the strip of land had been granted and they had discussed the possibility of building it themselves. It was at this meeting that they decided definitely to sell it due to the huge costs of bringing gas and electricity to the site as well as water supply and cesspit.

They had met Ray and wondered about showing him the details of the latest permission, as he had spoken to them about the flats he was close to completing in Wanstead. I felt a little awkward, as I knew the drainage was going to be the expensive item of this new build and still no soil tests had been carried out. Although when purchasing a property or land, it was the responsibility of the buyer to ascertain all relevant information and I knew it would be Ray's responsibility, if he bought it, to carry this out, I felt concerned that we knew it was going to be an expensive build and perhaps he would not factor this in. Chris said we could only warn him and then it was up to him. He had asked us to keep a look-out for places to develop, or land, so we passed on the message that J & J had recently gained consent on a parcel of building land close to Stanstead and decided to sell it. I tried to tell him there were unknown elements but he made his own decisions. He agreed that when the flats were sold and he realised the funds he would buy the land.

He eventually sold the top two flats and kept the lower ground floor unit for himself, but rented it out to someone so he bought the plot, then decided to sit on it until the property values rose and meanwhile, flitted about still trying to re-woo his estranged wife. He told us he'd got a puppy and it was sweet to hear the stories. He avoided receiving a traffic speeding fine when he was stopped on the North Circular, bobbing and weaving about the lanes at an almost dangerous speed in order to get back to the pup which was all alone in the house.

The policeman actually took pity on the animal and Ray and let him off, but warned him not to drive like a maniac again.

After a few weeks, he came in one day, quite crestfallen, to say that his wife was seriously thinking of returning to him but she didn't like the dog. I asked him if it had been house trained. 'Yes,' he said, 'I put some newspaper down on the kitchen floor when I have to go out and he goes on that.'

We talked among ourselves. No.3 wanted the dog. He promised to take him for walks. He promised to feed him. It was a Springer Spaniel, not known for their docility and as crazy as could be. But apparently, he tolerated cats and ours were loved and established so it was a factor in his favour. It was sweet and friendly and gentle and he was trained. Reportedly.

So, about a week later we took temporary custody of the dog. We made it clear to Ray that this was a week trial only as he knew how busy we were. We took his bed, his lead, his dish and bowl and a few spare cans of dog food and packets of biscuits. I resolved to take him to puppy training classes. Springers were intelligent, I knew: they were trained as sniffer dogs at the docks and airports so they must be bright and obedient.

There was great excitement. Alvin and Mary came to see him and loved him. They had their little black terrier thing and the two jumped around each other in delight. He loved being fussed and took no hesitation in leaping half across the floor onto a lap to be petted. This was especially endearing when holding a cup of tea or reading a book.

No.3, unfortunately, for all his promises and efforts was unable to control him on the lead. This became my job. The first evening he made a mess on the living room carpet which had to be cleared up, by me. We supposed it was due to excitement of being at a new house and new people and strange layout. The next day he did it again, in the kitchen. I thought his walks were not long enough so took him for miles but he certainly didn't equate being out with going to the loo and squatted the minute we got in, so I had a heap in the hall to clear up. There clearly had to be a reason for this. Of course, he missed the newspaper.

I made a big show of laying newspaper down in the corner of the utility area and tried to bring his attention to it, but instead he thought I was inviting him to play with it and skidded about, pawing it into shredded pieces. He obviously had no idea what paper on the floor meant so I telephoned Ray, who laughed like mad.

In his house, he had a small kitchen area and he covered the entire lino surface with newspaper so reducing the damage of defecation. How funny, he thought, our lounge carpet, our hall laminate, our painted kitchen floor not yet finished and all those hours walking around trying to get him to go.

'Sorry, Ray, it pains me to say it but we can't cope with that. Even poor No.1 got up one night and cleared up a heap at the bottom of the stairs. You said he was house-trained. He is nowhere like it. You haven't bothered and I don't know how to teach him as we don't have time.'

He didn't care. 'Bring him over. Stel's changed her mind anyway. She's not coming back. She likes living with her mum and didn't really want to get married, she just likes being taken out.'

I think she saw the young dog as a rival for Ray's attention and I hoped he wasn't confused. Poor Bimbo went back. We truly felt sick to see him go and I hope he wasn't mentally damaged by his short holiday at ours then being ejected back again. I know animals suffer from depression and feel rejection and I was angry at Ray's ignorant indolence of an animal's fundamental needs.

**

We were visited by two builders known as A and E, who had actually built our original little office within the parade before we knew of it or them. The mid terrace premises must have been in dreadful condition to be demolished and rebuilt, so Mr Clooney must have acquired it for a song. They slated the character of the owner/landlord and thought he had been out of order in his treatment of us. We thought that after all it had given us the best outcome as we were extremely happy in our present office, our young teachers were happy in the flat above, Denny was happy at his patchily rented desk and we had built up a client base of such diversity, providing us with work and rich experiences, that we seriously believed it was a blessing.

They wanted some engineering calculations for an extension in Walthamstow and promised a steady flow of jobs to do. We helped E when he changed the window lintels of his own flat and neighbouring units in the block. When A bought his ex-council house we helped him when he needed a beam at the back entrance to a conservatory. Then they bought a small infill plot in E17 that was just the right size for four maisonettes. There was a central external staircase to the first-floor units and beneath the steps Chris drew useful storage cupboards. Our ex Landlord Mr Clooney ran an estate agent's in the area and he sold them from his office. He also had a sister business near Clacton and we had prepared plans for a project down there which had been successful.

**

At last work began on the extension of the batching plant in Tower Hamlets. Our young concrete mogul wasted no time and was energetically organising the plant for the excavations of the footings. Chris made a flying visit to wish him good luck then rushed off to a different site where a couple of young men wanted a conditions survey of a building carried out, in order to take a lease.

I was intrigued to learn that a gruesome discovery of heaps of bones had been discovered on the industrial estate which had once belonged to rough grounds adjoining a field which could have been hospital or church owned. The Environmental Health department at the council had been called and they pronounced it to be a plague pit, commonly found throughout areas of London. There was a small element of panic from the workers, who feared that the plague disease could be released into the atmosphere now that the earth above the bodies had been shifted but the experts said the enzymes would have died out long ago, unless the tests showed the cause of death to be Anthrax which they said lasts for thousands of years. Apparently, many former excavated mass graves like this, were found to have been caused by death from TB or Typhus and even Salmonella, once scientists had examined the bones. The whereabouts of many pits are known as parish records had listed the names and sometimes accurate death explanations but others were unknown, as frightened people, often terrified of contracting the disease themselves, just dug the hole and tipped the people in. So many thousands of people died in England, in heavily populated areas that it must have been difficult to keep track. In Walthamstow, in St Mary's church yard there are two such pits. One has a commemorative plaque but the other is unmarked and exact position is unknown. At the side of the church is Vinegar Alley, so called as the locals tipped vinegar into the ditches to the side of the walkway in an attempt to repel the disease.

A halt was called to the building works while the bones were removed as gently as possible and taken away to a specialised pathology unit. The specialists, known as osteologists, I presume carried out tests on the bones which usually happens, which often show not only the causes of death but diets and even districts of origin. There have been cases where the evidence produced indicated the remains to have been from foreign nationalities. The unknown bones were re-buried on consecrated ground and the local clergy held a short service and everyone carried on as usual. Just a sharp reminder of difficult times the population endured and hopefully not to be repeated, although there are newer diseases in circulation proving to be as horrific for medical science to produce magical cures.

We were introduced to another Sikh family, who knew the ones involved with the building for application to a nursing home. These three brothers bore no likeness to each other and personalities were different. They worked together relatively well because they allowed the middle brother to call the shots. From humble beginnings by their father and uncle, who ran a sweat shop type of clothing manufacturing concern, they had taken their half over and the business had burgeoned. The elders had possibly quarrelled and the huge factory building they had bought from their local council was divided into two for the cousins to run their own empires. The manufacture of outer wear, anoraks and trousers, fleeces and padded jackets and coats, and distribution to outlets all over England was their main concern. As they became more and more successful, they bought properties and developed them. Some they kept and rented out and some they sold. The buildings were purchased with a view of attaining as many residential units for rental as possible and they had acquired a sizeable portfolio. The elder brother still ran his stall on market days and weekends in the East End, as he loved the camaraderie of the other stall holders and organised building contractors working on their sites. The middle brother bought clothing articles from popular shops and travelled to Hong Kong to have copies made and prices calculated for manufacture in bulk. The variance in price by just a penny per article made a difference to their costs and profits. He spent a great deal of time travelling, sourcing his fabrics and organising the goods for manufacture in Hong Kong; shipping to the UK then delivery from the docks to their building, which had gradually morphed into a warehouse with very few machinists working. The building was a hive of rooms and a staircase, leading to a vast open space on the first floor where the sewing frenzy used to be carried out.

I have always been interested in the rag trade, mainly for children's wear, and fabrics and the production of garments I found fascinating, especially hearing some of the tales involving the travelling and customs of the people, making and producing the goods, organising the transportation of the boxes of assorted outfits and finally making the sales and receiving the payments. Most of the garments were destined for markets and the vans drove to wholesale outlets, who would then sell them on.

Inside the factory, which is what they called their building, there were hanging rails displaying the current lines and often local tradesmen would call for oddments to top up their stock. Their memory of the prices for each of the examples was impressive and in many cases, we found them to be generous. Almost every time that Chris called to show them their latest drawings, the meeting turned into lunch and someone would go for kebabs. These were made of cooked, spiced, minced lamb in sausage shapes, with a little salad and pickles with a flat bread rolled around and held in the hand to eat. Little No.3 often went with Chris and he loved these kebabs. All of our children wore padded or rainproof anoraks or a fleecy top, given to them by one of the brothers, some of the garments were from their own stock but some were from the odd expensive samples. Of course, nothing comes from nothing and we tried our best to achieve the outcome they wanted from their projects and sites.

Once we knew these industrious brothers we also added their friends and acquaintances to our client base and more and more, we were meeting people who were closely attached to someone who we had worked with before. One person telephoned us and said that four different people from different sources had recommended Mr Chris, so he thought we were quite famous.

It was easier too to obtain deposits and balance of account fees and bouncing cheques became rare as, we supposed, nobody wanted their family or friends to hear adverse remarks or complaints from us. There was of course the odd hiccup, where a stranger ignored our advice or quotation and offered an insulting alternative.

Once, at about four-thirty, a call from an unknown person came in. He introduced himself and asked for a price to measure up a building that Chris was familiar with. He wanted to apply for a mezzanine floor to be installed. As Chris knew the building, without actually knowing the owner, he was able to tell him straight away. He said that it was reasonable and asked if he could see him right away so Chris and the boys took a drive over there. No.1 told me afterwards that the man was arrogant and once they had all shaken hands he asked how soon the job could be started.

He said, 'Can you measure it now?'

Chris looked at his watch and pulled a doubtful face, to which the man said, 'It's easy. It's just a square, won't take long and it'll save you coming back.'

He looked at the boys and they both agreed, 'We'll help you, Dad.'

They started. Laying a fresh white sheet of paper on the pad he carried, he sketched the rough shape and marked the details, windows, doors, radiators and marked the positions of the beams up at roof level.

As he passed the end of his tape to No.1, the client suggested that the fee quoted was excessive and suggested an insulting amount instead. This was a fraction of the quoted fee and Chris asked him what he was playing at. 'We discussed this earlier, Mr Q. This is my fee.'

'But it's simple, a child could do it. Look, yours are.'

Chris was so angry, he swore at the person for wasting his time and said, 'Come on boys. We're leaving.'

The boys were so proud of their dad. They told everyone that would listen. I hoped it didn't get bandied about the school, much. Bad language was rarely spoken in the family and they considered it was just and proper what their dad said. Word must have got about that kind and helpful Chris Prentice actually was not a pushover and the annoying haggling that we experienced from some of our clients did reduce slightly.

A common introduction to a fee quotation went like this. 'Mr Chris, my friend, I will come to you for many jobs later, so you can give me a discount.'

'Nice idea, but I don't know you and this is the first job you have discussed with me.'

'But I have brothers and friends and I will send them to you.'

'That doesn't mean I can give you a discount on your first job.'

'There will be so much work later.'

'Sorry, I have to pay my bills now and I'm not able to wait for jobs in the future that might not materialise.'

'Ahh, Mr Chris, you are not my friend. I thought we would have an understanding.'

'We have. You pay my bill now and when I have a successful introduction from you, I will give you commission.'

Sometimes, after they had received their quotation we heard no more and they went away when we refused to take cash to avoid paying the VAT. Sometimes the job went forward but often stopped halfway, after the deposit had been paid and work continued to prepare the plans for application, we heard no more from them when we asked for the balance of account. In our earlier days, we had made the submission and unfortunately not been paid. We were learning.

Once, we were involved with a job acting on behalf of a group of surveyors in Ilford, who were linked to the housing department and were handling an improvement grant job in a different borough. The fee was fixed and not by us and we would receive commission from the group. We prepared the initial report and met the council operative, as well as the prospective builder to handle repairs. The house was in poor state and the family were also unfortunate. They barely spoke English and had sparse furnishings. We felt sorry for them and glad that their home was to be improved. Secretly we wondered how they had managed to obtain a mortgage and pay the monthly instalments, as well as run a car and pay other family housing commitments. But this part of the remit did not involve us.

The wife had mental health problems and sometimes thought the police were going to arrest her if they knew where she was. She blocked up the letter box. She tried to explain to me how the Pakistani police were coming to take her away. I wondered if someone threatened her with this fate or whether it was part of her illness. I believe it was a kind of schizophrenia or "persecution complex" as it used to be called. The small children were hyper, shouting and chasing about and the smell of incense burning got down my throat. I had a headache each time we were obliged to visit. One day, to our horror, the husband cut the wire of a tumble drier situated on the landing, as he said his wife used it too much and it was expensive to run. There was no washing line outside in the garden or clothes horse inside. She went almost hysterical and the children went wild. One of them snatched my tape recorder and started yelling into it. A spokesman for the family demanded a present from us to denote thanks

196

for being allowed to handle the job. I told him the percentage of the fee granted to the group was not awarded to us. We merely handled the visits to oversee the work. He was quite threatening so I told him we would report him to the authorities.

We had some furniture in store, which we were intending to sell via an advertisement in the local paper, but seeing the state of the house had already decided to donate it to the family and arranged a van to deliver it. It consisted mainly of a sofa and armchairs and a television and we thought they might be pleased. The only furniture in the entire building was mattresses, a filthy cooker, fridge and broken tumble drier. Instead the husband who barely spoke English was inside when the goods were carried into their through-lounge, rubbed his thumb and fingers together and said, 'We want money, not this.'

We didn't want extreme gratitude but we were both affronted. Chris looked at the poor woman and asked her if she wanted the goods and she said, 'Yes.' That was enough for us and we turned tail and left. The Oakshot Housing group were told that we did not want to be part of their concern again.

The very scruffy house was situated near a relative of mine, so we used to call in to see her for a cup of tea when in the area. She lived alone, was slightly disabled and was retired so a chat about the outside world was welcome to her. I used to call her first to see if she needed anything and she looked forward to seeing us. She had worked in a draper's shop, a bus ride away since the war, when she proudly remembered being in the Land Army. One day the bus swerved while trying to miss a dog and crashed into the side of a shop. She was flung out of her seat and projected towards the driver's end, finishing in a heap in the gangway and seriously breaking her leg in several places. Luckily there were few passengers and an ambulance was called for her and she was taken into Whipps Cross hospital where she remained for about six weeks. I was in the same hospital for some weeks when we got No.3, so I visited her ward a few times, dressed in their fetching nightwear. When baby No.3 finally arrived, I took him to show her and she was delighted and called out to tell everyone else in the ward. I had to hold him up and turn around so the other orthopaedic patients could see him. Her leg was in traction and had a pin through it and altogether she had endured a painful ordeal. Her shop manager was sympathetic and the staff all visited regularly, knowing she had no immediate family. He was also instrumental in obtaining her compensation for which when it arrived, she was grateful and spent it on a new washing machine and taking the entire staff to lunch at their local pub.

I knew the staff quite well and when the owners decreed a twice annual sale they used to ask me if I wanted to help for a couple of days. I was home with the children then, so a couple of days working in a shop selling diverse objects was welcome to me. Not only was I privy to the items going into the sale but they allowed me a further staff discount on top. I bought curtaining, sewing materials and goods, bed linen and a measure of pale blue towelling that I made into a heap of little pants for my first two children when they tried potty training and dispensed with the nappies.

Chapter 15

We received the disappointing rejection notice for Mickie's application. We had drawn the exact shape and size suggested by the planner and altogether it was upsetting in several ways to be rejected in this way.

I went to the council offices and spoke to the duty planner at the desk. He looked at the application notes and the drawings we had produced and looked flummoxed. He confessed to not knowing why this had happened and asked me to wait while he went to discuss with his seniors. I waited and he came back to the desk. 'The suggestion is that a bungalow would be more acceptable,' he said. Really? I thought. That would make it more obvious and not blend in with the street scene at all, but as there were other bungalows scattered throughout the borough on infill sites and bomb sites I thought I could see a parallel, however unsuitable in my mind. I thanked him and went back to the office to pass on the advice.

A pretty bungalow, using the flank wall of the existing house was drawn, obviously using more of the garden but still complying with the guidelines and re-submitted. A second go was free of charge. There was now a delay of a further three months while the officers in the department went through the drawings and documents, waited for 21 days to receive adverse comments from neighbours and finally made their consideration. They resigned themselves to further waiting.

**

A relative of Jeff Gold, basement owner, contacted us to visit his jewellery shop. We were busy during their early closing day so agreed to go on a Sunday and we arranged to go for lunch on the way back, to a restaurant of the children's choice. They chose a hotel close to our home, where the Sunday roast dinner was usually very good. They also did a range of dreadfully wicked desserts and children's "pretend" cocktails which the younger two loved, collecting plastic animals on sticks and miniature umbrellas. Apart from the dining room, they had a reading room equipped with bookcases stuffed full of books of all sorts and a lounge equipped with dozens of random chairs and occasional tables, and a couple of machines which played quizzes, a jukebox and a fruit machine.

We arrived at the shop and were shown around by his wife and Chris discussed with them the ideas they had for the first floor. It comprised two rooms with a kitchenette and bathroom and although tiny, was beautifully fitted out. Their workmen were two brothers from the Philippines, who were working over here temporarily. Goodness knows where Ed and his wife Jo had met them, but the purpose built wardrobes in the bedroom and shelves, not forgetting the kitchen, were beautifully hand crafted. They had decided to try for a family and wanted a further level to be added to the shop, as well as a balcony and a weird sort of turret on the top. Chris referred to it as a folly to me and the draftswoman but agreed to take the challenge, thinking they would throw out the turret if they didn't throw out the upper extension, as adjacent shops in the parade did not extend this high. Imagine our surprise when the application sailed right through the process and was granted. We went back to the shop to discuss the second stage of building control, detailed plans and engineering for application and while there he said we could have a generous discount on any goods we chose from the shop and Chris bought me a garnet and diamond eternity ring, which I still wear. No.2 chose a gold chain from the display case and proudly wore it home. There were no DVD films or Airfix aeroplane kits in a jewellery shop so the boys declined and he gave them some change to spend instead, for which they grinned their thanks.

By the time we reached the hotel, the chain had broken and luckily she caught it as it slid down her front and landed on her shoe. I think it had been hanging in the display case too long and had weakened, but that was another job for me to get repaired at our local shop. This was duly carried out during the week but over a few months it broke over and over again, so she traded it in for a small pair of silver ear rings. The links of the gold chain did not look weak or fine but obviously, it was substandard or it would have been strong enough, but we never told our client. No.3 asked anxiously if we thought the gold was stolen and had a curse on it and we told him obviously, there was no chance of that. But, it was surprising what little ears picked up and the origin of the gold had struck me too as dubious, but cursed? No. Just inferior, but couldn't complain.

We had our lunch and settled in the lounge to relax for a few hours and the children wandered off, No.2 to the book shelves and the boys to play quizzes with their change. After a while we thought we'd round them up and head off home, where I had their school shirts to iron and PE kits to pack up. There, we were amazed to see them clustered around the fruit machine with intense faces, playing like hardened gamblers and with a large heap of silver change on the side. They pooled their coins from Mr Gold and to their delight, a couple of foreign holiday makers checking out of the hotel for the ferry, presented a heap of English coins to the boys, cheerfully wishing them luck. Luck was on their side and they gathered up a tidy sum to take home. I wondered how they would have fared if we had left them longer as they certainly seemed to be on a winning streak. It made me laugh to think of us playing the penny machines in the arcades along Southend seafront, carefully sharing out a pound's worth of pennies each, and there they were playing with about twenty pounds' worth of silver.

**

We picked up some work in Stoke Newington. The first was a devout Muslim man who had a doctorate in microbiology. He met an English girl and she converted to Islam and he married her. They had five children and seemed to be a happy family unit. For reasons unknown to me he had trouble finding and keeping a job, which obviously caused problems as their house needed repairs. He wanted to convert the loft, which would have given them several more rooms for their burgeoning family, to an already large dwelling and managed to find our costs. They had their builder lined up and he started. Over several years, he carried out extensions, the recent loft conversion as well as routine maintenance, but instead of paying him they gave him a holding in their home. By the time we completed these building works he owned about forty per cent of their building. I presume these transactions were legally binding and the deeds became annotated but I feared for their futures, seeing their ownerships reduced so. The builder was a black Caribbean man and very pleasant. He must have had a silver tongue to inveigle such a huge slice of real estate and a ladies' man too, going by gossip, as at the last time of our meeting he had reportedly fathered eighteen children. Unfortunately, in spite of his business acumen he never took fatherhood seriously and just went from day to day, loving and leaving these silly women, who produced tiny black babies as if on a production line.

The second project we had was for another black man. He was an entrepreneur and owned a shop in the High Street which had been let out for wet fish sales. His living quarters was over the shop and accessed by a separate entrance door from the street and an escape stair at the rear. The ground floor opened out like Doctor Who's Tardis at the rear of the shop, spreading into a large rectangle with communal parking for the shops in close proximity. At the first visit, we got no further than the shop premises, which were still furnished as a shop, with counters and shelves but the middle section leading to the rear was cluttered with fridges, freezers, plastic crates and bags of unknown goods. A clearance company had failed to arrive and the piled up disused white goods created an impenetrable blockage.

A follow up appointment was made and Rog promised to get it cleared out.

When Chris went back to carry out the dimensional survey, he luckily took the boys. The majority of the disused white goods was still there and completely blocking up the access. He thought they would have to go around the block and enter by the communal area but had no key; instead he lifted No.3 and gave No.1 a leg-up and they swarmed over the barricade like the Gibraltar apes. Together, this survey was carried out and Rog turned up at the rear with a removal van and a couple of willing men who emptied the shop and store and took it all away. We all went up to Rog's flat where we drank bottles of a delicious malty liquid labelled Dunn's River. Rog told No.3 if he drank enough of it he would develop muscles like his and be enormously strong. Of course, he believed that and pestered for a bottle of it wherever it was noticed.

Rog's idea was to convert the ground floor to a night club. He was a jazz enthusiast and knew many musicians. The front shop was to be the entrance, selling Caribbean comfort food by day, with the storeroom behind for coats and cloak rooms and the rear exit was ideal as an emergency fire escape route and led into the night club.

Of course, as the proposed club area was tucked behind the shops with only a few flats above, one being Rog's, there were no complaints or adverse comments and he received his permission. The planners haggled over the opening hours but as he had always been of good character, he was granted his liquor licence and granted his choice of opening hours until 2am. We had to return to the premises to carry out a survey recording all details for his fire insurance certificate and the transformation was incredible. The stage area had specialist lighting above and a dance floor around. There were two bars and plenty of comfortable seating with tables. With a colour scheme of black, red and silver and wall mirrors, plush leather chairs and a black tiled floor, the venue could have been in the poshest part of London.

We had been invited to the opening night and had a hugely enjoyable evening. The programme for the coming weeks was displayed and he had secured advance bookings of known musicians.

No.3 asked if we drank Dunn's River malt drink and we agreed that it usually is what you drank at jazz clubs.

Someone, I believe Mickie, introduced Erlich to us, telling him we would help him in a report for his investment house in Hackney which he rented out as a HMO, house of multiple occupation, which he needed to modernise by means of a grant from the council, who also supplied the tenants; and a loft conversion at his own house which was large and beautiful. Erlich was a rabbi and he had a glass fronted bookcase in his side room filled with large red leather bound volumes of the Torah and plenty more besides. He thought Chris was also Jewish and was surprised when he denied this, believing that his parents must have changed their faith to avoid persecution. We found it easier not to argue and Chris murmured, 'Who knows? Actually, we believe in allowing everyone to believe what they want; the Ten Commandments sum it all up really.'

Then I said, 'And there is only one God, so why should it matter what he's called or how people worship?' earning a hasty 'No, No,' from Erlich and a glare from Chris.

Over time we made several visits to Erlich's home and his wife showed me the two kitchens she ran separately. Milk must not be stored in the same refrigerator as meat. She gave us a piece each of the most delicious homemade cheesecake and explained some of the rules and customs they followed.

Their son had married and left home years before so the house was large for the two of them. He lived abroad, I think, with children of his own and had a well-paid position in an investment bank.

Erlich gave lessons in one of the rooms, for Bar mitzvahs and Bat mitzvahs for girls as well as teaching the religion and Hebrew language, spoken and written. His wife ran a ladies' boutique from another reception room and had dress rails holding the most beautiful gowns and suits for special occasions. Customers called regularly, even while we were there carrying out the dimensional surveys and they conversed in Yiddish and paid large amounts of money for their garments.

Erlich told us their son and his family had recently been to stay for a few days and poor Erlich had been severely criticised for allowing them to stay in inadequate rooms. He told him he didn't expect to visit his parents, who had a position to upkeep, and share cramped quarters. He was told to get attic rooms with en-suite facilities installed for when they returned at the next Jewish holiday. He was an elderly man, probably in his seventies, and used to get quite agitated and was upset to know his son felt ashamed. I thought that it was rude and disrespectful to speak to him in this fashion. They could have sat reading all day at their ages but chose instead to keep working and were highly thought of among their contemporaries.

His roof rooms were constructed. Fortunately, his chosen contractor had been recommended by grateful former clients and the results were lovely. The ungrateful son and wife had a lovely room, lined with wardrobes and new furniture and a gleaming white shower and WC. The two boys had an equally pleasant room with twin beds and their own bathroom and we told them the décor and finishes were excellent and good enough for any Swiss banker.

The investment house, however, did not have such a happy ending.

It was an end of terrace house on a corner, with a front entrance door from one road and a back door and side gate to the pavement around the corner, quite spacious and having only the kitchen diner as a communal area and a single bathroom. We had prepared him plans, showing a couple of separate WCs added to the first floor and one with a lobby at the rear of the kitchen by the back door and obtained building control approval for him. He handled his own application and he had been awarded a sum of money towards the works. He also had been given a list of three approved contractors and told he had to obtain quotations. The cheapest one would be the contractor who would be awarded the job. A cheap price usually means poor workmanship or cheap materials being used, in my experience. Unfortunately, the council stipulation was the guide used by them all at the time and the chosen contractor met us at the house with Erlich. He seemed a pleasant personable man. We all felt reassured. As well as the showers and toilets he was to install small wash hand basins in the rooms, paint the interior and exterior joinery, which was in such dire need of decoration the previous paint was flaking off, install another serviceable kitchen and a single mist coat of emulsion paint was to be carried out to the whole premises.

The work started and very soon the stage payment was invoiced for, authorised by the representative from the local authority.

We were out, near the area so Chris decided to call round to meet the contractor and Erlich. We walked in with high expectations but very quickly disappointed. The standard of the work was poor. The plumbing for the new sinks in the bedrooms was messy and untidy and not even straight. Glue oozed out at the joins of the plastic waste pipes and the plaster making good of the walls could have been carried out by schoolchildren. We criticised the finishes to the builder and he nodded affably, listening to our complaints. To my astonishment, he agreed with me. He walked around with us looking as we pointed out each area of substandard work. We told Erlich to withhold the payment until the standard had improved and he got himself into a state of nerves.

I called the council to advise that the work was inferior, they ought to make an inspection and remove him from the approved list but I don't think they bothered. I was told by an unseen ignorant woman that, "What do you expect? Cheap quotes don't give you the Ritz."

The next stage payment and inspection proved as bad and the final completion visit and balance of account equally disgusting. I have never forgotten the bland agreement from the builder that the standard of the plastering, plumbing, installation of the kitchen and wash rooms, painting and final clearing away of old packaging was appalling, and failure to order his men to rectify it. In my opinion this was a total waste of taxpayers' money as well as the balance of account from Erlich. The undiscerning tenants moved back and probably in no time the standard was as seedy as before, but the building complied with the guidelines of the day and no-one cared about utter absence of decency in their greed. We never came across this company name again but if we had I would definitely have vetoed it.

Still in the same area, we handled an insurance claim for another Jewish family. They were orthodox like Erlich but different in their dress and thoughts. They always wore wigs and we never saw their hair. The men wore black hats as well as a Yarmulke, a type of skull cap. The men also had ringlets of hair hanging in front of their ears. The way of life was historic, still following age old customs and segregation, compared to the openness of Erlich's family and associates who also covered their heads and followed their religious guides, but they were open to Westerners and tolerant of differences as far as I could make out.

This family had lodgers in a couple of their upper rooms who were suspicious of us, as English and "different". When we had to enter the upper rooms as part of preparing floor plans of the building and to inspect for movement as noted on the ground floor, a saucepan of something foul smelling was simmering on the stove. The woman hid a knife beneath the folds of her overdress. Did she think we were going to hurt her? I think her English language was non-existent but it would remain so if her self-imposed segregation continued. Our client said she was strange when we told her about the knife and she would be glad when they had enough money to move out. Allowing other people to live in rooms as a start to married lives seemed to be common and I wondered whether it was part of a Jewish brethren custom or friendly help.

All of these children went to the special Jewish School, for which we also gained a planning consent for an additional classroom. Even tiny boys wore a yarmulke or kipah to cover their heads after their long hair was shorn at the age of three when education begins.

This family believed they should have as many children as possible and certainly had a brood. The wife was an excellent housekeeper and cooked and cleaned for her family, taking her responsibilities seriously.

The front section of their double fronted house, having a two-storey bay window on each side of the front door, had subsided by a few inches. Although the movement was obvious, the insurance company insisted on going through the process of applying monitoring over the fractures and taking note of the gaps which had appeared at the joints of the skirting boards and sloping floors. We had made a few visits to check whether the movement had continued and it appeared to be static. A workman had excavated a pit close to the bay wall to inspect the foundations and it could be seen to be fractured down to formation level, which is the start of the footings. It was proposed to underpin along the entire front wall. Chris worked out a sequence. It was not possible to dig out and underpin the whole area at the same time, as removing the ground below would undermine it and the whole thing would collapse. The length was divided into sections of approximately one metre each and allocated numbers in sequence. On the first day all sections along the distance marked "one" were dug out to a depth of about a metre and ready mixed concrete poured into the pits. These were allowed three days to go off, or set solid. On the fourth day all the sections marked "two" were treated in the same fashion and also left to set for three days. The remaining sections were treated in the same way until the whole wall was underpinned. We advised piping in a product known as "expanding grout" at the top of the solid concrete mass which seeped to fill in all crevices between the original foundation and new concrete mass and expanded slightly: this ensured that the reparation works remained solid. The works were inspected at all stages by the council engineer and a certificate issued at the end.

Tree roots damage to the sub soil drainage was usually the cause of this type of movement, or broken drains or leaking from a rainwater downpipe if maintenance was not followed. Bay window constructions during C1910-1930 were often built with shorter depth footings than the main external walls, that is the reason why distorted front bays are frequently to be seen along terraced houses of the age. A two-storey bay will be distorted full height but often a three part angled bay at ground floor has two sash type windows above and they can be seen to slope either downwards at the ends, giving the appearance of surprised eyebrows, or have jagged fractured brickwork below which needs to be repointed or in severe cases completely re-built. Another common short cut is that the party wall between houses is often founded on a shallower depth, as the builder relied on strong main walls footings to help support it.

When the structural aspects were completed the builders moved inside and made good all the fractures noted, fixed all the joists back and laid the floorboards over and re-attached the skirting boards. The usual insurance remit is to replace or repair the damaged parts and not to improve any aspect. The family were disgruntled that when all the timbers were replaced, the floor surface was not level but still sloped. I reminded them that we recommended three different builders who each provided an estimate of works and purely because they valued their good names and enjoyed providing an excellent service, would have gone the extra mile and adjusted the floor timbers level once more. They had heard of a company who often worked in the area who they heard were cheaper and insisted they were awarded the work if their quotation was less. Of course, their estimate was considerably cheaper but the work just reached adequate and the finishes were disappointing. An old mantra, "You get what you pay for," sprang to mind.

She was cross at the results but thought she was being careful with Insurers' money which they had paid over the last twenty years. There was nothing we could do. A cheaper contract price also reduced our agent's commission, being ten per cent of the whole which meant all our site visits, subsidence underpinning drawings and calculations and liaison with insurers' loss adjusters, local authority and contractors were carried out at reduced costs and barely covered our expenses. There is a limit to watching every penny, especially when it affects others.

**

Our young concrete mogul was progressing well with the site works after all the unfortunate remains were removed and re-buried in hallowed ground elsewhere. It was interesting to visit from time to time, to observe the gradual changes implemented and to watch the large concrete trucks drive in and enter a bay where the special chutes tipped the measured materials into the moving mixer and off it went again to deliver to a waiting site somewhere. It reminded me of measured ingredients going into the bowl to make a fruit cake. The heavy steel blades swirled the concrete mix easier than I did the Christmas cake and pudding mixes with a wooden spoon.

At busy times, there were several trucks waiting to enter the loading bay, idling in a line until the one before it pulled out.

These works were creating larger storage areas and a different chute or conveyor belt arrangement to reduce waiting times and therefore running costs.

While in the area we travelled down to Forest Gate to meet David Mozan. A shop that he used to use as an office while running his estate agency business had been turned into a glazier's. He retained the rooms above for his own use and we sat up there having coffee. A redundant photocopier and typewriter remained with a couple of sad looking desks and a fan. He seemed quiet and thoughtful and I wondered if all was well.

The shop was an outlet for the glass of all descriptions and people used to drop doors and window frames in for the staff to cut the glass to size and insert it correctly. There were office doors having Georgian wired glass put into them and frames wanting coloured glass panels to be made. Even pictures were being framed and I realised this part of the business was an overspill from the factory in Hackney. I particularly liked the coloured mirrors and geometric designs that cried out for 1930s or off-the-wall modern displays.

We had a neighbour living about eight doors down who was extremely artistic. While a teenager he applied to study at the Royal College of Art and was accepted but his father died and his mother made him start work instead as she couldn't afford to let him go. He trained as a silk screen printer but created Tromp-D'oeil designs onto blank walls and painted pictures on to mirrored glass. His murals were brilliant and created the illusion of space and distance, pictures showing Roman pillars and rolling hills, waterfalls and statues. His skills became known and his name passed around. He attracted very wealthy people who commissioned him to create these works and sometimes was flown out to work on their foreign homes. He should have been wealthy and I don't know how he was cheated so often, but they lived virtually hand to mouth sometimes. His wife worked as a cleaner, rushing from one house to another to earn her housekeeping. She had bought many of my little dresses for her girls when I ran my bespoke kids' clothes enterprise, before I returned to the bank. I always gave her mates' rates as I knew she worked so hard. He painted a picture of Donald Duck on a piece of mirror, which No.2 had over her little bedroom wash basin and was admired by all her friends who saw it. I rescued it from their rubbish one day when I saw it lying on the top. 'Nobody wants it,' he said. 'It was an experiment with paints on glass.'

She was reliable and we took turns to collect our children from school sometimes but he let us down when we took the small office. We commissioned him to paint the shop sign and various bits of information on to the glass shop front and door. We bought the materials he said he needed and waited for him to turn up. And waited. And waited. When he came the first time, he fixed an elaborate silver strip around the edge of the window which we hadn't requested and told us it would look like security installation to prevent us being burgled. This was unexpected but hey ho! He was creative. It would have looked a bit more authentic if the strip actually went somewhere when it terminated at the front bottom corner instead of trailing off as a floaty little end, all frayed and tufty. After Chris had stayed late to wait for him several times and different appointments were made and broken, I strolled down to the house to confront him: he had been paid a deposit. To my surprise, he was out again and she was packing cases as they were off on holiday in the morning. When I asked her why he kept making dates to do our work and then failed to turn up she feigned ignorance. This suggested to me a possible reason why we heard stories from them of how clients let him down and thought he may have let them down too. We never had the shop sign finished and intentions flew away when we moved next door, which was eventually painted by a friend of No.1 with the three names of Denny, Ray, and ours in the centre.

When they asked us to prepare them plans for a two-storey side extension for planning approval and for building control we did, at a very reduced rate and received payments in irregular instalments from her, collected from her cleaning round. Much to our astonishment, before we had been paid for the construction drawings he hired a few labourers to start excavating the footings. All three were obviously totally ignorant of actions and reactions and their neighbours noted with horror that their garage footings were exposed and were in danger of collapse onto the building site. They shouted at him to stop and called for Chris, who was less than pleased. He told them how to shore up the garage and the correct way to position the trenches so that adjacent buildings were not affected or put at risk. He also quietly asked him how he thought it was acceptable to commence work before he had actually paid for the plans. He had given the money he should have paid to us to these odd job men to dig out the footings. We were paid in painful little amounts and the extension shell gradually took shape but not internally. It would be years before the dream became completed. They spent much of this time without proper plumbing, plastering or wiring, having wonderful visions but little forward planning. I always felt so sorry for their stoicism, sorry for the family who gradually were becoming resentful of living in this way while the parents, who should have known better, drifted along in denial. The eldest daughter spoke to our children one day, telling us how the bath was not connected to water so had to be filled with buckets from downstairs. Bits of hosepipe masqueraded as copper pipes. Electrical wiring trailed around the place, fixed behind furniture with Sellotape. Suddenly in the midst of all the chaos he announced that he was moving the staircase. A grand timber fabrication was brought into the house in several pieces and put together. It then had to be installed. This involved removing the original installation, changing the landing, changing the bannisters, obtaining a new handrail for each side of the grand confection and balusters ornately carved. The grand construction finally was fixed in. It wasn't painted and only showed in more graphic detail the shambles around it. The large amount of money showered into this latest grandiose idea would have been better spent in my opinion completing the main bathroom and kitchen and installing approved electricity and plumbing. Two of the bedrooms had no windows for years and the effort of plastering was ruined by adverse weather action. Efforts to fill the voids with stiff plastic were in vain. As time went by we saw the installation of mock Doric columns at the front with a timber roof over to form an open porch. Of course, the timber was not painted and became rotten: bits of architrave loosened and fell off. These imaginative whims, although shown as visionary drawings more suited to film sets or wealthy people's palaces, were totally incongruous in our street and did nothing to detract from the annoying views of cardboard over windows and heaps of unused building materials lying among the overgrown wild grass and weeds pushing through. It was part building site, part scrap heap, self-induced residential nightmare. Years earlier, we had a garage built to the side of our house and the original prefabricated concrete garage was disassembled and stacked in the front garden. We intended advertising it in the local paper. 'Can we have it?' asked Will.

'Of course, can you come to collect it then? We'll help you, it's heavy.'

Each strip was extremely heavy and with great effort, it was all moved to the front behind the hedge and several weeks later it was still there. When I saw Pen after school one day, I checked with her that they did still want the pieces and would be able to re-erect it at the end of their garden to use as a den for their children. She assured me that they wanted it. At the weekend, we got No.3's old push chair out of our garage and carefully stacked a couple of strips on to it and wobbled down the road to their house. They were sitting in the garden, enjoying the sunshine and initial greetings and grins changed to awkward frowns when they saw the load on the buggy. The atmosphere was almost tangible, definitely perceptible and we couldn't have cared less. They prevented us disposing of it weeks earlier and may have deprived us of a few pounds in a sale, then casually sat around doing nothing while we strained to help them. 'Why are you doing this now, Chris? We could have done it another day?'

'Make hay while the sun shines, ay? We'll get it done then we can all sit in the garden,' muttered Chris.

'Many hands make light work,' I added and they duly searched out an old pram and followed us down the road for the next loads. What a lot of rag tag gypsies we looked but it was done. We adults pushing baby carriages up and down the road while seven children ran between and in front in excited play. Our front garden was clear and all the pieces of concrete planking, door, windows, up and over entrance door with the automatic gear and corrugated strips of roof were now safely ensconced at the end of their garden. I gave them a separate bag of nuts and bolts for the fixings: we even offered to help them erect the thing when they were ready. As time went on, the state of their unkempt garden worsened and when a family of foxes settled close by, we secretly thought they were living there. We believed they had made a den down in the stacks of materials which over time had increased with sheets of fencing and sides of sheds gathered like jackdaw's finery to be used one day. Stacked up as it all was could have provided shelter for the creatures. One day during a very hot summer time, we left our front door open in the evening and Chris had gone up to the side room which we used to work in at the time and called me very softly and gently, to come up slowly and quietly. I knew it must have been a creature up there and picked up a large towel out of the laundry and crept up the stairs. Chris was in the far corner standing completely still and I slid through the door. There, looking utterly adorable, sat a fox cub on the photocopier. I wished I could have photographed it and picked it up for a cuddle but knew better: besides Mum or Dad may be close by. We all regarded each other solemnly and the cub jumped down and ran down the stairs to freedom. Baby animals have bendy little legs and soft fluffy fur and loads of fleas, added Chris when I expressed regret at not touching it. I didn't need the towel. We occasionally saw foxes strolling up and down the road but never ascertained their actual den and never dared to ask Will, who would have thought we were hinting at his lack of progress. The neighbours down that end of the road denigrated their ineptitude and lack of achievement and it was a shame. As people, they were lovely but life for them could have been easier.

If they had suddenly had a windfall it probably would have been spent on a trip to Disneyland, a couple of weeks of fun and pleasure and more years of deprivation and pandemonium to follow. During the school holidays the family could be seen venturing out on repeated trips to Thorpe Park. This involved five or six train fares and entrance costs as well as activities inside and this was repeated over and over. She saved relentlessly throughout term time in order to blow it on re-runs of the same day out. We of course also took our tribe to the attractions of the day but they were also happy to meet friends at High Beech or Wanstead Flats or Valentine's Park in Ilford, where we shared picnics and played games of cricket and hide and seek and fed the tame squirrels. There was a paddling pool in the park where they tumbled and splashed and I truly think they gained equal enjoyment from spontaneous fun and mixing with friends.

We often took the train to parts of London and walked huge distances. A former school friend with children about the same age as our first two and I would take them all over, showing them museums, palaces and the grand parks. There is a wealth of activities in London and historical facts going back to Roman times and the children all became quite adept at reading the underground signs and sorting out the correct platforms to reach the different stations for the trip of the day. They all loved the Museum of London and this outing usually involved a reverent visit to St Paul's Cathedral first. Once inside the Museum and No.3 was fascinated by the display showing a tiny London in a glass case, picturing how the Great Fire started in a baker's shop owned by Thomas Farriner and patronised by the king. This swept through the closely built streets and timber houses, wiping out homes, shops and probably the vestiges of the plague as well, finishing at the site of Pye Corner in Smithfield. The monument is 202 feet high and 202 feet away from the site of the baker's shop where the fire began. The monument was designed and erected for this reason by Sir Christopher Wren, who also re-designed the City of London as well as the beautiful St Paul's Cathedral to replace the original, also destroyed in the fire.

Charles II, who had fled London to avoid risking the plague, returned when the fire was reported to him and set about planning and designing a new London to provide a better place for his subjects to live. This information always made me think that he couldn't have been such a bad king, leaving aside his many and diverse interests, such as Nell Gwynne.

The Barbican was within walking distance of the museum and my friend's husband had been involved in the heating and ventilation of the construction, transforming a bomb site to an arts centre. We had many an enjoyable trip there, watching films, listening to concerts, eating meals and generally looking at the displays. Within the fairly close walking distance we visited the Globe Theatre, watching Shakespeare's plays and once went to Regents Park to see *A Midsummer Night's Dream* in the open-air theatre.

During the summer weeks, we used to go over to Wanstead Flats sometimes, near to where my friend lived, and meet up with other mums and their children from their local school. Those children never resented ours and we never noticed any bullying or segregation when they all joined in the races and played together. These were events costing nothing more than a drop of petrol to get there and the cost of the picnic type lunch that we all got together. Sometimes someone brought a large tin of cakes or biscuits. I remember the ecstasy of an afternoon when No.2 won the welly throwing contest. This innocent contest awarded her great pleasure and she had a garland of delicate daisy chains hung around her neck. To quieten everyone down before going home we searched for a four leaf clover for luck while we finished up the drinks and packed up.

**

It was about this time that we worked on our first mosque. As our client list grew and acquaintances mushroomed, we were requested to meet at a small mosque in Leyton to give them advice about providing a fire exit. The leaders of this building never disrespected me. We took off our shoes when we entered and placed them in a pigeon hole and walked on carpet through to the back. There we were given tea or coffee made in the small kitchen and shown around the premises. This building seemed peaceful and innocent in its simplicity. They ran a women's group and play centre and discussed cookery and meal making which was in no way different to my own pre-school activities. They had several classes to teach women English and how to read and write it. Obviously, there were classes to study the Koran and teachings of Mohammed. There were no anti-white posters about and nothing inflammatory in all our times there. Over the years, we returned several times to this building and were involved in all the extensions, purchase of the adjacent building and enlargement of their premises. The main leader of this Masjid lived in Essex Road, Leyton, almost opposite where St Paul's church once stood. It was sad for us to go to his home and see that the church where Chris and I were married had been demolished. I remembered as a child there had been fund raising to pay for a new house for the vicar. I remembered going to the newly constructed house to discuss the Bible and having lessons in order to understand the meaning of religion and admission of being a Christian in order to be confirmed into the Church of England. That was my dad's idea, as he had been brought up quite devoutly and in his remote village the church played a big part in his life. When my sister reached 13, however, there were no lessons booked for her and she was never made to be confirmed, possibly as by then I had stopping going there. They were days of my early teens when I taught a Sunday School class and talked to a couple of old biddies about being a missionary. I was quite an impressionable child and had read about brave women and yearned to be similarly driven having recently learned of Gladys Aylward. My feelings were reversed totally when we returned from a holiday and when I turned

215

up at the hall to take my class I saw that I had been replaced by another girl. Her family was very involved with matters parochial, her father a part-time lay preacher and mother on various committees and I think I saw with sudden clarity their hypocrisy. I have never lost the realisation of the fact that religious people are often not nice. Those two faced characters who had deliberately usurped me in favour of that simpering young woman showed me how a veil of holiness can hide double dealings and corruption.

This was the start and over the years we became involved with several major religious buildings in Leyton, and also Ilford and Leytonstone. Only in the Ilford mosque did I feel unwelcome. We were there to comment on the roof over one section and I wandered about in the large entrance hall while Chris went with several of the members to investigate the possible problem. There were notice boards within glass fronted frames on the walls which were filled with informative papers as well as advisory notices and all sorts of promotional leaflets. One notice was addressed to the young men of the worshippers. It advised that hair should be kept cut neatly and not of the stupid styles shown in films and having names such as "short back and sides". I thought how ignorant that poster was. A short back and sides was the haircut of respectable middle aged men at the time, businessmen and most certainly not a cult style. The poster went on urging the young men to resist the bad habits practised by the men of the detestable west. Now I agree that many of our men of all ages let themselves down as well as their country, but to call the United Kingdom "the detestable west" I thought inflammatory and grossly unfair. I am sure that nobody took these people and forced them to live here so if it was so detestable why did they stay? For many years that poster infuriated me and I wanted to report it to someone. I never knew who and so I never did.

**

Our young concrete man was going from strength to strength. He had bought a shop along the high road in Forest Gate and was carrying out a refurbishment program. Above the shop were a few rooms of living space. We applied to provide a separate entrance in order to self-contain the rooms above and to add roof rooms with dormers to add height. Three dank and miserable rooms were transformed into a whole small unit and the loft rooms above although slightly smaller replicated the layout. He reached a level with the work for the building inspector to approve and sign off the property and then proceeded to add a few more details, like an extra kitchen and bathroom and suddenly there was a delightful bed-sit situated in the roof space, with panoramic views over the High Road in one direction and a plethora of back gardens from the other. The kitchenette was adequate, the shower WC room was adequate and the main living room changed status at night by pushing the table and armchairs over a few feet and pulling a bed out of a wall space. While two people could have turned murderous while being confined, it proved to be a twee weekend bolt hole for a rural couple or working week pad for a business man who went home to a remote pile in the wilds to wind down.

**

A couple of developers who we had known for a while, introduced by our concrete mogul, introduced us to an Italian businessman who had a pub in London, near Waterloo. He was a colourful character and we built up quite a friendship. He told me a few facts about himself. He was an undischarged bankrupt and everything he did was actually in the name of his wife, although she was merely a figurehead and spent most of her time running her own pursuits in Italy. She unfortunately apparently died and the purse strings of the business and family fortune was then held tightly by their daughter who also resided in Italy. Giacomo spent a fair amount of time complaining of the unjustness of his dizzy-brained daughter, now authorised to control his affairs.

Talks had been going on about constructing the joint venture of the tunnel under the sea. It was now accepted that it would come to pass. Of course, this was a joint venture with the UK and France and called the Channel Tunnel and the Eurostar train service is a regular and popular route.

Giacomo, with an eye to the future, was convinced that the train would emerge near Folkestone, the main motorway route was the M20, and the high-speed train would hurtle through the Kent countryside through fields and villages to finally come to rest at Waterloo. This, he reasoned, would bring him additional business. He wanted to improve his pub in readiness and plotted to convince his daughter to release him the funds to achieve it. We never met her but were regaled with tales of her lack of sense and difficulty of dealing with her while she was stuck in Italy. Perhaps she had inherited clairvoyant gifts regarding the future or his business sense was well known to her.

He had called in to the office which by now was a sort of staging post for so many people who just came in to say hello, to pass on some good news or bit of gossip and said his daughter was coming and he was going to meet her. I wished him good luck and off he went again in a very cheerful mood, waving out of the car window.

Our day progressed as usual with the usual mild emergencies from Denny, endless telephone calls asking for updates from clients, a visit from the Yugoslavian team who missed lunch and had a biscuit instead and a lovely long conversation with my sister.

Chris went to collect the children and brought them back to the office and they went to choose a takeaway from Mrs Chin. No.2 was sitting on the floor in a doorway eating her Chinese food and No.3 was chatting with Denny. Suddenly the front door burst open and an enraged Giacomo came in. He was red in the face; his eyes and mouth were furious and he stamped and jumped over the floor. We all stared. Then he started waving his arms and tried to explain what had happened in his stilted English. He had arranged a place to meet his daughter and went there himself quite early. He just sat there in his car when eventually he saw her driving along in the traffic and hooted so that she spotted him. She waved and somehow got into the wrong lane and went back towards the Blackwall Tunnel. There she was unable to turn around or get off and he saw her car disappearing back into the distance. I think I have never seen an angrier person. He shouted, 'Stupid' over and over, stamping and waving each time then as he got faster it morphed into 'Stupidastupidastupida. Stupid girl. Stupid girl. Stupidastupidastupida.' This was accompanied by torrents of Italian, punches into the air and paces around the room. Eventually he realised we were all staring at him silently and No.2 had a fork poised mid-way to her mouth and we all burst into shouts of laughter. Luckily that dispersed his fury and I got him a cup of tea. She had his address, of course, but I think they were going somewhere else first and he was unable to contact her, he had no mobile phone as they were not common then. Also, it would be getting dark. I don't know why he came to us except it was somewhere between his home and the Blackwall Tunnel and he needed to have a rant out of his car.

All worked out well eventually and he managed to persuade her to release him funds so that his pub kitchen could be up-graded, new windows could be installed and some new seating.

He was the Italian who reassured me when we had all those calls threatening Mafia intervention, convincing me the caller had no connections with them. Those who did, he smiled, kept quiet about it. There was something in his eyes as he said this that made me wonder, just a bit. You never really know about a person.

**

My friend in Manor Park, my sister-in-law, my sister and myself having children of varying ages passed around cast off garments to help each other out. We had a laugh when I told her we had just been deluged with white shirts from both of the others and No.3 was telling everyone he had thirteen new shirts. I warned her that in a year or two she would receive about seventeen white shirts, a bit like one of those chain letter things where you were supposed to send four postcards out and in about thirty days you would receive hundreds. I never received any.

Among the bag of assorted hand-me-downs passed to us there was pair of black plimsolls used by Chris's sister's youngest boy, a cousin to our children; these were used by No.3 for a while and sent on to Hampshire to my sister. One day when they returned from school her son asked in puzzlement who John Brown was as he'd been wearing his gym shoes and didn't know where they came from.

Chapter 16

I was alone in the office one day when Professor Hussein came in. Due to being very observant of his faith he never shook hands with me. I didn't mind.

He was very sad and as he passed me a cheque settling the balance of his account, he told me his wife had left him and taken all his five children, one was a young baby. He said they had all gone to his wife's parents, who had finally persuaded her that he was no good for her. What could I say? She had apparently taken his faith, that much I knew: she always had a hijab on her head and always wore trousers, she always looked very straight and was abrupt in her speech and I had never seen her smile. She may have been shy and perhaps unhappy. He by contrast seemed friendly, was polite and smiled at us. I thought privately that it was a pity the parents, if it was indeed their doing, had not managed to convince her of this fact before they had produced all these children together. I also wondered where they lived as to suddenly accept their daughter back after eight years and all the disruption a young family would bring to their home would be a tumultuous change in their living standards.

He told me they had tried for eight years to get her out of his clutches. They called him a madman. They said he forced his will on her, he was suppressive, he was lazy, he was a religious freak. It was uncomfortable hearing for me, having no interest in any religious propaganda and I felt sorry for them all and the mess they were now in.

To make things worse, their genial builder owned half the house and had moved in.

We received a second rejection notice for Mickie's application for a second dwelling. We had prepared drawings this time for a bungalow from advice from the planning group leader. Mickie was distraught. On my way home I called into the council offices and waited to speak to the officer and when he strolled round to the desk I smiled and waved the envelope. 'Thanks for the advice, Alan. It only took hours and hours of work and printing costs, map costs and all. Not worth anything really, was it?'

'No, sorry,' he agreed glumly. He just stood there looking at me.

'Let's go over it,' I suggested. 'First attempt and your advice was: Go with the existing street scene and follow the design characteristics so it blended. Look at that, Alan. Side garage with dormer window for the bedroom over; double bay and front door with fixed glazed side panels; a chimney stack and rainwater downpipe exactly the same as the others; soft red brickwork and sandstone cills to blend in. This was duly rejected by the department but no advisory comments. Second attempt, you clearly stated to me you had discussed it with your team leader and the head of department and you wanted us to change design altogether and produce a bungalow which screams "I'm new! I'm different!" and certainly won't blend into the street scene. It's lower in height but uses more of the amenity space, which you always endeavour to retain for garden, washing lines etc. How am I doing so far?'

'Yes, you're right,' he said. 'Chris, I've got nothing to say.'

What an admission and we taxpayers paid their salaries.

I was on a roll now, especially as he had put up no resistance or excuse, I knew it must have been pressure from the moany neighbours which was wrong as they should look at schemes for their merit and if the criteria fit the complaints, should be overruled. The planners knew that and I thought the objectors must be extremely voluble or influential people, or perhaps related to one of the councillors, that was usually the case. 'Your team has wasted six months of all our time and wasted a lot of money. Our client had most of the materials ready and the manpower. He is struggling with financial issues due to this quagmire. You know the objections are based on prejudice and have no planning advantage at all.

You know Chris doesn't draw stupid greedy schemes and is sympathetic to the surroundings. So what do you think about it now? Shall we apply to the secretary of state as an appeal? It will take a year but won't look good on you or your department when they know the bum advice you gave, twice in fact, or shall we discuss a third application scheme which will be accepted and approved?'

'Yes,' he said. 'Go back to the first idea, Chris, an end of terrace addition, just change the roof a bit and we will approve it.' It was done.

**

We had booked a day trip on the ferry from Dover to Calais as we all loved walking around the shops, bars and restaurants by the front and enjoyed the enormous hypermarket where we intended to stock up on wines and beers for Christmas. We always managed to get lost somehow on the way to Mammouth or on the way back and never knew which way to go, finding our way by accident. We always drove off the ferry in a line of British cars and started following the familiar number plates in front, which were mainly on their way for cut price alcohol, like us, then suddenly we would realise that they were all gone. No-one ever noticed that somehow everyone else evaporated or spotted that we were turning off the road but it had happened every time. A few times we had become so completely lost in a maze of back streets that we had to pull over and send No.2 into a shop to enquire. She was quite shy and preferred to leave us behind in the car so that we didn't witness her attempts, which always seemed to be accurate as her translated instructions would magically direct us to the hypermarket or back towards the port.

Anyway, full of enthusiasm and blind faith we got ourselves ready and motored down, eating our breakfast journey sandwiches by the time we reached the Blackwall Tunnel and looking forward to the bacon and eggs on the ferry but we arrived too late, just in time to see someone drape a thick red rope across the end of the line, which prevented our entry to the ship. There was still twenty minutes before the ferry left and it was hard to see the cars in front of us dribble on board but leave us on the shore. Other vehicles had followed us down the waiting area and feelings were quite vocal so we asked the time of the next ferry, thinking it was a waste of time charging around to get down to the harbour only to be barred. The girl in the ticket office said it would be over an hour later but as we had booked on a special day trip price, we couldn't change ferry times and would have to pay again.

Nobody wanted to go home but we certainly weren't going to pay full price for a day trip with the car when it was supposed to be a special offer which had been paid already, so we decided to go to Canterbury. It was some years since we had been there and would be a new place for No.3 so he was quite pleased when the others were telling him an exaggerated, gruesome version of how the old Archbishop of Canterbury, Sir Thomas Becket was murdered on the altar steps.

'Was he very old?'

'No, I mean it was a long time ago, in olden days.'

'Was it on television?'

'No, they didn't have television then.'

'How do you know about it then? Was it in the paper?'

'It's history. When you're older you'll do it in history class. It's written in books. I don't know about newspapers then. Mum, did they have newspapers then?'

Me: 'Groan. No, I don't think many people could read then and they didn't have printers or typewriters even. I think it was word of mouth. Handwritten posters perhaps.'

'What's word of mouth? Anyway, why did four knights get sent to kill him? King Arthur's Knights wouldn't kill an old Archbishop. They did good deeds, didn't they?'

'That was the idea, I think, yes, good deeds. But those four knights just went rushing off and killed him without thinking about it. The king wasn't telling them to do that, he just had a moan about him and the knights misunderstood.'

'Perhaps he was a horrible old man and the knights were trying to help?'

'It's still murder. Isn't it still murder? What happened to them then? Were they hanged?'

Chris, wearily: 'I expect they were sent to bed without supper. It was eight hundred years ago, kids, don't worry about it. We'll have an interesting day, we'll go in the cathedral, we'll have some nice lunch and walk around the old cobbled streets.'

'I'll show you where Auntie J and I used to come when we visited our grandma,' I said.

My father came from Kent and we visited his family often. I remember my sister and me climbing Dane John in the park which seemed like a big deal. It is a grass covered mound with a winding path round to the top and I told the children how we could see Stephenson's engine, the *Invicta,* in the park and they could climb the mound. It was a bit of a let-down because the engine was gone and the mound, in reality a Roman cemetery, seemingly large to us as children, appeared to have shrunk over the years. We managed to park quite easily and set off around the historic town centre. Canterbury being famous and close to the coast and ports has as many sightseers and foreign people shopping as people from England going off to France.

The visit for us wasn't a history tour, so we didn't traipse around the other sites and apart from telling them that the museum contained artefacts from Roman times, Anglo Saxons, Norman, Plantagenet being Henry II and the famous murder, we stopped first for drinks all round and discussed what we would do next.

I love to see Elizabethan buildings and we strolled the narrow streets with the shops festively decorated and wondered where we would eat lunch. We settled on a pub and had hearty beef and ale pies with a variety of vegetables and didn't mind missing our trip to Calais. Not too much.

Of course, we went into the cathedral and walked around. Christmas music was being played inside and everywhere else and they bought a few odds and ends in the shop.

The air was turning frosty and we went into a large BHS and bought a dinner set. It was white bone china with a fine gold line and we decided to buy the whole range as our dishes, plates and all had become quite assorted over the years. Restricting ourselves to the plates alone was sensible as we had to carry it all to the car, so decided to travel to a local store to buy the rest on another day. It did in fact look inviting, laid out on the table once we had accomplished the feat. It was all dish-washer safe but the gold paint would spoil if it went into the microwave.

While we strolled about we noticed a restaurant housed in a narrow building, squashed between other tall ones that served fish only. Apart from the timeless, ever-popular fish and chips they served chowders and pies, prawns and crab. We all love fish. Lunch seemed a while away so we felt we could force a few of these delicacies down before the long drive home and it had become quite cold outside so, carefully storing our bags of boxed plates underneath the table, we studied the menu.

They made the most amazing chowder that had smoked haddock, prawns, cockles and a little potato and leek, with brown rustic bread and they wedged a whole prawn on the edge of the bowl, along with a mussel. It had a rich creamy flavour with a hint of cheese and I produced my own version afterwards, which has gone down well ever since.

The waitress was a young girl, very friendly and knowledgeable about fish. We had a conversation about my chowder and several other dishes and I asked her if she had eaten oysters. She had of course, but admitted they weren't for everyone. We thought it applicable how people's diets usually depended on the availability of fashionable foods, being plentiful or scarce, depicting changing times as well as seasons. Once oysters were the food of the Romans and nineteenth century poor, bought from street vendors also selling pies at a penny each and people drank gin or beers like porter as the water was so dirty; as the pendulum swung they had become expensive: poorer class people dismissed oysters as disgusting and turned to packaged prawns for their luxuries, linking oysters with champagne for celebrations.

I confessed to never having tried an oyster and she brought me one to try. She shucked it, forcing the shell open and asked me if I preferred lemon or shallot vinegar. I of course had no idea so she squirted lemon juice on it, then handed me the lower shell case with the oyster in it, lying in its own juices. 'Tip it all in your mouth, give it one little chew and swallow it down.'

I did and loved it. I asked all the others if they wanted to try them, as I would have bought a few, but that day I was alone. All of us liked fish, prawns and crab meat, jellied eels for the boys and cockles with vinegar and pepper.

Over time we went again to that beautiful restaurant spread over three floors and reached via rickety narrow stairs and one Sunday when the children all had a school thing, we crept off, taking my mother for a civilised long lunch. What a crushing disappointment it was after I had enthused so fanatically to her for so long, only to find as we reached the door at last that they never opened on Sundays. I think we ended up in a carvery, where we could have gone any day. Mum was pleased anyway, as it was a treat for her to be taken out and she didn't care where, so the hundred mile round trip was enjoyed by her at least. I resolved to check availability in future.

**

A pair of businessmen came into the office one day to discuss an idea. They were young, with an underlying confidence and an easy manner probably derived from a background of financial stability all their lives. D was dark haired and spoke with a drawl; M was fair and laughed easily. They apparently owned a two-storey building in the High Road, which was constructed in a Georgian mansion style and painted an attractive deep cream.

They had an idea, quite innovative then, to install a receptionist on the ground floor who would answer the telephone. Anyone going into the building would stop at her desk first and she then would buzz the visitor through to the relevant room or suite.

All calls went via the central switchboard and everyone paid their account monthly, along with the service charge and their rent. This was proving to be popular and a cheaper way to rent a private office without all the extras loaded on top, like council rates, heating and water bills; telephone, cleaning and secretarial work, with printing and postage costs included. It was a starter scheme which, once proved workable to a budding entrepreneur, allowed him or her to go on to greater things, including additional rooms or premises, equipment and staff.

In recent years, the local authority had authorised the construction of several tall blocks of flats along the main road and D and M's idea was to add a mansard roof level to their building which would provide the building with eight more rooms for rent.

They had done the rounds of agents already known to them, and nobody wanted to touch it. 'Over the top.'

'Planners won't have it.'

'Too central, they won't allow the height.'

'Oh no. It's too dominant a building. They won't allow another level on that.'

'Right then, Chris. What do you say? Do you want to have a go?' from grinning M.

Chris regarded the pictures they had brought in showing the subject building and the immediate street scene and announced that he knew what he would draw and felt confident of a good result. He asked if the fee was dependent on a successful outcome and they said it wasn't, they were grateful to find someone who accepted the challenge and understood that not every application had a happy ending.

The deal was done. Chris arranged to go around there to take the dimensions that were needed, to buy the Ordnance Survey map extracts and to generally get on with the process and they promised to drop their deposit over. 'How did you hear about us?' Chris asked and they mentioned several other people that we had met. Our fame was growing and it was becoming exciting.

**

From time to time we had become involved with another pair of developers. J was a builder and his partner V seemed to secure the work. A brother and occasional workman made up the team. Chris would hare off to meet them to give his opinion on the stability of a property and likelihood of it gaining permission, which would transpose it to another level if the works were carried out. If they bought it and the relevant permission was gained and building works were completed to effect a profitable sale, this obviously covered all expenses and building costs and landed them a large profit in order to engage in another venture.

One day over a year previously they had run out of work and were at our house for a cup of tea and a chat. A few years earlier we had extended the first floor of our house to the side, for Chris to work in at the time. This airy room became the bedroom for No.2 when we took the office and enabled little No.3 to have the box-room. The extension was supported on piers which formed a parking area beneath. While we chatted, they walked around, looking at the construction which was quite innovative and J suggested they could fill in the sides of our parking area to form an extended kitchen or dining area and construct a garage in front. The price he came up with was apparently three weeks' work for his brother and mate and included the cost of all the materials, he said. The idea of carrying out this work had not occurred to us as we had our hands full of the other projects, but he swore the stated amount of money would be sufficient and could start in a few weeks. It was an amount of money we had managed to accrue, and leaving the cost of our holiday aside, we could just stretch to.

We instilled into both of them that the sum they mentioned to cover materials and three weeks' money for the boys was in fact all we had and unless they were totally positive, we did not want to embark on any expensive projects at this time. They promised the stated sum would cover the materials for a timber frame garage with roof over and to infill the existing side wall between the piers, some plaster board, a door to the house, garage doors and Bob's your uncle.

We were due to go on holiday and they pitched up the week before. This week was full of enthusiasm to start. J's brother then had a car crash which although left him absolutely physically fine, prevented him working because he mooned about his car to such an extent that he sat about drinking tea and constantly phoned his girlfriend for sympathy. The work as such was carried out by the worker and another one roped in from somewhere else. The side wall was filled in as far as the garage front and some demolition to the kitchen which they said was necessary.

I was caught on the hop when asked for the first week's money, which was considerably more than a third. J explained that it was for materials, wages, really only the worker's wages because A did virtually nothing, but I found it very awkward and difficult to refuse.

The next week we had arranged for a neighbour to come in to feed our cats while we went on holiday for a week, and she had the key for the building team to get in and construct the floor of the side room and timber joists for the roof over the garage.

We had borrowed a three-bedroom apartment in Nerja, Spain, from a client and thoroughly enjoyed ourselves, anticipating how good our home would look after week two had been completed and arrived home full of expectation.

Instead we had a disappointment. No further work had been carried out. The site was a complete mess. Monday morning arrived and no sign of any builders appeared and Chris called V to ask if there was a problem. I think they had suddenly landed a profitable contract which made our piffling little infill an irritating nuisance but eventually they returned.

We tried to pin them down over the costs as already having more than the initial third of our money and achieving less than the expected level of work seemed more than a trifling worry and we reiterated again that we had a fixed sum only, now depleted.

They returned and at the end of the second week J didn't wait for us to get home, he came to the bank where I was working at three o'clock and demanded a second instalment. This was a little more than the agreed third and left the final instalment very diminished and a huge amount of the work outstanding, not forgetting the cost of the garage doors and roof materials. I had the embarrassing experience of trying to speak to him quietly at the enquiry desk, while also feeling close to panic at the state of the property and the financial situation. He seemed completely nonplussed about the whole affair. I am sure he thought we were lying about the money and really had a big bag of it somewhere and I eventually gave him the cash he wanted and tried to reiterate that next week's money was half of the previously stated amount, because he had already taken it at the end of the first unproductive week. Of course, at the end of the third week the end of the project was far away and we handed over the remaining cash and watched his face become completely blank. 'What's this, then? It's not a week's money.'

'No. You've had it, remember? We told you we only had this fixed sum.'

The conversation repeated a few times in similarly worded sentences until he finally realised the cupboard was now bare.

He pulled off site and we surveyed the state of our home in dismay. There were gaps in the wall revealing the insulating foam that had been piped into the cavities some years earlier, a lump of the existing kitchen ceiling was down exposing an ornamental timber surface above, which also was damaged, the kitchen floor covering had been removed, ceiling plaster boards had been fixed to the proposed garage joists but no roof covering installed over to make it weatherproof, so a recent rain storm had damaged a couple of sections which were now torn and hanging down and we needed a concrete screed for the garage floor, as well as additional works to the electrics and new garage doors. Not much less in the scheme of things as we had needed at the start of the project, as perfectly good areas had been damaged in their initial gusto. We dismally knew we had to gather together as much money as possible in order to hire the relevant tradesmen to complete the work gradually but as fast as able. The first one was a roofer. A skilled worker, tradesman or craftsman makes a difficult job look easy and this man created a beautiful flat felted roof over the doorless garage one afternoon which cheered us all up.

This worrying state of affairs continued for quite a time. As we saved a little it was spent immediately on the next stage of reparation. There were no full height doors so the side of the house was visible to anyone who walked by. We only had the side gates which hid nothing of the proposed garage area and items stored there were in constant danger of being pilfered.

After a while we noticed that No.2 had developed a cough which refused to budge regardless of medicines, syrups, gallons of lemon and honey and several doctor's visits. Finally, she was sent a hospital appointment, which Mum took her to. The consultant decided she must have developed an allergy and set about a series of tests. As the weeks went by with no break-through we went from being slightly worried to nail bitingly frantic, then Chris heard a pertinent programme on the radio. It had been discovered that properties in some kinds of wall cavity insulating foam contained irritating chemicals which caused varying symptoms of chest problems to some people. We immediately hired a couple of men to repair the damaged wall in the kitchen and create a new kitchen ceiling. Once again, our coffers were bare but our daughter healed immediately and we felt sadness at our trusting incompetence and their greedy irresponsibility.

The story didn't end there because J sent V around week after week asking for sketches, site visits and calculations to act as repayment for the money he insisted we owed them. This went on for a while and suddenly, one day Chris got annoyed and told him where to go. Chris once annoyed is not a pretty sight and I think they finally got the message. V admitted that J and his brother had performed the same act on his sister and their estimated job eventually cost double. Due to our mortgage, office costs, school fees and ever escalating bank charges, accumulating a lump sum was not easy for us and it backfired for them because he believed our resources to be elastic. All in all, I think we got off the worst as we had to use many different trades to finish the job off, but they lost an honest surveyor and engineer who also produced very good drawings. One of the last jobs that Chris did with them was to accompany J to a house for a visual survey of structural integrity. The house was isolated but in a nice area with a large garden and good aspects. It was a house that J wanted to buy for his own home and not for development. They drove up and parked to the side where the estate agent waited with the key. He unlocked the front door for them and asked if they could securely shut the door upon their departure, which they assured him they would. He drove off and Chris went into the house with J.

The house was about a hundred and fifty years old, with leaded light windows and timber panelling. It had a small room with shelves to use as a library. They slowly walked around inside, Chris was testing for dampness ingress readings and examining the timber flooring for signs of beetle infestation. The kitchen was old fashioned with an early Aga type range and a corner copper in the utility room to heat the water to wash the clothes. They went out the back door and strolled around the outside, with Chris looking intently for signs of movement to the foundations and walls. Older properties often have shallow footings and there were many trees around the periphery.

Once back inside they walked up the staircase to the first floor, when suddenly a blast of freezing air almost knocked them off balance. The temperature plummeted and they stood quietly looking at each other, then started to go into the bedrooms. They both felt the hairs on the back of their necks start to rise, a sensation I had not experienced myself and thought it was just a saying: then both turned as one and leapt down the stairs, along the hall and outside, slamming the door behind them. Chris said they both felt wobbly and J had gone a pasty shade of grey and they

231

drove away. I have no idea where that house was and who finally bought it, but Chris has never been fanciful and I believe they really experienced something evil that day.

We never liked a relationship souring but learned a bitter lesson and dented our trusting natures.

When we give a client an estimate of costs we always send a letter and our client has time to accept the terms and conditions.

Now we urge all clients to obtain a JCT agreement, which is a binding contract. Building costs will have been calculated by a quantity surveyor and a document produced known as a bill of quantities and the contractors will have provided their estimates according to this document. This does not mean that an emergency or unexpected issue will not arise but it helps to safeguard both parties.

It also helps to have a look at other works that the relevant contractor has carried out before and received recommendations. Picking a name out of the phone book, although hugely practised, is never a good idea.

So, Christmas was rapidly approaching and it had taken us nearly two years to finally complete our house, which looked nice at last. We heard via the grapevine years later that J and V were very successful and drove expensive cars and I think it must have been lucrative buying and selling that earned them their fortunes, rather than carrying out or partially carrying out small building jobs as much work like ours would soon bankrupt everybody.

**

The school was launching their usual shows and concerts so our children were busy and we had more taxiing about, dropping them for rehearsals and picking them up afterwards.

No.1 was showing great promise with his technical drawings and art subjects as well as becoming the champion for running, 100m and 1500m races. Our pride was quite massive when he beat the school record and his name was engraved on the cup.

He never took part in school drama productions of any sort, saying he felt a fool pretending to be someone else or wearing stupid clothes. Plays by Shakespeare or worse, Chaucer, he hated with a vengeance; thees and thous, hither and thither and prithee, soft! caused him to roll his eyes and pick up a Donkey Kong or Mario game.

No.2 however enjoyed taking part in choral displays and helped backstage with the scenery as well as occasionally taking a character role.

One year I was asked to lend a large metal cooking pot for some reason, which I did, and to buy a bottle of Moet for her particular gang of cronies to present to the drama teacher, which I also did. At the end of the production my cooking pot vanished, somewhere presumably into the dark storage area beneath the stage. It had morphed into a prop for future productions probably and someone dropped and broke the bottle so not only did I lose the family soup pot, I was never reimbursed for the booze.

This year they were doing a play about Al Capone and the stages in his life, which managed to include some singing and evoke a light hearted take on it. She had the part of Al Capone's mother which involved her yelling the same phrase at intervals throughout the play. His parents were Italian immigrants, speaking with heavy Italian accents and he spoke with a Brooklyn drawl, having been born and raised in New York along with a tribe of siblings, hard living in the early 1920s for the Capones. His parents were ordinary, hard-working, law abiding citizens and nothing like the gangster that he was to become, amassing an empire with a fortune of over sixty million dollars by the age of thirty.

The first time, she rushed onto the stage dressed as a poor Italian, wearing an apron, curlers in her hair with a head scarf on and waving a rolling pin, probably fresh from the pasta kitchen. This was when he became a father while still a teenager, which would have angered his devout Catholic parents. He married the young girl and went to Chicago where he changed from young father and husband to gofer, errand boy and Mob leader. After he was involved with a gangland shootout which the police were unable to prove, they managed to convict him for tax evasion. It was during the mayhem that followed that she carried out another shouting episode. She was dressed a little smarter although still an immigrant mother and delivered her telling-off in strident heavily accented tones.

He bought a mansion in Florida where he continued to enjoy his high life and thuggery, primarily involved with the illicit liquor trade during prohibition. Finally, when he was thirty-one he was charged again for tax evasion, having omitted to file a tax return a few years earlier and during the scene where police, mobsters, family, assorted children and all were generally panicking on stage that suddenly her raucous voice rang out again and she was pushed onto the stage in a wheelchair. She had told us nothing about the play so we were as surprised as the rest of the audience and her angry persona, dressed for the part and still trying to rule them all from a wheel chair, brought a huge roar of laughter.

Al Capone died in his forties, his body rife with the effects of venereal disease but his wife looked after him in his declining years. He was one of the first prisoners to reside in Alcatraz and is probably the most famous gangster ever, his charity donations softened his overall brutal image but responsible for a chain of death, drugs and prostitution misery in his wake.

A couple of the schoolboys playing major parts actually were from Italian families and their accents and singing were marvellous. Over the years, they played predominant roles and I often wondered what happened to them in the ensuing years.

No.3 had a small part of a scruffy street urchin playing as he liked to be anyway, aimlessly kicking a ball, with rakish hair and wearing patched old jeans and jumper.

**

Denny introduced us to a friend of his, a quiet young black man paradoxically called Mr White. He ran a television repair shop and needed a valuation for his bank in order to obtain a mortgage to buy the shop freehold which he had been renting for some time. After this had been accomplished we met him a few more times to draw him a kitchenette and WC room on the ground floor and later to self-contain the shop to create a separate dwelling over.

Another friend he had known since college who worked for a surveying company as a quantity surveyor was a frequent caller. Like Denny, he had never completed his studies and his degree was elusive but he worked hard and steadily and was an asset to his company. He was instrumental in coaching No.1 with various aspects of surveying and along with his sisters, remained a friend as well as an associate when he introduced us to colleagues that needed building or structural advice. His older sister was a teacher and his younger sister worked for a children's charity.

**

Our valuations for our bank were going strong, two or three a week and as staff were moved around they took our names and details with them, so more and more branches put us forward to carry out the surveys. It started as a favour one day for the branch where I worked. Their usual surveyor was unavailable and an urgent loan was in need of sanction. The accountant at the branch asked me, 'Please, Chris, would your husband look at this for us?'

'No,' I said, 'he's not a qualified valuer.'

'It doesn't matter. We know the place is worth a bundle. The manager has been there and there's a crack on the side wall that he's concerned about. It's the wall that the manager needs looking at, the rest is academic. Please ask him.'

'You ask him then,' I replied. 'Tell him what you need and see if he agrees.'

He did agree and that was the start of it. Now I went with him sometimes but mainly he went alone. These valuations consisted of measuring the floor space in order to calculate the insurance required and the re-building costs in case of need. Any necessary repairs were noted and any adverse features likely to affect the granting of the loan would be stated. Loans were granted then at no more than eighty per cent of the estimated value and there were always similar properties advertised for sale in estate agents, so an accurate value was attainable.

One afternoon he arrived back at the office in a strangely quiet mood and waited for Denny to go out before he told me what had happened.

He arrived at a house to carry out a routine valuation as the owner had asked his branch manager for a top-up loan which he needed for business purposes. The customer's wife let him in and left him to inspect the outside structure and wander the ground floor as his usual practice. He went upstairs and to his horror, the wife had undressed and was draped over the bed, wearing a diaphanous nightdress only and beckoning him over.

I gasped at him and asked what he did next. He said he ignored her completely and carried on with the inspection then when he'd finished he left. The loan was obviously important to her if she was willing to bribe the surveyor in this way but conversely, a refusal could have enraged her and she could have accused him of indecent behaviour or worse. We wondered if the husband had put her up to it and how he would react when he found out Chris had spurned her. Or maybe he would believe the offer was not rejected or did not believe his wife.

The property was worth the amount that they had applied for and obviously, the bank had accepted it in principle, but if they were granted the loan they could think it was her behaviour and Chris's acquiescence that had clinched the deal and if it had been refused we were sure she would cry "rape". This was a predicament which could have dire results for us.

We decided to tell the branch manager so they had it on record. He was a person that I knew and he took the information gravely. Apparently, he called the couple in and told them in no uncertain terms that the bank, he and we did not do business in this way and he had made a note in their records so that if any further untoward behaviour on their part was ever brought to his attention he would close their accounts.

A valuation carried out less than a mile from our office caused distress to the prospective buyer. The mid terrace house was fairly modern with square windows, plain front entrance door leading straight into the living room from the pedestrian walkway, with no front garden or off road parking space. There was no garage or garden shed and a tiny back garden. The roof space was too shallow for a loft conversion: the property was in reality a basic starter home. There were other similar estate properties on the market which highlighted the ordinariness of the structure and style but the asking price was considerably more than the others. The owners had spent a large sum of money on plaster decorations, ornate ceiling roses, double coving to all the ceilings and wall panels framing pictures of cupids and bowls of flowers. The walls were painted pastel colours and the plaster works were white and extensive, it gave the impression of being enveloped in a wedding cake.

It was difficult explaining to the tearful couple who wanted the property that the size and type of house was only worth the same as all the others and decorations were not a permanent fixture and can easily be installed: it was like paying too much for a building because you liked the carpet. A silk purse out of a sow's ear sprang to mind.

Another time when I went with him, we picked up the key from the estate agent and let ourselves in. Chris unlocked the back door to go into the garden and carry out his inspection of the exterior when a cat hurtled down the path, leapt through the doorway and jumped up at me, mewing and scratching my boots. I was glad at that point I had worn them that day as the claws scored such runs in the leather that my legs, if attacked, would have been seriously hurt. The fuss was quite considerable and we guessed it was hungry, so I looked in the fridge and found a tin of cat food which had been opened and had a plastic lid on. To my disgust the food inside had mould on and I refused to give it to an animal, which would make it sick, so I threw it away and opened another. I also put some water in the bowl and watched the cat lap it up and wander off outside again. 'Blimey, Chris, I hope it's not someone else's cat,' Chris said to me. I hoped that too.

When we had finished, we drove back to the shop and I took the keys in and explained what had happened and showed him my boots. 'I'm sorry the owner might be annoyed as it wasn't my business and I had no right to touch her fridge or tinned food but I just couldn't ignore it. Look at my boots.'

The estate agent I think agreed with my sentiments, but he said he would have to tell his client as I expected he would but I was unprepared for her extreme reaction. She telephoned the branch manager and went berserk at him. 'How dare the surveyor accuse me of starving my cat? How dare they have the cheek to touch my fridge and open a new tin,' and more, and more. I actually didn't care. It must have been days since she had opened that can of mouldy food and there was no sign of any biscuits or treats. I hoped the cat wandered away and found a new home. I hoped she would think about it and feel guilty. Why do you keep a pet if you don't look after it?

She couldn't sue us for pitying her cat but I secretly rang the RSPCA and reported her. Probably nothing happened, as I had experienced a few weeks earlier with a case of reported cruelty.

I saw some youths tormenting a dog over Wanstead Flats, they were lifting it and making it hold on to a branch with its teeth and then hitting it. Obviously, it held on as it was afraid of falling. I rang the institution and the local police but nobody came. A police car driving by actually passed them and ignored them. In the end, I went over to them myself and told them they should be ashamed of themselves. Their actions on the dog were to get it ready for fighting, training it to clamp its teeth on the branch or another dog and not let go even though it was being hit. They told me to go away or words to that effect and I went back to the office and tried the police again. I never told Chris I had approached the gang and was aware it was a foolhardy action, people get stabbed for less.

Another valuation we carried out on a mansion flat in London achieved a knock-on effect. The marble topped stairs with carved oak bannisters led to the garden flat below and three floors above the common entrance hall, comprising five storeys: the beautiful building included a residence on each level with the caretaker's room and store to the rear, beneath the landing. Over time structural changes had been carried out and Chris noticed stress fractures at the ends of a beam over the staircase, which had been installed probably a century before. We suggested the beam was probably of timber, which had become rotten and was now deflecting and noted a section of the front elevation where concealed rainwater drainage was thought to be leaking into the structure from a small ornamental balcony to the first-floor unit. Our remit was for the ground floor unit only and we did not have access to the flat above or permission to climb a ladder to inspect the other areas. Our valuation document stated our thoughts and the sale halted. We were gratified that the freeholders did not ignore our observations and instructed the management company to investigate and carry out the remedial works as required. We heard back a few months later from the client that the leak to the balcony structure had been strengthened and rainwater box gutter had been replaced, as well as a steel beam replacing the damaged timber one. Apparently, the freeholder was a major land owner and owned the strip of buildings and enlarged the program to carry out inspections of the other, similar blocks.

**

Christmas was approaching fast now and we all went to a party where Santa would be making an appearance and giving all the children an early present. This involved each child approaching the grotto and, accompanied by an elf, having a short meeting with the Santa of the day. Little No.3 was still full of the magic and believed in Father Christmas but wondered how he could have been allowed to come away from Greenland so close to the actual event, when he should have been organising the toys and production line and sorting out his routes. Obviously, he listened to us when we pored over maps. When it was his turn he went into the makeshift cabin and scrutinised the poor man. 'Who asked you to come here? How did they reach you? We write notes and put them on the fire but we don't know how to phone you? How does the magic work? What do the reindeer eat? They don't have wings, do they?'

I think he answered as vaguely as only a qualified Santa can and our sceptic accepted his gift with thanks, but later, when everybody sat with a plate of buffet food to watch a magician hired for the event, No.3 poked me in the side and pointed out that a man sitting over there had stolen Santa's boots.

Chapter 17

We rocketed towards Christmas and the longed-for break where hopefully everybody gave up all thoughts and aspirations of property purchases or development for a few days at least, which would allow us to relax with our families.

All the presents had been wrapped and secreted away, recipes written out and shopping lists for special foods stored in the side of my bag and I tried to bring our records up to date and tackle our accounts. I was trying to prevent my annual last minute rush, whereby everybody else got blasted at New Year's Eve parties but I was desperately finishing the quarter's VAT and paying our annual taxes.

We had carried out a valuation on a new house in Hertfordshire by a famous developer and to our horror, noticed that a support pier had been omitted from the detached garage. Garages are not classed as residential and the walls are usually of single skin brick or block work but strengthened by a pier at the front and rear corners and half way down the side walls. Obviously, this was brought to the attention of the site foreman who had directed us to the plot, as he and his team were busy constructing similar houses on the estate but he just shrugged. We wrote out the detailed form and mentioned that the pier must be installed prior to the completion as it was not safe in adverse weather conditions. A heavy snowstorm or sustained winds could affect the stability of the building and the clients were very upset, but the company, when the bank brought it to their attention, immediately ordered the installation of a pier which had a roof support fixed and the sale went ahead as planned. This afternoon I had a telephone call from the jubilant buyers, to tell us all was well and to thank us for noticing the error. A structural defect such as this could go for years with no problem, then suddenly in a freak weather storm, collapse, causing destruction and possible serious threat to life.

The children had broken up for the holidays and were lolling about the office so they took it in turns to go with Chris to hold the tape.

A few months before, he had carried out a valuation on a council owned flat, which a young lady at a neighbouring bank branch lived in and wanted to purchase under the Right to Buy Act. Her parents had been council tenants for years and she took the flat over when they died. The length of the tenancy would allow her a huge discount on the purchase price, which was a maximum of 50%, but selling price could not be below the actual cost of the building construction at the time. She had applied to her manager for a staff mortgage and had been approved so our valuation was the last thing in the chain. This was duly carried out and it went ahead with no complications. No.1 went along and helped to measure the place for insurance purposes but the policy would have to form part of the council's own. They went on to include the communal areas on the ground floor so a lease plan could be drawn for her if it was needed and form part of her mortgage package. Roz and I often spoke on the phone afterwards: she was grateful to Chris and our help generally and she put people on to us whenever she could. Apart from that, she and I had a banking background and had much in common. My mother had lived in a similar council owned block of maisonettes and although she moved after Dad died to be nearer her cousin, we had embarked on a similar project to buy her flat for her, so being the same council I was able to pass on my experiences.

This afternoon he went to a commercial unit in South London and took the younger two with him, while No.1 went out with Ray to look at an old house he was thinking of buying for development.

I had a relatively peaceful afternoon with my figures and decided on Mrs Chin's fish and chips all round when they got back.

Ray had sold the last of the Snaresbrook flats and had resolved to sit on the land that he had bought from our lovely gay estate agents, but decided to buy the old house in North London and asked us to pencil it in our diary for as soon after the New Year as possible, to be measured and drawn and submitted for a flats conversion. It would be far more profitable to market and sell three housing units within the periphery of London than a single house in the outskirts, even if it was near the airport. He estimated that it would transform quite easily into three large units, with parking spaces and a huge garden and No.1 excitedly told us that Ray said he could do the lease plans when they were ready to be marketed. He was looking at about nine months in the future but we didn't want to dampen his enthusiasm.

Chris had a reasonably good meeting at the leather store and discussed a revised scheme the owner wanted to carry out at one of his houses. He had worked on several schemes and ideas for him before, but had to persuade him that flats units have to be correctly worked out with regulation size kitchens, bedrooms and living rooms, roof height below a beam and ceiling height over stairs and width of stairs. In this case it was a loft conversion for his children, to allow them a larger bedroom, a much easier scheme to be drawn and constructed but also a re-draw for a tatty terraced building he used for his workers. He purportedly liked children and was friendly towards ours, giving No.3 a colouring book and some pencils to take home.

At last a revised scheme was decided upon which Chris would submit for discussion.

**

I had taken a call from an estate agent from Ilford who wanted drawings to self-contain the rooms above his shop. There were two levels and once the planners had approved the scheme and the work was carried out, he would have two decent sized flats above the offices. The premises were in a busy shopping parade and close to the station, convenient and highly marketable. 'If he decides to sell them,' I told No 1, 'there will be more lease plans for you to get your teeth into.'

**

We were asked by a plumber we had known for some years if we would intervene on his sister's behalf, outlining the problem that they had and he introduced us to her and her husband. He was a greengrocer who ran a shop and had a market stall several days a week. There was a problem with the house and the insurance company was proving difficult. They had tried to make a claim for the movement of the rear kitchen, which had suffered subsidence of the footings, but his insurers refused to take any notice.

In those days, a householder was entitled to use a surveyor to act for him and in this case after he almost gave up due to his insurers' intransigence, he asked his brother-in-law if he knew anyone who could help him to dislodge them from their static position. We agreed to try, not that we savour a challenge but we felt they were being unfairly treated. The first one thousand pounds of a subsidence or heave claim is deducted as excess, therefore monies a claimant spends within this sum will be deducted from the total as long as the insurance company accepts the case as a claim, otherwise it becomes an expensive exercise.

We sent them our report and also phoned the office. We also chased them a few times. Our client paid his premium via an agent who called monthly to collect the fees, and he also reminded him several times over the weeks.

Finally, our client received an ex-gratia offer of a thousand pounds as a full and final settlement and a friend of his who worked in the industry advised him to accept it. We thought not. We reckoned if they were prepared to offer a thousand pounds when their own representative or loss adjuster had not even been to site, it was a cop out.

We wrote on our client's behalf that we were getting ready to contact the Insurance Ombudsman to intervene and enclosed another copy of our survey, a copy of a tree specialist report and a CCTV report on the drainage along the side, which clearly showed tree roots encroaching into the pipework and causing sub soil leaching. We knew why they were trying so hard to escape from this claim as it threatened to be messy. The drainage pipes crossed the party boundary beneath the fences from the next door premises and the trees which were identified as the perpetrators had also encroached from next door, therefore the insurers would have the added aggravation of making a counter-claim on the neighbour's insurance company. On one of my chase-up telephone calls I couldn't help remarking that I considered it disgusting that they took people's premiums very willingly indeed and then did their utmost to duck out of a claim that had manifested. It was one of the office workers who I had expressed my opinion to, but she must have felt a prick of conscience and spoken to someone of suitable importance because she called back and said they would be sending someone out and due to the excellent evidence we had collected, the claim had been accepted. Also, taking into account the length of time our client had been battling, they saw no reason to wait the usual twelve months for the seasons' tree growth to be monitored and would authorise for new drains to be constructed, as well as contact with the neighbours to liaise about their own drainage and trees treatment and finally, to pay for underpinning work to be carried out along the flank wall. We received no commission for this work but the greengrocer and his wife had paid us for our survey and sent us a basket of fruit. Whenever any of the children passed his stall they were invited to take an apple, which they did.

A frustrating case had been completed and he remembered us when they wished to move from the house after the work had been completed. His wife had been badly affected with the worry and could not settle afterwards. She could not relax and was looking constantly for signs of fresh movement so he finally told her to look around and when she found somewhere else that she liked, he would ask Chris to look at it for them.

They found a lovely semi-detached house a few miles away which was given a clean bill of health and they moved, changing their insurers out of principle.

**

A couple of shops with living accommodation over had come up for sale in Walthamstow. A young developer we had become quite friendly with bought one of them and asked us to apply to obtain change of use permission, from a shop to a residential unit, and self-contain the upper level on his behalf. The builders lined up to carry out the building work were the Yugoslavians that we knew very well. The permissions were granted within the eight weeks and gratefully the work was started. There was access around the back of the building, being formerly one of a parade of small shops, which was useful for the delivery of construction materials and allowed a decent sized garden for the ground floor unit. When the works were almost completed they were put on the market for sale and we were surprised to be requested to carry out a valuation on the upper flat for mortgage purposes, which of course we carried out. We had also prepared the lease plans which would be used for the mortgage package and lodged with Land Registry.

The young owner had retained the end piece of the rear garden for his own use and the builders built him a block work shed for storage purposes. We had not been aware of this at the time. This was to be rendered over and painted white. Several other similar buildings were treated in this way and this stretch of the main road became purely residential.

A few months later the young man came into the office and asked us to help him. He had been sent a planning notice telling him to demolish the shed he had built on the land. He asked us to apply on his behalf to retain the building and this we did for him. The decision came a few months later refusing the request. We rarely carried out appeals to the secretary of state in Wales but had heard that a town planner working in a different borough was taking them on for a set fee. He agreed to take this one on and stated that he felt quite confident. Six months later, however, the appeal was rejected and our client was forced to demolish the beautiful little building. Information on the grape vine a couple of months later was that a local publican who was reportedly racist had complained about the illegal building and made a fuss. He went around the neighbours getting them to sign a petition and the offending building was duly removed. Our client asked the flat dwellers if they wanted to buy the land to extend their garden and the land went up for sale. Some time later, when we passed the premises on our way to a site we noticed to our amazement that a store, of similar size and appearance had been rebuilt on the land. We wondered who had built this and if they too would be obliged to remove it.

Some months later we met again with that client, who knew what had happened. He sold the scrap of land to someone who knew someone else and he finally received a pittance for it, being useless apart from parking a vehicle on, but later learned the publican himself had obtained it and immediately resurrected the building he had been instrumental in removing. Our client was wryly accepting of the chicanery carried out but we were yet again dismayed at the double dealings by some of our town planners and blatant prejudice.

Planning rules have changed and the Freedom of Information Act enables people to see the relevant file and look at the messages, letters, emails which divulge the names of objectors and their reasons for making the objection, so they cannot hide behind anonymity. Further changes to their regulations, currently government led, mean a householder can now build sheds and stores over half of the garden without formal planning consent as long as the criteria regarding position, size and height is complied with, depending on green belt, village position and of course, the ultimate use.

**

When Chris first worked at the smaller office next door, he began to build up a client base and a pool of people who used his services. A person he met worked mainly for an Ilford based team who I have referred to already and he knew many people, who gradually were introduced to Chris for his help with surveying or engineering. It was he who introduced a young woman to him to help with secretarial work when I was still working at the bank. It therefore became a little awkward when we realised that she was systematically dipping into the paper, envelopes and tea bags, sugar and even biscuits. Her husband was a self-employed painter and decorator and we asked him for a quotation to paint our window frames externally at home. He must have thought they were on to a good thing, with her steadily pinching the goods and then the mugs asked for a quote from him. He presented us with an eye watering estimate that we believed even he thought would never be accepted and didn't bat an eyelid when we declined. It was after that we noticed the supplies dwindling.

Chris told Ewen what had happened when he called in one afternoon but he had enough to worry about in his own life. He was about our age with a beautiful little daughter. His wife had been a depressive with unpredictable behaviour and had to take daily medicines to keep her steady and for a while she had seemed calm so, believing that he could keep her in this level state, he agreed for her to leave off the medication in order to try for another child. They had a boy. After a short while, even though he ensured she was taking her drugs the bizarre behaviour started. She would call him incessantly while he was at work, worrying and needing reassurance. He often worked from home, preparing plans and due to caring for the baby, ensuring his daughter was looked after with school lunches and general routine and mollycoddling his wife to keep her stable, his working hours became erratic. Although he was freelance with his drafting, he mainly worked with and for the company mentioned. Things got to a head for the family when due to her medical state, she worried constantly for the welfare of the little boy and drove everybody else crazy with her constant calls to the nursery, then school as he grew, until their daughter, now about fifteen, left home to live with a friend's family because she refused to put up with her actions. She told her dad she was too embarrassed to bring friends home and felt no attachment to her mother. She blamed him for not leaving her in hospital where she was sent from time to time, saying he should have refused to allow her home. I am not sure that he could have done that but I was exquisitely sorry for their plight.

We then took on a girl we had met at karate class. The family were down to earth and her mother confided she longed for someone to give her a part-time position so she could say she had work experience in an office and this would help her to get a good job. I've always been a sucker for a sob story and want to help people so I showed her the ropes one Saturday morning and she willingly tried to act like a secretary.

Her handwriting was laborious, with painstaking loops and twirls and took her a long while to do. Her typing was a slow, two finger operation, like mine, but not especially accurate and although she was a sweet girl she would never be the quick-witted asset to Chris's budding concern that he needed. It was with regret that her industrious efforts were ended when he told her I would be leaving the bank to help him. Her dad telephoned and I thought he would go mad at Chris for rejecting his little girl, but in reality I think he knew she wasn't the sharpest knife in the drawer because he just thanked him for giving her a chance, which again made me feel awful. He was self-employed, making tarpaulins for lorries and large marquee tents for weddings and ceremonies, so I guessed he must have understood the ups and downs of the roller-coaster ride that working for yourself brings. He also had his children at his factory sometimes, so probably expected that her part-time employment would be short-lived.

Another person we met at karate became a client several times over. His main money-making concern was the buying and selling of cars and scrap but he also dabbled in property developing. He was up-grading his home in Chigwell and Chris helped with the engineering and building control details. He brought his little boy to the class, who tried hard to carry out the moves and emulate his dad. He was a miniature version and looked amusing when he stood near him.

The second job we did for him was to extend his car lot in Newham which was achieved on plan, then to give advice when the little office was being built. He gave us some details of a piece of land in Essex he owned jointly with another person and asked if we could get permission to erect a building. We drove out to look.

The land was close to Bradwell nuclear power plant but closer to Bradwell on Sea on the Blackwater estuary. We noted the very old St Peter's Chapel and rural village aspects. At the time buildings were restricted due to the proximity of the power plant and we found the strip of land marked on a map quite easily. Our client had hoped to build a bungalow mainly for holiday rents on his strip and had a couple of other pieces ear-marked to obtain, but the council planning office gave a resounding 'No' to our enquiry. They did not want the land to be used even for holiday chalets, let alone permanent bungalows. I suppose they bought the land purely for speculation, like so many hundreds of people who spot the occasional advertisement in a newspaper for the sale of a strip of orchard land. The entire orchard is gradually sold off and the new owners become the proud holders of some grassy ground and a number of fruit trees. The planners review their grand plan for their county every five years and occasionally make changes under pressure to areas marked as commercial or farmland to residential in their quest for building land.

These orchards would be highly unlikely to be granted change of use for decades so the gamble often works out to be the purchase of a picnic area, as no sheds can be erected and usefulness is limited to a possible apple harvest.

As the years have passed Bradwell power plant, which closed in 2002, is gradually being dismantled and possibly the holders of the title deeds mentioned have been able to obtain a worthwhile use but I don't know. The nuclear plant was built on a previous airfield with the ground level raised and in spite of fear of the unknown and threat of nuclear leakage, had operated well with no known adverse results. The new plant is reckoned to be built on adjacent French owned land and is viewed sceptically by many for the threat to the ecosystem, wildlife, marine life alone.

The partner in this land gamble was a world-renowned gold dealer, a million miles different to his car dealing buddy. He came into the office once. dressed in a floor length fur coat and announced he was catching a late ferry across the Channel and driving his sports car all night to reach Italy, to surprise his girlfriend on her birthday the next day. I thought how romantic that was and secretly wondered if he would give her gold jewellery as a present. My mother used to say, "It's not a big deal to give someone buttons if you own a button factory." A gold piece of jewellery when you own bullion, I countered, was not quite the same thing.

**

Still reminiscing about the people at the karate class, I thought of the Sensei and his partner. They had a baby girl and brought her to the class to be admired by all. The mother was only slowly returning to training as it was so soon after the birth but she did the warming up part of the session and then sat talking to us in the waiting area. My own children were entranced with the baby, all clamoured for a hold and cuddle. No.1, surprisingly, was the most loving and affectionate and sat for quite a while in the interval gazing into her tiny face and touching her fingers.

They had moved into their house which had been sold via our gay estate agents' banner and seemed very happy there.

The latest mission from them had been the request to measure a certain piece of land in a fairly rural area of open ground and a few basic brick built dwellings. They looked like they could have been local authority houses. When we arrived, it was deserted and sections of it had been loosely separated with wire chain-link fencing installed with posts. It was impossible to discern the piece of land that we were supposed to survey and when a door opened we both stepped forward to ask the man stepping outside which piece of fenced off ground belonged to the number we had on our records.

To our complete surprise, he bellowed at us to get off the land before either of us had said a word.

We both spoke at the same time, asking him which piece was the subject property and he raised a shotgun to his shoulder and took aim.

Chris quickly grabbed my arm and dragged me back to the pavement. Of course, a quirk in my genes won't comply with prudent behaviour and I stared defiantly at him. 'We only asked you where number whatever is. We're not taking it away.'

'Come back here and you're dead,' the stupid thug shouted, still aiming his shotgun.

'For God's sake get in the car, Chris,' and sensible Chris pushed me in the back.

Still the thug pointed the gun and told us the land was owned by a member of a renowned South London gang and he would tell him we'd trespassed.

I did a "V" sign at him and got in the car. Knowing the mixture of characters that Jonny Pearson cavorted with and thinking of just the ones that we had met, I thought it likely that it was the very same gangland character that had commissioned the site visit and dimensional survey.

We went back to our office and rang J at the estate agent's

Instead of laughing as I expected him to do, as he managed to turn almost everything into a humorous topic, he sobered immediately and advised that we forgot the whole incident. He asked us nervously not to report it to the police, to which we agreed reluctantly. We were never quite able to forget it, however, ardently wishing low-life thugs like that could be locked up and the key thrown away.

**

To our surprise, the latest cheque from Ali's cousin with the leather jacket warehouse bounced, marked in red lettering, "Refer to drawer, please represent." This in banking terms advises the recipient, in this case Chris, to contact the drawer of the cheque and to pay it in again. It means loosely that the funds are not in the account at the moment but are expected to be shortly, so it's not a seriously detrimental remark. We thought it was a hiccup and he was probably waiting to be paid for a leather jacket delivery.

His latest scheme had been badly received by the planners and we had revised the drawings to reflect their advice to make the proposal more acceptable but we knew he was not ecstatic, wanting the size and volume of the original application. It was the first time he had messed us around over money and we tried to call him to discuss to no avail. He rarely answered the phone and whenever Chris or I called we were told he was out. Strangely the accent swung deeply into the vernacular when they knew who it was on the line.

A couple of days later Roz called us to discuss a valuation that Chris had carried out for one of the customers and she spoke to me. After I had confirmed her query she became a bit hesitant and said I was to read my own conclusion into her words, because she wasn't allowed to discuss another person's account and I said, 'Okay.' I knew this certain client banked at her branch and listened to her words as she said, 'Chris, if you were thinking of paying in at this branch today, come to the counter and ask for me.' I knew she must have been referring to our bounced cheque as we didn't usually pay in at her branch, but I decided I would at those words. I drove the slightly longer distance and went to the desk and my credit was stamped. Roz told me to ask my own branch to call them in the morning to ask the fate of the cheque. It was paid and we received an angry call from Tariq a couple of days later, complaining that an important standing order had been withheld for his factory rent as his bank had honoured our cheque instead and he was upset by this as he had paid in especially to cover it. What could he expect us to say to that?

Needless to say, that was the end of a short relationship but we tried our best and you can't always get what you want.

**

Chris agreed to carry out a partial inspection of an empty house on the outskirts of Clacton for someone and we all went along. The house was freezing cold inside and the cold crept through our shoe soles and made everybody restless. It was a Saturday, almost Christmas and we thought we all deserved a treat as we had put ourselves out so near to closing the office for ten days, and so I took the car and the children and we went into the town centre while Chris walked about with his tape recorder in the icebox. We went to Marks and Spencer and I bought us all a new outfit to wear on Christmas day and then returned to collect Chris to find somewhere for dinner.

On the seafront, there was a large hotel and on the spur of the moment Chris turned into the car park. 'Wait a minute everyone, I'll be back shortly.' And he went into the reception area.

He returned wearing a huge grin and announced, 'Everybody out of the car. I've booked us in for the night.'

We had no luggage, only the new clothes I had just bought, no toiletries, no razor for Chris, no cleaned shoes, but who cared? The lovely receptionist gave Chris a throwaway shaving set and there was a selection of shampoos and such in the bathroom. I couldn't believe the availability of the suite but apparently, it had been booked some weeks previously but just cancelled and the deposit was non-refundable, so we had a double discount. What the children did not know but were delighted to learn was that the rooms were to be used for guests partaking in the dinner and dance that evening, which included a cabaret. Probably few people would dream of allowing children as young as eight to attend but they would only drink juices and water and were all very good eaters and generally well behaved, so we thought the idea of Chris's was brilliant and cheerfully made our way to the rooms.

We all warmed up after a hot bath and dressed in our new clothes. 'Try not to spill stuff down the front, everyone, as these are supposed to be for Christmas evening,' I warned.

The dining room was set out in long tables and we were positioned at the end of one of them, nearest the dance floor, the band and the entertainment. They all beamed at us and I felt so proud. I loved to take them out and show them off and to give them opportunities and new experiences.

The band played the usual mix of show tunes and carols as the drinks order was taken and the bowls of soup were brought round. The waitresses all wore little black outfits with frilly white caps and aprons and called the children Sir and Madam.

The next course was a beef dish swimming in dark gravy with carrots, roast potatoes and the inevitable sprouts, quite tasty for the amount of diners they had prepared for, with a simple choice of Christmas pudding or trifle for dessert and cheese and biscuits with a glass of port to finish. In between the courses many people got up to dance and when Nos.1 and 2 showed off their version of the Twist and the Cha Cha they got many smiles. I don't think we noticed one bad look or overheard criticism about the youngsters and they received many encouraging comments.

There were special children's cocktails which we ordered before dinner and liqueurs prepared with youngsters in mind when our coffees arrived, but they were too young to crave or miss alcohol and it was the atmosphere we wished to impart. We knew that No.1 was growing up and there would not be many more family outings that he would wish to join. In private we allowed him a small glass of wine or cider and he often tasted the various beers we had, as we believed there would be no need to over imbibe once he was away from us if he knew already his limits and the effects and dangers involved with drinking too much.

He still helped with the Saturday Wine outlet behind the launderette and was beginning to know the types of grape and when they were drunk and the food which called for certain types or vintages to accompany them. He donned a black shirt with black trousers and with a long white type of apron tied around his waist, looked like a posh French waiter when he helped out at the occasional parents' ball or charity do at the nearby public school, which luckily was not his own. This activity of working with alcohol, pouring wine into jugs and serving at the trestle table bar would definitely not be lawful nowadays.

The evening lasted from seven thirty to midnight and the kids lasted out too, with no sign of a yawn and certainly no flagging on the dance floor. We all dissolved in giggles when they played a few country dances and the caller told us how to do it, words of, 'Take your partner and swing her round and do-si-do and bob to the corner,' he sang out as the band played ever faster and we all got confused and turned the wrong way until there was a massive huddle of bobbing people in the middle and we had to filter back to our starting positions. Hugely enjoyable for a dance evening or party. I was to remember the ridiculous fun of it when as a member of the PTA I suggested that we organised a barn dance as a fund-raising exercise a few years later and No.1, some years further still, chose the same event for his own 21st celebration.

The other guests at the dinner-dance were so kind to all of us. So many stopped to chat to the children, I think we were the novelty that evening. The head waiter told us that they had families stay for their summer holidays and school breaks and children obviously ate there with their parents and watched the entertainment, but many were annoying to the other guests, crying and screaming during the cabaret acts and running across the floor when serious people wanted to dance. Their regular dinner dances were hugely successful but usually frequented by older folks, there never had been children there before. No.2, who could spend her whole life at a get-together, asked him if they would be allowed to go again and was delighted when he brought her a free children's cocktail with a cherry and umbrella in it with a leaflet advertising the forthcoming events. She begged for us to come again another time and I told Chris he'd better start saving, as the bill when we checked out was eye wateringly expensive, even with the discount. I suppose we did spoil ourselves.

I learned the next day that the receptionist was dubious about letting the rooms to a family at first as they were specially reserved for the event, but Chris had begged for a couple of rooms as we needed to be in the area the next day and he couldn't possibly drag the children and his pregnant wife all the way back to London only to return again tomorrow. It was lucky that I had been unaware of his blarney at the time, but when I thought about it the staff had been very solicitous, although I did get the odd straight look when my wine glass was refilled, again and again ... I was glad that none of the children had overheard as I didn't want that rumour glancing around the school, true or untrue.

We often took one of their friends out with us if they were staying over and most weekends we had a few. No.2's best friend at the time begged to be allowed to go with them to an early morning site trip because she knew Chris would take her to a Little Chef breakfast and she loved their pancakes.

**

We took No.3 and his friend to Selfridges a few days before Christmas to see Santa in his grotto. The underground was packed but eventually we walked along Oxford Street and made our way to the store. The windows are always splendid and this year they didn't disappoint, and we managed to look at a few before the plaintive moans got the better of us and we went in. To our horror, the queue snaked around the toys shelves and crept along at snail's pace and it took two hours before we reached the biggest let down of our lives. I don't know why but they didn't get to see Santa. Perhaps he had left or perhaps he never was there. They were given a gift by elves and the scenery was beautiful but we were all expecting something more. I had to go through an elaborate tale of explaining that he couldn't be everywhere at once and he must be helping out somewhere else, but I thought Nana knew a garden centre that managed to get him to visit sometimes and I would ask her if she could arrange for us to go there.

Poor Mum, she joined in the conversation when we told her and the next day we traipsed off to the local place and he managed to visit Father Christmas in his sleigh. He clambered in and sat next to the elderly man in disguise. We laughingly cringed when we heard his plaintive voice telling this Santa how his mum and dad took him and his friend Matt all the way up to London to see him and he wasn't there. 'Do you know how long that took?' he asked. 'Hours and hours and then we lined up in that big shop and it was so hot with nothing to do and all we saw was a few fairies and elves.'

'Sorry,' mumbled the fraud, 'I have to keep going from place to place. It's a busy time of year.'

'We were really, really hungry too and had to line up all over again to get a burger and then we got squashed going home on the train. If we'd known you were at another shop, we would have gone there.'

I felt a bit sorry for this pseudo Santa hearing No.3, who was never backwards in coming forwards, berating him unfairly but he did very well with his replies. When his turn was over and he climbed down, clutching his present, Santa leaned forward to see him go and gave us all a cheery wave, we could see he was laughing.

It was the last year that he believed in Father Christmas and another little bit of magic vanished. Strangely the belief in the Tooth Fairy lasted far longer, but that may have been just a nice custom or the lure of money.

**

Christmas Day arrived and the usual knobbly sacks of gifts were left at the ends of their beds.

We had tiny bits and pieces hanging on the tree as surprises and a few beneath it to be shared when we collected Nana, or Grandma and Granddad arrived and a spare box of chocolates if someone turned up unexpectedly.

I had made mince pies and a cake with almonds on the top the week before and Chris peeled all the vegetables for me. Mum had made our Christmas pudding, an annual undertaking, making about six to distribute round. It had always been a ritual, all our childhood, when the whole rigmarole took about a week. First, she bought packs of dried fruit: currents, raisins, sultanas, prunes, mixed peel, cherries and I don't know what else. One by one these separate fruit packs were painstakingly washed and dried: she said you couldn't trust the suppliers to make sure it was clean, even if it stated "Washed" as they could be dusty. Then she went through each variety, checking that there were no stones or spiky little stalks. Then they were chopped by hand as there wasn't a chopper available. Nuts were blanched of their skins and chopped and added to the bowl. A small bottle of brandy and a bottle of beer or ale or barley wine, the liquor varied year by year, was purchased along with yards of greaseproof paper and string. The sugar had to be dark brown or molasses, farm eggs with rich yolks and bright yellow butter and various pungent spices thrown in by the tablespoon. Combining the whole was extremely hard as the mixture was so stiff. She always used the same yellow mixing bowl and huge wooden spoon and we all had to stir it and make a wish. A local aunt and uncles and Granddad would all call round in the week before the mixture was poured into basins, to stir the enormous bowl. She never put silver threepences or sixpences in the mixture because you never knew who'd touched them and you mustn't scrub them or soak them because then the detergent would contaminate the food. When the rich mix was transferred to the white china basins, differing sizes depending on whom they were for, each one had a little spirit trickled over the top and was wrapped completely in the paper and each basin was

256

steamed for hours to start. As the years passed, the top layer of paper was changed to foil. The largest was kept back for the close family, because we all congregated at one house for the magic day and my granddad, an uncle and my mum would play the piano and we would all sing carols and the old songs. As we children grew and the elders passed on, so basin sizes changed as the venues also changed year by year.

Our table was set and Christmas records playing, we had white wine chilling and a bottle of red "breathing" when a double ring on the door bell brought my neighbour into the hall in tears.

Halfway through the roasting of her turkey her oven had broken down and she realised the bird had stopped cooking. 'Have you any room in yours, Chris?' she begged.

So, we went to the kitchen and rearranged the food on the cooker shelves. Their turkey was small as there were only four of them and she brought in the trays of potatoes, stuffing and sausage meat, prepared to go in a bit later. Luckily the gas rings on the top were unaffected so she was able to continue with some of the other things, like steaming her pudding, making the gravy and vegetables.

We invited them in to eat with us, as it seemed that it would all be ready about the same time and the mood was quite jolly, although strange as there was a constant stream of us charging backwards and forwards with chairs, saucepans, plates and dishes and there was a sort of "Blitz spirit" when we all finally sat down. It took about three days to finally return all the crockery and china to the right house, every now and then someone would fish a renegade teaspoon out of the drawer to be taken next door and they would find the same.

Our pudding had had about three hours' simmering on the top and we made a huge pan of custard and No.1 whipped the cream. I turned a blind eye to the copious dashes of brandy he swirled in. The pudding was turned out onto a large platter and brandy poured over it. We scattered a few raisins into the liquid moat and turned out the lights in the dining room. Chris lit the brandy and the children tried to pick out the raisins from the blue flames, screaming with delight and mock fear as their little hands stabbed in and out.

It was a busy, fun-filled day that year and the parents stayed over. Chris's brother-in-law would arrive about eleven thirty for a mince pie and tiny sherry and take the Prentice parents back to their house for Boxing Day. We dovetailed this, transporting them backwards and forwards to spend Christmas at alternate places. It was a bit of a palaver but they liked to see the children and this meant they would see all of them, spread over a couple of days. Chris's brother lived in Devon and his son was quite grown, but he liked to stay at home resting after his hectic time, preparing hundreds of geese and turkeys and roasting joints for the people of Torquay.

My sister lived in Southampton with her family and our mum spent many Christmases there.

Boxing Day was a quieter affair, with most of the food already cooked and ready for bubble and squeak and a selection of cooked meats, sliced.

The older children had new bikes and No.3 had "inherited" a larger one from his cousins, so we all walked, mum and I slowly bringing up the rear, to the pond across the green to feed the ducks. We had heard that too much bread was bad for them so we took carrot and parsnip peelings too. The ducks showed no preference though. Many families were strolling about, their children proudly trying out their new presents and we all cheerily greeted each other, many we knew or recognised from the local school and neighbours from the estate.

After the first two hectic days, I cut all the turkey off the carcass for pies or freezing and put the bones into a large cooking pot and poured about a pint of boiling water over them. The pot was simmered for about half an hour and the bones removed from the stock and discarded. Any remaining meat usually fell off at this stage and was returned to the pot, with chopped onions and vegetables and some of the remaining gravy.

I made a few turkey and ham pies, adding diced potatoes, chopped carrots and perhaps a few peas and my lovely rich gravy was poured over to moisten the filling: a lid of shop bought pastry then topped them off. These were frozen in this state and used later in the year when we had forgotten all about them. My turkey stock was turned into soup by adding lentils, pearl barley and vegetables and the remainder of the leftover turkey and bacon. These rich soups were always a favourite of all of us and sometimes included chopped sprouts and chestnuts and pigs in blankets and cranberries. In extra chilly weather a small dumpling was welcomed too.

**

It wasn't long before the work enquiries started again but we tried to dismiss all but the urgent until a few days after the New Year. Amazingly, many people used the celebratory time to start knocking walls about.

A few of our clients from Chinese or Asian background thought we were hypocrites, as they stopped their work and spent time praying and observing their cultural or religious beliefs while we followed no religion closely and spent our religious breaks by generally eating and drinking, playing games and watching endless films on the television. They asked if we went to our church at these specific times and were horrified to learn that this was not always a given. Of course we attended the school services, we contributed to the food collection at harvest festival, we gave toys for sick children, we prepared food parcels for needy pensioners, we added coins to rattling tins for war injured, flood victims, starving people left with no food or water due to battling despotic leaders, we sent money for animal welfare, tried to prevent animal cruelty, sent letters to deserving causes to try to prevent endless ghastly practices worldwide, too grisly to mention.

All these arguments made to counter the accusations of being heathens in our own land went by the wayside. We all have our own ways and cannot often accept others'.

**

My accounts were up to date and cheques written out for the VAT collected and our company tax, as well as personal tax, by the last day of January.

Chris spent a few hours daily to prevent a rush of queries the following week, even though people thought we were dozing by the fire watching a third-rate film.

We picked up mum and drove up to London to see the Christmas lights and went for supper somewhere and another day, when incessant adverts spurred us to go to Harrods while their decorations remained, we drove to Knightsbridge to check out the sales.

While we were looking at men's clothes and marvelling at how anyone could afford to pay the inflated prices of even simple things, we noticed we were standing next to Charles Aznavour who was also turning over a heap of sweaters. We had recently seen him performing his well-known song, *She,* among others on television and the children were quite thrilled to see a personality up close. Chris suggested they asked him politely if he would kindly give them his autograph, 'But don't be surprised if he is too busy.'

No.2 volunteered and we watched her approach him with a scrap of paper rescued from my bag and she asked him the question. 'Of course,' he said. 'What is your name?' she told him and he scribbled his message and signature. She beamed and thanked him and we all walked to get a drink in one of their numerous food and drinks outlets.

As they drank their milk-shakes she looked at us in exasperation and said, 'Oh I was slow there.'

'What do you mean?'

'Why?'

'I should have asked him if I could be in his next show. I won't have that chance again.'

Chapter 18

We were intending to have a mini celebration on November 5th as that date was the start of our venture in our office, the day we completed on the purchase, but all sorts of other things interrupted it so we had a half bottle of Champagne in our own lounge and toasted ourselves, but saved a few fireworks and sparklers to celebrate the New Year instead. In previous years, the local church where No.3 was baptised held a display of fireworks in the rector's back garden and while some volunteers barbequed sausages and others served soup, there were others lighting the rockets, Catherine wheels and muted pretty fountains and still others going around with collection buckets. Being animal lovers, we were against the whole shebang, knowing the traumas the noisy affairs cause, day after day for hours to all creatures, domesticated and wild. People gaily letting off these mini-bombs have no thought for terrified pets or hens or farm animals, many of which have enhanced hearing, so we celebrate this macabre occasion sparingly and try to buy ear-friendly versions.

**

The school term started again and off they went all muffled up to beat the chill. Sadly, for us, they all joined sports teams, the boys for football and No.2 decided she'd like to have a go at hockey. Goody, more driving backwards and forwards, and hours of standing around the edge of muddy fields watching groups of them bashing a ball about. Then more sports clothes washing which is always fun, scraping mud off when it's dried then soaking and scrubbing, boiling and finally ironing. Gratifying when it's all then stuffed into a bag as if it's last week's newspapers. I got her some shin pads but she snorted derisively, saying nobody wore those awful things nowadays. From distant school memories of my own I remembered some pretty vicious thumps from wayward hockey sticks wielded with callous enthusiasm by the opposition.

**

The plaintive calls started from people with power cuts, asking questions about their insurance policies, or burst pipes, wanting us to recommend a plumber, or the heating wasn't working and could Chris do it? No, he's magic but he's not a magician.

We finally received the awaited planning permission for Mickey to build a new house, attached to his own semi. We had visited them just before Christmas and enjoyed a typical Serbian meal and drinks. He didn't seem very pleased to finally receive this approval notice, which surprised me a bit but I think we had been disillusioned over the first two results and instead of euphoria we just felt underwhelmed.

He had started importing metal objects, bedsteads and hearth surrounds and fire guards and then tried to sell them. I don't know who bought them from him, he knew many people.

He had become quiet and kept ringing up asking for work to do, which was a problem. If it is known that workmanship is good and the costs are fair, we can recommend but not guarantee and perhaps his estimates were becoming too costly to be acceptable. He seemed to be on a treadmill of needing more and more and we waited to hear why his situation appeared to have changed.

News was trickling through to us in the UK that since President Tito of Yugoslavia had died, the regions held tightly together under his control had started to pull away and the earlier wars of 1980-1981 had only brought economic crisis. Albanian Nationals demonstrated in Kosovo and the Muslims' uprising in 1983 had started to inspire Serbians to expel Croats and vice versa. They all decided to form their own separate countries. No-one could have foreseen the violence and cruelty that would transpire over the splitting of the regions and disgusting religious hate crimes that occurred in their thousands.

Mickey, while the times had been good, had been investing in property and business back home. He routinely drove overland to visit family and cohorts and presumably took money with him to finance the ventures. While the situation in his country had been stable, he spent his money acquiring a fairground among other things, and presumably was paying for it in instalments but due to the gradual slowing down of business in England and turbulent times starting over there, it was proving difficult for him. The crux came when the splitting of the countries happened and boundaries formed. His investments and concerns were over the border and he could see his dodgem cars flying wildly round the track and was powerless to intercede or obtain the proceeds. He had effectively lost a fortune and someone else was reaping the benefits.

His workforce consisted of men from all creeds, united in the language and ability to construct a well-built extension or conversion and we never experienced a sideways look or sharp word, but could tell they were all concerned for their loved ones back home.

From time to time Mickey would make one of his overland trips to his own area, with his van laden with foods and clothes supplied by a charity group who paid the expenses. We were not aware of the destination or the precise contents of his van but he was regularly stopped by armed police and soldiers who went through the van, presumably searching for arms. He always got back again so obviously, nothing was ever found, if ever transported. A three day round trip, wear and tear on the vehicle, rising fuel costs and insurances ensured this was a pricey enterprise. That a cash strapped person would perform this exercise on a monthly basis for expenses only was laudable but not likely, I thought, but who was I to question or judge?

**

We were contacted by a man for whom we had carried out a bank valuation and he had gone ahead with his house purchase. He had obtained our details from his branch as he wished to use our services to apply for an extension and internal alterations.

The day that Chris went to visit him was freezing and there had been heavy snowfall, so the entire garden had a thick white covering over. Nevertheless, the dimensional survey was carried out and the Ordnance Survey map purchased.

They had discussed the fee and come to an agreement.

The plans were prepared, printed and sent to him and he responded happily that he loved the design that Chris and our lovely draftswoman had prepared for him and his wife. He called into the office and paid his fee in cash, winking like a demented lighthouse as he went outside.

We paid it in and sent him a receipt. The planning had been approved and the next step was building control, which he said he didn't want or need as his builder knew how to construct this scheme without instructions, so he could save the money. 'Okay,' we said. 'You will need calculations for your beams when you get that far, so give us a call later.'

A few weeks later he called us. His tone was creepy and threatening and he blamed us for his builder's mistake which he told us had cost him thousands.

The builder, who knew how to build and didn't need detailed drawings, had constructed a new drains run and series of manholes which the building control officer had questioned the need for, as there was an existing manhole under the compost and the drainage already ran along the side way. 'You should have marked the drains on your plans,' he sneered. 'I gave you cash and I'm sure the bank manager will be very interested to hear that. I bet the tax man will have something to say too. You'll pay for this and compensation.'

When somebody made an accusation that our work was defective in any way and you got this thrilling news over the phone, your heart gave a flip, your stomach contracted and you momentarily felt a small surge of panic.

I told him I would let Chris know and we would get back to him.

I meanwhile retrieved the file and retrieved a set of the plans which I spread over the desk. These were planning drawings only, which at the time did not require detailed drainage to be shown but Chris had clearly shown a note by a downpipe on the side elevation that all drainage was to be confirmed prior to starting the excavation of the footings. This comment was also made in our letter.

I looked up our quotation letter and checked my paying in book and to my delight saw that we had paid the whole amount into our account, so he was unable to report us for tax evasion or not declaring the VAT.

Still with a loudly beating heart I waited for Chris's return and explained the situation.

Chris gave a wry laugh and told me that he had a feeling he was up to no good. Only a fool plays games with their accounts and cash payments and the fact that the ground had been covered with snow, completely obscuring gullies and manhole covers, ensured notes would be marked advising that the drainage runs would need to be identified, absolved us completely.

He rang him back. His silky tone was worth recording but of course I just listened, mouth agape. 'Mr Jones? Good afternoon. I hear you have a problem?' Continuing with, 'No. Mr Jones, it is your problem, I'm afraid. You see, you are building your extension with a planning drawing and due to the impossibility of spotting the manhole under the snow I made a comment, you'll notice it, ringed in red, that's it, on the left there, to tell you someone would have to look for the drain run in order to join the new pipes to it.'

I don't know what the odious man said next but Chris continued: 'Ahh, no problem there, I'm afraid. You received a receipt from Chris and we marked it in our records, so there was no cloak and dagger stuff or jiggery pokery as you put it. So, would you like me to inform your bank manager of the outcome of this matter? No, because you didn't call him? And what about the tax man, Mr Jones? He might be concerned to know that you paid us in cash because he might misconstrue your motive, mightn't he? No, just a silly mistake. I don't think you will want me to do your beams, do you? By the way, paying a bill in cash to avoid taxes is a crime by both parties, not just the receiving person. Goodbye.'

That was a potential disaster. I thought it lucky we had entered every penny paid by this client: not that we often took cash as we needed the money in our account to pay all the expenses.

Another testing situation was a phone call from a stranger who had apparently been given our details by the gay couple from Bishop's Stortford. He told me the whys and wherefores of his proposals and asked if we would make a site visit and prepare a report with rudimentary drawings for an enquiry to a neighbour and the council. He asked me for an estimate and I spoke off the top of my head, with a rough quote.

He hummed and then asked if we would take cash and if that was a usual practice of ours.

I told him that we didn't do business that way. He said, 'OK, I'll be in touch,' and got off the phone.

When I saw J and J a few days later I recounted the incident and they looked horrified. 'Blimey, Chris, that was a close shave. He works for the Inland Revenue and he's an absolute bastard.'

O Good, I thought bleakly,

That was a second averted disaster, maybe a Guardian Angel was watching over me that week.

Mohammed, for whom we obtained established use approval on a property into two flats the previous year, was now going from strength to strength. He asked us to prepare drawings and apply for planning consent to construct a loft room in the roof space of his house and his in-laws next door. In those days, an extension in the roof space had to be awarded permission and there were criteria to fulfil, like coming away from the party boundary and the chimney stacks.

We went first to his own home and met again his young wife and their daughter, who was now a bright toddler with a tiny new sister. We measured the house and enjoyed a cup of tea and a chat. The house itself was shabby and needed maintenance but a great deal of his work and earnings had gone into the investment property nearby and he was clawing his way back. We made arrangements to return the following week to measure up the adjacent house and returned to the office, via the school to collect the younger two children and finish our work for the day.

The following week we returned and entered Mohammed's in-laws' house where his wife was also spending time. The front room had her two young sisters, two huge boxes of envelopes, heaps of papers and another almost empty, even larger box into which they were stacking neat piles of addressed mail for collection. This soul numbing activity earned them little more than pennies but it was honest and they were able to watch the children and carry out their college studies and domestic chores at the same time as watch television programmes and chat amongst themselves.

This house was measured up in the same way and we arranged to return the following week, with both completed schemes ready for their records and comments and to collect the deposits cheques for our fees and council costs. The applications could both be submitted then as both families were looking forward to having their new bedrooms in the roof constructed.

The ground floor of Mohammed's house was the next item to be discussed and we told them they could prevent doubling up on council costs and share the Ordnance Survey fees if the kitchen extension was submitted on the same package. Once the approval had been granted and work commenced, the entire scheme would retain permanent permission indefinitely.

From then onwards we carried out drawing and engineering work for Mohammed on numerous developments, for him alone or in conjunction with a partner and as a family concern; single storey extensions, planning permission to self-contain shops and offices with living accommodation over to the first and sometimes second floors, a single new house, a flats block, a small housing estate.

We saw his first baby girl grow, followed by three other daughters and they all integrated into British life, having college qualifications or university degrees in due course. They never tried to censure the country, the government, or our religion. They never attempted to indoctrinate us with their religious beliefs or influence our customs and we ate in each other's homes occasionally and met in several restaurants in London, meeting relatives and friends of all ages.

**

We heard again from the builders, A and E. This time they had acquired another infill site on which A wanted to build a house for his own use and his maisonette had been put on the market. This was agreed with A, who had himself carried out major changes to his own home and they gave us instructions to proceed. The site was not wide and we incorporated a garage on the ground floor as off-road parking was beginning to become a premium in the borough. The house comprised three storeys with the garage, a kitchen and shower room on the ground floor; reception room, WC and office on the first floor and two bedrooms with a bathroom at the top. He was like an excited puppy with a plethora of wagging tails when he saw our creation and the house sailed through planning with no adverse comments or conditions, so that we progressed straight away with building control details and Chris prepared the engineering for the foundations, drainage designs and roof construction.

We made the occasional visit to see the building project rise from the ground like a phoenix. The site had been part of a bombed-out carcass, compliments of Mr Hitler and we took pleasure in seeing his beaming face as the various stages were reached: footings, drainage, damp proof course and brickwork to the lower level. The upper levels were built with blockwork and rendered over. The window frames and entrance door were stained timber and all appeared very attractive.

We did not see or hear from them after the house was finished, apart from helping him to apply for the Zurich insurance package for developers and self-builders. Then a few years later he came round with a woebegone expression and asked for help as the house had developed subsidence to the front corner. We helped him fill in the forms and enclosed a copy of the relevant approval documents and in due course he received the permission to carry out underpinning that supported the foundations. The road was sloping down towards the main road and the neighbouring homes were at risk of sliding down the hill, taking his home with them and a complicated strengthening scheme was carried out.

It was after this worrying time for him that we heard a disgusting scrap of gossip about his partner, A, who had been sent to prison for illegal under-age sexual relations with his step-daughter, who apparently was only thirteen at the time. When the man in these situations is in a position of trust and bleats in his defence that it wasn't his fault, are we all to give him our sympathy and agree it was all OK? He said she had been in agreement and even suggested it so he didn't know it was wrong. After all, he reasoned, she wasn't his daughter.

Our bank valuations and surveys continued and client base widened even further.

We were visited by an associate of Mr Clooney the landlord and also Ewen, known as P and he regarded himself as a sort of catalyst in property deals. He acted as a purveyor of tradespeople. When someone he knew found a property to buy, he arranged for a quick look-see survey, with us as the amenable surveyors to carry out a visual inspection, point out any obvious faults or areas which could need work or strengthening, and provide them with a verbal synopsis and possible costs for reparations. As these visits were usually accompanied by him, proudly leading the way as well as up to three or four would-be purchasers together it was almost like leading a guided tour, sometimes around a small flat, with Chris pointing out bits and pieces and they all scuffling around to have a look. He was very pleasant and absolutely huge and loved the position of leader in these charades. They never wanted a bill but just stuffed a present in Chris's pocket to express their gratitude, but as it was usually a cheque we obviously had to pass it through the account. We often crammed into a local café for a cup of tea and the situation was hilarious.

He seemed to know so many different people, one of whom was a writer, television producer and director whose name was often spotted in the credits. This person owned an enormous house in a swanky part of London and wanted to convert the basement into a lawful, residential flat. I loved to accompany Chris on these visits as I tried to imagine where walls would be removed and installed and the position of the different rooms. I loved to see their homes too, and type of furnishings and décor. It was a bonus when during the construction works the builders wanted Chris to pay a visit as they had found some renegade drains which needed to be bridged over, or the client wanted to change the layout or had gone ahead with this and was now haggling with the planners or other flats' residents. It was a known criterion with flats buildings that when the units were constructed, a bedroom was positioned over or under an existing bedroom. It was not allowed to situate a bedroom on top of a living room. This was known as "stacking". Obviously, this was an attempt to prevent late night revellers from disturbing the sleep of the family above or below. For this reason, there were several types of materials for sound proofing

269

as well as fire-resistance that were fastened below the ceilings or within the floors to reduce the noise of thumping feet and ordinary living, which can resonate and vibrate causing real disturbance and distress.

The planning rules for houses vary to those of flats buildings. A formal planning application must be submitted for a flat to extend at the ground floor, or top flat to convert their loft, but if the planning laws are followed an extension or roof conversion for a house does not always require this. A structural alteration wherever the position or situation must be submitted and approved by the building control department. It is amazing how many people carry out illegal works to their homes and usually these anomalies only come to light when a move of house is proposed and the prospective buyer's surveyor mentions the beams or building work and asks if permission was granted, and suggests the solicitor investigates. A retrospective application can be made to both departments at the councils to obtain legal documents, or an insurance policy can be purchased should an alteration prove to be onerous.

The lure of money is usually the reason to create an illegal dwelling by installing a timber studwork wall to form a bedroom in a garage or even garden shed and more and more cases of inadequate housing have been discovered, then as well as now.

Unscrupulous landlords who own or run multiple occupation homes do not always follow the strict government guidelines and many properties are not legally constructed or safety procedures followed. It was gratifying for us to have been involved with clients who endeavoured to provide adequate facilities for people who were in unfortunate situations and unable to have funds needed to house themselves in chosen establishments.

**

The builder who introduced us to his brother in law, who we managed to help win an insurance claim, asked us to prepare plans for his own house, their first home together. This was a tiny terraced cottage which was listed so he was limited with possibilities but we managed to get him a small kitchen extension. After him came his wife's brother, who wanted a loft conversion with a dormer window on the roof. We applied knowing that the planning laws were under discussion and hoped we could achieve this for him but it was denied. His ex-council house had a park at the back of his garden and this was considered the reason for the refusal. A public right of way at the rear negated the right to have a dormer window in the roof.

Planning rules are constantly being reviewed.

We felt bad about his refusal, believing that if we had not been so busy and had sent the application sooner we may have beaten the deadline for the change which came into force during the consultation period. He never blamed us for the refusal though and we continued our good relations with the family.

The next job connected to his wife was for her sister and her husband, Lexi. Chris inspected a house for serious defects, i.e. dampness, movement of the foundations or fractured walls and he asked if we would prepare some plans for a shop he was buying for his business.

This was an ordinary mid-terraced building which needed a new shop front and to add a separate door for the rooms above, which required planning consent. He already had one outlet a few miles away and wanted them to look alike. Luckily the local authority agreed with his application and work started. The window and door were removed ready to install the new larger window and shop sign when his builder noticed the Bressumer beam, which was the main support above the front window, was completely rotten. With haste, they installed acrow metal props to hold up the front to prevent collapse and ordered a new steel beam. The rot had spread to the timber floor joists of the front bedroom, which involved stripping out the defective timbers and replacing them as well as carrying out anti-beetle infestation treatment to the remainder of the shop.

The work was completed and the pale blue paintwork was distinctive in a row of the usual black, appearing clean and fresh and eye-catching.

The next time he asked us to carry out the same exercise within the same borough but a different town, the planners argued. The wanted him to use brown paint instead to blend with the other shops instead of pale blue to stand out or they threatened to refuse the application. He involved the aid of his local councillor, who called a meeting to discuss the case along with a heap of other cases. This was held one evening at the council offices, usually a monthly affair and served to take the decision away from the planning team and to have the councillors make the decision. Rather than to have a refusal sent out he welcomed the meeting and went along himself. This was allowed if you were an interested party and he had booked a time slot to put his case to the committee. He explained that large companies always used the same colours and shop signs so that people recognised them among a crowded street and quoted a well-known burger outlet.

Although he was eloquent and his councillor supported him, the rest of the committee, comprising a few planners and other councillors sided with the decision and he was forced to use dark colour paint. When completed the shop looked super smart. He used black and white, which also was not brown and had a man in an evening suit illustrated on the window glass. His business went from strength to strength. We always thought he was a brave young man, taking on long leases on buildings to carry out his dry-cleaning work. He obviously had faith in himself and his wife backed him up.

When they got married we were invited to the evening reception and met the rest of his family and hers too. He was a Greek Cypriot and his family owned a café and they retained a villa on Cyprus. His young wife, the sister of the lady we knew already, was Irish and had been brought up in privileged circumstances. Their father owned a factory in London which made components for engines and he had his own private plane and chauffeur. I have never met a more grounded family, no pretentiousness, no hedonistic behaviour. Everyone had a job and never expected special treatment and never boasted about their parents' position. Even having the solid security of a well-founded family, they believed in giving and receiving value for money. They were an entire family of well-adjusted persons and we were proud to be associated with them.

One day the home of the Greek parents was burgled and jewellery, silver and crystal glassware was taken. Lexi believed he knew who had carried out the burglary and he went to the police to tell them what he knew. They said they had picked up finger prints but they were not listed on the police register and without real witnesses or reports, had no reason to interview his suspects. He knew where these villains lived and drank so he went to the local pub and watched them one evening. When they got up to go, he carefully put their beer glasses into plastic bags and took them to the police station.

He could not believe the words of the police officer on the reception desk, who refused to take the glasses for testing. If they had their suspicions they could have taken them for evidence, he said, but not allowed to accept items from a member of public. The family were furious about that and the thugs, because thugs they were, got away with it. Luckily the elderly parents were insured and recompensed but that's the reason why insurance is expensive. Thieves raise the living costs for everyone else.

**

Chris's sister and husband had a caravan berthed at a park on the Kent coast and they tried to use it often, to give their children a taste of freedom and during good weather there were rolling fields and the nearby beaches to enjoy.

She had a check list pinned on the inside of a kitchen cupboard of all the things that would be needed for their weekend trips and referring to it ensured nothing was left out or forgotten. We thought of doing something similar but our finances couldn't stretch to the same, so when we spotted an advertisement in the local paper for a campervan with awning we went to look it over. It wasn't new, of course, but had been refurbished and we couldn't spot any rust on the gleaming yellow and white paintwork. There was a tiny kitchen with sink and oven, high level cupboards, a pull-up table and side benches which housed the sleeping bags, blankets and the awning. The backs of the seats pushed down and somehow it all pushed and pulled to create a sleeping area over the entire back, avoiding the hand brake and steering wheel. The awning was erected to the side by fitting it around the van doorway and slotting together the metal rods which fixed to the roof, forming walls. The plastic floor and canvas tent also joined together and after considerable difficulty, with general ineptitude, plenty of cursing and bad temper, the wretched thing stood in its green and white glory, providing us with a reasonable sized square of usable space. As we had just started out on this caper and never fancied camping before we had no equipment, no fold down beds or chairs and poor Chris and No.1

slept out there, tucked up in their bags with no vestige of creature comforts. The wafer thin sliver of foam euphemistically called a mattress, could not in the widest imagination be called comfortable and huddled together like canned fish Nos.2 and 3 slept beside me in the van. We were enthusiastic, it was new to us. How a family could live like this and tour around vast areas for weeks on end was beyond me but we wanted to give the children as wide an experience as possible and we all smiled and drank our lukewarm tea and planned our trip.

Of course, those in the fixed caravans had none of this fun and adventure and we had more than a few amused spectators, both when the appendage was erected and when it was dismantled.

Chris's sister and her family arrived and loaded their food shopping inside their six-berth caravan and she began to cook us all breakfast. The usual delicious food appeared as if by magic and we tucked in gratefully. In cold blustery, dreary, weather as this weekend was, any breakfast other than the greasy spoon full English fry-up just doesn't cut the mustard.

Only a few stalwarts had braved the open air that weekend and much of the field lay bare and empty. To my astonishment, I noticed Max's car coming down the muddy side way, thankfully slowly, being confidently driven by our grinning No.1. I had been coaching him with gear changing for some time, explaining the old-fashioned term "biting point" and he understood the concept of gears and the clutch. We also had verbal driving lessons on the way to football or back, when he learned how to judge the probable actions of the car in front and behind us but also to read the road ahead. He was very excited to have driven their car and very well too, I judged, so we proposed to take him to a disused airfield we had heard of where young and inexperienced drivers could take the wheel without a licence.

The rest of the weekend was taken up by team games of rounders and such, between meals and trips out. Together seven children with the intermittent addition of parents made two reasonable sized teams. The children liked the responsibility of going to the small camp shop for provisions, feeling trusted and very grown up to return with a newspaper or bottle of red sauce, and usually in the case of the younger ones to be praised for collecting the correct change, if the change was remembered.

This trial weekend was the first of several more when we took in the usual sights and amusements: Dymchurch Railway, Dover Castle, Canterbury and Dreamland at Margate. After decades of becoming run down and little used, it closed down in 2006 when idiotic arsonists caused damage. After lobbying and receiving a financial grant for refurbishment and modernisation it re-opened during 2015, retaining some old rides and pinball machines as well as many more modern additions, the Grade II listed cinema and timber roller-coaster ride remain being the most historic and iconic.

I cooked a meat pie, roasted a chicken and a beef joint and wrapped them all in foil and froze them in advance and these defrosted over the weekend. These formed the main ingredient of some meals while away on our jaunts and we added simple things like chips or tinned vegetables. I never got over the amazing meals that Chris's sister conjured up for all of us when we were together, in such a poky little kitchen with hardly any preparation or serving space. She did have a full-sized oven though, whereas mine in the camper was little bigger than a shoe-box.

**

A cousin of one of Mohammed's connections had married and moved to a different East End borough to live with her in-laws. When fractures appeared in their front wall and gaps in the ceiling and wall joins, they knew there were problems with the front bay structure and the young girl suggested that her parents in law contacted us to help confirm the cause of the movement and help them with a possible insurance claim. They listened to her and we were called.

I went with Chris to jobs where reports were required, as I spoke into the tape recorder. I found it easier to type them up into reasonable sense when I had actually seen the points noted. Previously, before I joined, when Chris recorded a survey it was punctuated throughout by noises where he was jumping on the floor to test the boards and levels and knocking walls and timbers, opening and shutting windows and doors, all drowning his voice in a cacophony of din which punctuated the descriptions to such an extent that I refused to attempt the translations and attended the inspections myself. Many Saturday mornings were used for this purpose, while the children were at school.

We prepared our report as usual, which was the start of an insurance claim and the client paid for our services. The response came back that if our diagnosis was correct it had to be proved, so we had to proceed with organising tests. These were to excavate two trial pits in the front garden next to the front porch and in front of the bay window. If roots were found to be present in the sub soil they had to be sent for analysis to a specialist for identification, we used a laboratory attached to Kew Gardens. We also used a company based in Chelmsford to carry out a hand auger test when the soil needed to be analysed: this would prove whether the soil had become so dry due to root action seeking water, the moisture had been sucked out, leaving the desiccated particles of earth. The level of the sub soil being so dry sometimes at a depth of a metre or more, the building footings or foundations would naturally start to sink. Footings are usually formed of a concrete trench with bricks built on top, or corbelled brickwork which appears like tiny steps of shaped brickwork which narrows as it gets to the top and external walls are built on top. Movement at formation level of the foundations once these strategic areas are exposed is usually noted in the form of fracturing or the bricks rotating, causing distortion at low levels which had a knock-on effect by fractures emanating in the walls, usually at low level; gaps between floors and walls, gaps to the top of skirting boards, fractures in the corners of bay construction where walls joined, gaps between the top of ceilings and plaster decorative coving or the floor above.

In this case the loss adjusters employed by the insurance company insisted on using their own firm of investigators to dig the inspection holes. They were supposed to inform us once they were dug but when we arrived by chance, they had already infilled one and were in the process of filling in the other. The foreman was dismissive, saying he had recorded the details and would be sending them straight to his principals. The lady of the house came out when she noticed a small crowd in her limited front garden and asked us to please come inside. The excavation had taken a few hours from start to finish and unknown to the men, she had been watching as they reached formation level of the bay and heard one of them remark that the main front wall at the junction of the bay was "buggered". She was very reluctant to use the coarse word and whispered it to us, wincing as she said it. She had peered out of the edge of the bay through the gap in the lace curtains and said she saw roots in the earth as the spade lifted it out. She had actually looked into the pit by the porch and saw roots throughout.

We advised her not to pay the invoice for these fraudsters when it was presented and we contacted the insurers. They professed to be ignorant of the trick but agreed that we could carry out our own tests using our usual operatives, which we wasted no time in carrying out. We took explanatory photographs showing dry loose earth, distorted brickwork of the house foundations and roots. We sent the soil samples to Chelmsford for testing and roots to Kew Gardens and waited for the results.

The house owners will lose the first thousand pounds of an insurance claim as excess, so it was usual for them to settle the expenses and invoices of the people carrying out the tests, if these have been authorised by the insurers.

When the test results came back a few weeks later, the roots were identified as the council owned and controlled tree in the pavement, two metres away from the bay construction. The roots from the porch trial pit were from the laurel bushes owned by the next door neighbour. The soils showed an absence of moisture in the content and clay within the earth had dried over years to become a sandy mix.

We had arranged to fix small plain glass strips over the fractures, glued with super glue to the walls on either side and asked the family to let us know immediately if they noticed any of them fracture, indicating further movement of the wall. The glass strips we used were actually sold as laboratory slides and costing pennies rather than the more expensive counter type on the wall, which expanded or contracted with any movement. These had to be visited and monitored regularly, recording the readings over the course of a year. Of course, this method was accurate if regularly inspected, but we thought our simpler cheaper method was easier as the family was only too pleased to watch the slides and any minute movement immediately shattered the glass.

As the loss adjuster had been caught using cheats, of which they denied knowledge, they were in no position to try to spin this case out. Spring was rapidly approaching and tiny buds could be seen as nature was waking up. Trees, shrubs and plants of all descriptions grow new branches, leaves, blossoms, and roots seek water, from rainfall seeping down through the earth or in dry spells the roots spread deeper and further. We were authorised to obtain three estimates from companies to underpin the entire front wall and to repair the fractured bricks. The gaps in the bay structure were filled with mortar and steel rods were anchored at the corner joints and inside the fractures in the living room and hall were filled to level and painted over.

The council removed the huge cherry prunus tree in the pavement and replaced it with a sapling and next door's laurel bushes were reduced in height to about three feet.

In those days, we acted as an agent for householders or landlords whose buildings had become damaged due to movement of subsiding ground, damaging the footings, or heave, which was the opposite and caused by an excess of moisture in the ground. Prolonged extremely wet weather can soak the ground, leaking drains and removal of vegetation play its part and foundations may start to rise, causing different fracturing and problems to be addressed. Installing a soakaway can be useful to dispose of excess rainfall and various methods of drainage away from the house.

Chapter 19

A small group of business people known to Jonny Pearson booked us to carry out a dimensional survey of a small hotel in Eastbourne which they said they were taking over. They wanted to convert the building into five flats of varying sizes. Small areas could be tweaked, like a dormer or two added to enable the roof area to be utilised, a dormer window in the sloping roof of the garage, but no extensions to the ground floor.

I called them to arrange a date and we went. I had packed a small overnight bag with a change of underwear and toiletries, just in case I could tempt Chris to stay out as No.1 was helping at a dinner dance with the wine wizard and was staying overnight at his house and Nos.2 and 3 also had sleepovers with friends. It was a rare opportunity, I reminded Chris.

When we arrived the two owners of the hotel were elsewhere and a very pleasant middle-aged lady welcomed us in. We explained what we intended to do and said we would endeavour to complete the job in one day and keep out of the way of the other guests. She cheerily suggested that they had a small double room that was vacant and we could use that to store our bags and coats and if we felt like breaking off, we could stay and pick up the threads in the morning. 'What a lovely idea,' I gushed, as if it had never entered my mind. 'We may take you up on that.'

We worked flat out, measuring the grounds, gardens and garages. We started at the top of the building and worked our way down. We actually finished and it was about half past six. Chris wanted to go home as we were both tired but I wanted to stay to take advantage of the freedom.

One of the owners was by now behind the bar in the visitor's lounge and he gave us a beer. I asked him if the room was still available as his receptionist indicated and he agreed.

Unfortunately, the kitchen was closed as his partner, also a chef, had gone to visit family for some sort of celebration and would not be back until tomorrow morning, so offering many apologies, he said we would have to go out for dinner. He recommended a Swiss restaurant about half a mile away so, longing for food, we went there. The food was indeed delicious and we slowly returned to the hotel about nine thirty and after a quick shower we both collapsed into bed. Rarely have I been so exhausted but it was a substantial building to cover in one day, not forgetting the journey down and we woke up early.

When we arrived in the dining room for breakfast, we were surprised to note that we were the only heterosexual couple in the room, which was filled with small tables and most couples were male with a few females interspersed. We were not stared at or made to feel uncomfortable and the owner who presided over the dining room was pleasant and there was nothing tangible to make us feel awkward or out of place. We did though. 'Well done, Toots,' Chris muttered with a false smile around his mouth and narrowed slitty eyes.

He had wanted to go home and it was my idea to stay, thinking it would be a nice mini-break and rest for ourselves, taking advantage of our children being safe with others until about mid-day.

We ate the very nice breakfast and went back to tidy the room, collected our sparse belongings and went back downstairs to take our leave. There, grinning like a chimp was the owner, who handed us the bill for a night's stay and breakfast. Insult to injury: first no dinner, which forced us to go out and eat an extravagant, delicious main course with wine, followed by some sort of Austrian rich pastry and chocolate thing for dessert which had a flambé sauce poured over and whipped cream, coffee with brandies and petit fours all of which lulled us into heavy sleep and coshed our credit card for a week's shopping bill.

Taking the bill, which didn't even feature a discount for the fact that we had worked so hard the day before, I just flashed the plastic again and we left. 'I'll add it to the invoice, Chris,' I said. 'They should allow us expenses, it's a long way to go there measure up and get back in one day.'

'Mm. We did it though. I wanted to go home. What if one of the kids needed us?'

He was right of course, but no good crying over spilt milk. I resolved to try to recoup some of our expenditure, but we weren't forced into buying that bottle of wine over dinner which was so highly recommended but tasted just like Piesporter, or made to have that decadent chocolate, crunchy, nutty, creamy, boozy thing afterwards, or the brandies or soppy little cakes.

The hotel was drawn up as it was and transformed into five little units, perfect for holiday lets or bijou getaways. Each flat had a parking space. A bin store had been shown and a large garden store for the equipment and a bike rack. The application was submitted to the local council.

The next instruction for us from this group was to visit a beautiful Georgian building tucked away in a Hertfordshire village which we measured and produced drawings showing the existing elevations and floors to scale.

It had been used as a ladies' gym and beauty treatments centre including hairdressers. The lease had expired and the owners decided to sell the building.

Light snacks were prepared in the huge basement and drinks, which could be consumed in the basement or upstairs in the lounge.

While measuring the beautiful building, we took in the wrought iron decorative panels beneath the curved, polished timber bannister. The magnificent hall to be used for reception on the ground floor and lounge on the first floor each had an Adams fireplace, both in excellent condition. The ornate plaster covings, cornices and ceiling roses had not been damaged.

The rooms above were like dressing rooms of a theatre: mirrors had light bulbs fixed around the edges, and several vintage type bathrooms which were not original. A small door to the side led through the eaves to a narrow walkway around the edge of the roof behind the parapet walls. The views stretched to the corners of the village.

It had been decided to turn the beauty parlour into a restaurant, which required very little input from us other than to reproduce their ideas on paper and to submit the existing floor plans and elevations already prepared by us, and another plan showing the new kitchens installed in the basement, a waiting area full of sofas on the ground floor and a bar with another mini bar in the entrance hall. The first floor was to become the formal dining room and lavish cloakrooms for the diners.

Planning permission was granted in due course, as well as for the hotel to be converted into flats.

Somebody introduced the owners to a company who constructed beautiful conservatories. They had been in their village and got persuaded to add one to the restaurant. We assumed that everybody knew what they were doing and made a couple of site visits just to see the transformation and ensure that important listed features were not damaged.

The building inspector from the council told me that in days gone by there were tunnels beneath the building which led out to the streets along the main road. The building at that time was a house of ill repute, a bordello apparently and drinking rooms on the ground floor. When the chosen customer had probably visited someone in one of the rooms above and consumed enough alcohol to render him utterly drunk he was led down the steps into the basement to the secret tunnel to avoid the dangerous narrow streets and assumed safety at the end. Instead, these victims were knocked on the head, thrown into a hand cart, covered with sacking and taken to a holding cell. The impress gangs operated lawfully in this town and they waited at the end of the alley. The wasted paralytics would find themselves in the morning awake and thoroughly terrified upon a galley, either already on the high seas or too far away to swim to shore. They had been press ganged into the king's navy and many would be killed or injured during battles far from land, some never returning home, their families never knowing where their drunken husband or son had gone.

A similar term originated in China, called Shanghaiing which meant men were snatched to form a crew of a ship and probably never survived.

Finally, it was open. Re-named The Orange Tree it was beautiful indeed. The rooms now looked like magazine scenes, curtains spilled along the floor, made from an exclusive fabric; the walls were covered

282

with exquisitely patterned paper not to be seen in the local DIY stores and about a hundred gilded framed chairs, which were upholstered in some expensive cloth, littered the dining room and lounge. It unnerved me a little. The money that had been thrown at this hidden away building could have settled the debts of a small nation, I thought, and I hoped it would be a successful venture.

I suggested theme nights and advertising to make the venue known but they looked shocked. They wanted it to be exclusive.

They asked if we wanted to be included in the opening night and promised a free drink. We took our draftswoman and No.2 with a boy from her class. I remember T and Chris had lobster and were given little chrome covered devices to crack the shells. I forget all the rest of the choices. I was subdued that night as I had witnessed a road accident during the day, which meant I quietly ate my meal and observed the other diners in the room. One of the owners came over to our table and chatted with us for a while. He was very pleased with the number of diners and we wished him well.

They had given a dinner the night before for the builders, which I felt we deserved to have been invited to as we had carried out a lot of work over and beyond the requirements on behalf of the owners but never mind, we had a free drink!

I was hurt when he rang me to say that a snooty couple who sat opposite our table and barely spoke to each other, let alone smile, had reported to him that we on the corner table were little better than guttersnipes. God knows what we were supposed to have done. We must have offended them deeply because they left half a bottle of wine on the table and glasses half full, barely finishing their main course even. I have puzzled over the years as to what we were alleged to have done and it is a mystery. They did, however, get away with not paying their bill which is more than can be said for us.

The restaurant was hit with letters from the council. The planners issued a letter saying there was no planning consent and would be closed down due to lack of heat retention in the conservatory. Our clients believed that planning permission would not be necessary as so many people were having them added to their houses. We knew that the situation for a commercial building would be different but they had not wanted to listen, which is why we thought the conservatory company had dealt with it. I had heard of a new film which if applied to the inside of the glass would provide a sort of double glazing. These could be bought in a few different colours and had properties to allow sunlight in but block the heat seeping out again. I researched it and reported back to our clients, who were in a high panic, expecting to have to demolish a hideously expensive extension after just completing it and the scheme was accepted by the council departments. Specialists were engaged to cut and apply the sections of film which were barely noticeable. The fact that the builders of the foundations had dutifully called the building control inspectors for approval at each stage before pouring the concrete strips negated the accusations of failing to obtain the relevant permissions and the lovely room was saved. I was presented with a tiny gold brooch as a present to thank me for my efforts.

One day I took Mum out to the village for lunch and she enjoyed the meal and the tour of the building which the other few diners did not experience. It was expensive but beautiful and we both enjoyed it.

A couple of months later we drove out there to have Sunday lunch. We didn't telephone to book a table but the doors were firmly closed at midday and no lights blazed. I casually spoke during the week to one of the partners and he said they were going to advertise as no-one had turned up for lunch the previous Sunday. I didn't tell him at that point that we had tried and the doors were locked shut. I wondered how many others had done the same.

When I saw the builder of the place who had carried out such a good job, he told me that he had gone on a Sunday with his wife and as they turned the corner into the courtyard the two chefs walked out, carrying a couple of bags each and locked the doors closed. No doubt the roast beef was cooked instead in their cottage up the road. That was two weeks where the Orange Tree Sunday lunch didn't happen: two possibly lucrative sessions lost. I think they went to work but left the door closed and the welcoming ground floor lights switched off. Any passing trade went away and spent their money elsewhere. By eleven thirty when the beef joints and roast potatoes should be zinging in the ovens, they packed up and closed up.

We knew the wine waiter from a different source and he said mismanagement of the cellars was happening but didn't explain further. He said the partners refused to listen to him so he was leaving.

The builder told the partners of his experience, not forgetting ours too. There was a meeting called but I think the battle was lost.

The chefs were the couple who owned the hotel in Eastbourne. They were smug and arrogant. The sneers vanished from their faces when news reached them that the hotel had been re-possessed as well as the house they had settled into, just down from the restaurant. They thought they were on to a good thing, that because their culinary skills were so good, their future was golden and rosy. Not so. There were no freezers in the extensive, stainless steel kitchens in the basement to store ingredients or leftovers. The food was either cooked and eaten or wasted or taken home. They should have read the small print more carefully on the contracts and they would have noticed the bit where it said that mortgage payments and loans would be paid after wages and suppliers' bills had been settled. They pocketed their wages, sneaked out the best foods and believed the group partnership would be paying all the other expenses, including paying for their two buildings.

The kitchen was dismantled and sold. The furnishings and curtains, the cutlery and equipment, coffee machines, crockery and linens were all sold at auction for fractions of the costs paid out.

It was the end of a dream.

**

During a routine house valuation in Wanstead, Chris realised we knew the name of the client and he turned out to be the brother of the fruit and veg man mentioned earlier. He had lived there for about a year and had applied for a top-up loan to fund university fees for his son and to buy him a car. They had a nice conversation and both sent good wishes to the families. When I came to type it up I noticed a double coincidence as the house had been owned previously by a friend of my mother and she had no inclination to sell or move as far as Mum knew when she met her last. She was afraid that something dire had happened to her or her husband but had not heard anything. She rang the last number that she had and nobody answered, so the phone had obviously not been transferred to another address.

**

Since we moved into our house about ten years earlier, I went with a few neighbours to the church hall to attend an evening monthly wives' meeting. The chairwoman had headed it for seemingly time immemorial as nobody wanted to take it over. The AGM was held in March a few weeks before Easter, when almost everybody tried to attend. She read out the minutes of the last meeting, the state of the bank account and the various fixtures we had arranged. Suggestions for speakers were always avidly sought as it's quite hard to find an interesting person to speak for about an hour who would be satisfied with a small fee. Anybody could suggest someone that they knew or had heard of that would come and give us a talk or display and hopefully not cost much Most required little and then we could magnanimously present him or her with a small gift instead as a token of our appreciation.

We had a woman show us the basis of flower arranging, in this case a Christmas table centre. She had painted pine cones with gold paint, but said we could do equally well using silver instead and glued them at random places on the base. She stuck stalks and twigs which had also been painted into a lump of oasis and added a few sprigs of holly, some plastic ivy, a couple of white roses and dusted it all with glitter. 'There,' she announced, holding it aloft while we all sat mesmerised in our seats. 'You can of course use real holly and ivy and real flowers.'

Mmm. She had a heap of odds and ends on the table and suggested scraps of cotton wool and little models of robins would be apt for winter displays. Who had dragged this woman up? I hoped we weren't paying her. Children might like to paint cones and bits of wood, I supposed.

Another waste of time and insult to our capabilities was a cookery demonstrator who gave us some tips on catering and storage.

I worked full time, as well as looked after children and all the other lovely jobs that working wives and mothers do, like laundry and ironing, cooking, cleaning, shopping and thinking ahead as a trouble shooter so I was interested in listening to this woman, who I hoped would come up with some useful recipes.

She started with opening a packet of spaghetti. It was nice, Italian branded spaghetti and not a supermarket bargain price wrapped in a plastic bag, but we sat like dimwits while she told us how to cook the stuff. We had to bring plenty of salted water to the boil and carefully coil the spaghetti strands into the water with the aid of a fork. We were to simmer it, without a lid, according to the instructions on the pack: then, if we were preparing this in advance, we had to pour copious amounts of cold water over it and it could be frozen for another day. She had brought a camping stove and jugs of water and demonstrated the whole procedure in front of us and by the time it was safety wrapped ready to freeze, almost half our time was up so she verbally reminded us that we could cook and freeze rice in the same way. Mercifully a live show wasn't carried out for this culinary advice and she went on to explain the art of blanching and freezing some fruits and vegetables.

I was glad I wasn't the only one to think this was a pathetic effort as we weren't children just starting out and some of the older women had been preparing family meals for forty years or longer.

One speaker we had that reduced some of us to tears was a man who had been a prisoner of war by the Japanese. He was quietly spoken and the descriptions he gave were graphic, from the state of their huts, the jungle surrounding the camp to the treatment of their fellow human beings. I don't think anybody even coughed during his talk. They were forced to work constructing a road and beaten for falling over or working too slow on meagre rations of one cup of rice a day.

He said obviously, the health of all of the prisoners declined and some died, digestive problems being onerous apart from beatings or being killed. He told us during his captivity he became constipated for weeks, then suddenly had to rush for the trench in great pain as he had the worst diarrhoea he had ever known. From that day onwards he suffered from dysentery which only abated after he had been rescued at the end of the Japanese involvement of the war and had the relevant drugs administered.

This was the worst experience he had encountered and he wished it on no-one but oddly, he felt glad he had had the experience. He said it put into perspective the ordinary moans and groans from ordinary people living their ordinary lives and whenever he heard someone say they had been constipated for a day or two he laughed, as he knew what constipation really meant.

For several years running a group of us got together to cook Christmas dinner for everyone who could also bring a guest. The tickets for the dinner cost about a fiver and the profits added to our membership fees in order to pay for the tea, coffee, sugar and milk with assorted biscuits every evening meeting.

I volunteered to roast a turkey which I bought and they reimbursed me later. Another member did the same. Somebody else did mashed potatoes, another managed roast ones, another had the hideous task of doing sprouts and frozen peas, someone else brought stuffing and sauces. A different wife sorted out the puddings, mince pies and gallons of custard.

I managed to get a 35lb turkey in my oven and when it was cooked I left it to get cold on the worktop. Chris carved it into a heap which I divided into about thirty or more individual servings and placed them side by side in a large clean roasting pan. I carefully poured gravy over the whole thing and this was taken up to the hall for serving.

I didn't mind being one of the turkey cooks, preferring that to doing a hundredweight of spuds.

There was turkey over and this I wrapped in foil and put in my freezer for later.

When the carcass had been virtually stripped, I simmered it in a large pot of boiling water and made a soup which reminded the family that Christmas was only a few weeks away.

The volunteering cooks and their guests got to the hall early and were allowed an extra sherry. The trestle tables were set up with all the chairs around, plates wiped and cutlery and glasses got ready. There were two cookers in the tiny kitchen and these soon became fully loaded with the various foods. The dinner was timed to start at eight and by this time we were set to go. About six of us stood shoulder to shoulder behind the worktop counter and our diners took a plate and went from server to server until they had their meal, then took it back to their table and poured gravy and sauces on it as wanted. Surprisingly this only took a short while, some of the presentation could have been criticised but soon we all sat with our dinners which turned out quite well.

We then cleared away the plates, apart from a few people who volunteered to eat the remaining servings left in the pans.

The same system was carried out with the pudding and pies and we all had another glass of wine and the enormous kettles were put on for coffees and teas. Somehow the washing up was done and everything put away when the games started. This consisted of types of quizzes by identifying certain people as babies and mysteries concerning London stations, so we claimed our baby sitter needed to go home and slid off.

On the afternoon of the AGM I took the little parcels of turkey out of the freezer. I baked a few boxes of shop bought pastry vol-au-vent cases and opened a couple of Campbells' concentrated mushroom soup cans. I mixed the thick soup base into the turkey and spooned enough into each pastry case to allow a couple per person, including my family as I reckoned it to be chef's perks and took the rest up to the hall. I made about seventy. The first time I did this only our leader knew in advance and the unexpected snack replacing a couple of rich tea biscuits went down exceedingly well.

The ovens were switched on and by half time we all had a cup of tea or coffee and my thrown together delicacy. It didn't take a lot of imagination to concoct a quick treat and I repeated the exercise at their request, for the remaining few years that I helped with the Christmas dinner, leaving the club when my time became so short that I kept missing the meetings.

**

There was around the corner in a small industrial estate a company of steel fabricators. From time to time they needed a drawing or a calculation for an installation. We carried out a structural survey for each of the partners when they purchased their homes. To us they were gentlemen and patient with the children, who were eager to learn about all the processes.

They had come into the office with a couple of sketches and asked Chris if he would give them a price to prepare detailed fabrication drawings for a steel and glass atrium staircase for the grand hall of a sports club and hotel, and he quoted a figure off the top of his head. Some time later, when this project had disappeared from our minds one of them called us to say they had won the job and asked if Chris would go with them to the building site to carry out a few dimensional checks for Chris's work and the steel to be fabricated. On the day, only one partner was able to go as something urgent elsewhere needed attention, so I was invited to go too and readily jumped up into the dilapidated lorry which rattled and shook all the way out to the site in Essex. The whole site was mud, surfaced with the shell of the main building. Trucks, diggers, small cranes and gear for lifting heavy materials were everywhere. The site was quite hazardous. Glad to be wearing wellingtons, we picked our way through the plethora of men and machines to the inside of the main building and scanned the drawings, identifying the area where the staircase would be installed. I wasn't much use at exercises like these and left the men to do their measuring and squinting and making marks all over papers and strolled nosily around, studying the pillars and areas which had been worked on.

There was to be a separate building for indoor ball games such as basket-ball and badminton, football and cricket bowling practice as well as a swimming pool, showers and gym, several bars and restaurants, not forgetting the golf course itself and landscaping of lakes, hills and copses.

At the time of the visit it was a messy building site everywhere and we stopped to get a drink and burger or something equally tasty and nutritious on our way back from a roadside van. Chris said very quietly while D lined up that beggars can't be choosers, we were guests of Mr Metal and didn't he always take me to memorable places?

Our paperwork was done and sent and we issued our invoice in due course. The metal and glass bifurcated stairs, situated either side of a fountain, met at a landing and continued outwards in two directions to the balcony running around the floor above. This was reportedly "the business", I was told but we never saw it. The hotel rooms were all situated on this level and corridors led from the balcony to the blocks of rooms. There was a lift building also constructed with glass walls and sides for less fit or faint hearted people shunning the stairs.

Over time we continued to see the steelworkers but sadly, the company carrying out the construction at the golf club had gone out of business as the owners had folded and this had a knock-on effect with smaller concerns being the sub contractor's.

The boys often called around the metal works for a chat and to watch the things taking shape. I think they learned a new language. One day they came back full of horror and glee at a story one of them told them. A client owed them money, a fair amount by all account, which he kept promising to pay but never managed it. After numerous phone calls of promises and excuses they apparently ran out of patience and took a trip to their base and burst into the office. Unabashed, the villain jokingly said, 'Hello, boys. What can I do for you?'

D asked for their money.

I'm not too sure what transpired next, apart from hearing that one of the men's hands was stapled to the desk while he shakingly wrote out a cheque with the other. The metal men then telephoned their bank and gave the cheque details, asking for their manager to get express clearance on it.

One metal worker went to the bank concerned and paid it in, paying a small fee for them to call his bank advising that they had paid it in. His own bank manager then called the bank branch and asked if the cheque was in their hands and in order if it would be paid. The answer was affirmative and the cheque was effectively cleared. The cleared credit reached our guys account a couple of days later and they lived to breathe again.

Once these crucial calls had been made and the positive answers were given, the other metal worker released the injured man's hand. Drastic measures for drastic times I guessed.

A year or so later and we received a cheque in the post for our work on the staircase. The site had been sold. Contractors had resumed the building works and all the people who were owed money previously were apparently paid. This was not quite the end of the story. Many more years later after we had moved out of London to downsize as our children had all grown, we drove around one afternoon. We had had a telephone call from a girl offering gold cards to businesses which entitled one free meal for each meal purchased. There was no restriction on this and it could be used for any number of diners, from two upwards and lasted for a year. Included was a couple of free nights' accommodation and use of the golf facilities and pool, with jacuzzi, sauna, steam room and gym. There were treatments on offer for massages, facials, manicuring, several bars and restaurants and people stayed there for breaks and holidays.

This all sounded very nice and off we went. We parked and walked around admiring the buildings and went inside to the reception desk then to the bar for a drink. Chris suddenly said, 'My God, Chris that's the staircase I did for D.' It was. The owners who resurrected the scheme had changed the name and we didn't know the address of the mud quarry we had visited ten years before. The Sunday lunch was expensive, drinks even more so but the quality of the food and the choice was excellent. It was gratifying to see one of Chris's jobs lift from the paper and take pride of place in the beautiful hall. Most Saturday evenings and Sunday lunchtimes a pianist sat at a baby grand piano and played almost anything that was requested and we loved our visits there.

**

We carried out a valuation for a house in the high road of an East End borough and the unknown person went ahead and completed on the purchase. Unless there is a quirk in the property or a problem the matter gets filed away. In this case, it had been dealt with and filed away as far as we were concerned but it resurrected itself like Hydra, the many headed nightmare.

The owner contacted us and asked for help. Chris drove over there to meet him. The ordinary mid-terrace house was transformed. He had installed a new wall and doorway at the bottom of the stairs to self-contain the upper floor. This was an actual conversion of a single, family dwelling house to two flats and should have had relevant planning consent in order to make it lawful. Chris knew the authority would not have granted the permission, the criteria then and now required several definite factors.

Secondly, the ground floor had been converted into a barber's shop. It was well done, it looked nice, being all white with white ceramics and gleaming chrome taps. A shop sign had been positioned on the front of the bay structure and a couple of striped barbers' poles either side. The neighbours had complained to the authorities that the business had become successful and there was a steady stream of customers trailing in and out of the place from eight in the morning until late at night. Chris told him the best thing he could do was to dismantle all signs of the shop outside and strip out the shop fittings inside, reinstate the living room appearance by removing the strip lights and hope for the best, that they allowed him to keep the upper unit separate, as council tenants were living there, but this was probably being optimistic and naïve. He had only been paying a single residential council tax so unable to plead in his defence that he had paid one dwelling council tax and one commercial or retail rates amount.

The bank would have demanded that he reinstated the property to the description on the mortgage. He was annoyed as he said he knew lots of other people who ran businesses from home and they got away with it. Chris said they probably don't have moving lights and signs and a large illuminated window and many tramping feet to the front door.

A builder we knew asked us to meet him at a Chinese restaurant in Chingford. The new owner wanted to make internal alterations and to erect an extension at the front to create additional seating. He wanted sliding glazed doors to enable them to be opened in summer as the sun blazed directly on the front all the afternoon. The feature would also be attractive during the evenings. We advised a solid roof as opposed to glazing as conservatory type buildings can get unbearably hot. The application for the new front was submitted and he got on with the other aspects so that he could get established in time for the Chinese New Year. This date varies year by year.

The formation of new kitchens and WCs at the rear and inner partition walls removed to form a larger dining room was achieved and decorated and we were invited to the opening night. An invitation had been sent to everybody who had been involved, from the estate agent at the onset to financial adviser and bank manager to council operatives, all building and decorating contractors and us. We recognised a few of the people there and we all stood around holding a glass which was replenished by girls wearing bright Cheongsam Chinese dresses and traditional hair styles and make-up. These dresses are Manchu or Mandarin and usually of beautiful silk fabric. This is not the traditional dress of a peasant but adapted by wealthy 1920s Chinese people to have a Western influence. Trays of bite size appetisers were also offered round and certainly whetted the appetite for more. When we had tasted about half a dozen different dishes, more were left on the side tables and we were each handed a little red envelope. How intriguing, I thought, until I realised we had to put a pound coin in the envelope and feed it to the dragon which had leapt through the back door into the main area accompanied by a clashing of introductory drums noise. It was the nearest I ever got to being up close to a dragon. At the end, the dragon's head and body was lifted up and two young men stood grinning at us all. The gift was to wish good luck to the venture; I don't know who benefited the most, the owner or the dragon.

He received his planning consent for the front seating and this was duly constructed.

One by one the other restaurants along the street, an Indian, a Turkish, a Thai had front extensions constructed and the restaurant flourished, as did this little area of diners' paradise offering tasty choices and an attractive street scene, like a holiday resort.

**

I was pleased that my children had faith in me. I hoped it would continue as many teenagers go through a stage of feeling embarrassed by their parents and this develops into a reluctant tolerance due to feeling out of touch. If you're lucky these doubtful emotions turn back to love and respect again, but have to be earned.

No.1 asked me in a deadly serious voice if I would agree to hide a boy from school if he turned up here. 'Why would he do that? What's he done?'

'I don't know the details, Mum. He's scared for his life. His dad's in dead trouble.'

'So, what has he told you then?'

'People are out to get his dad so he needs to have somewhere to run to. I told him he could come here. I knew you'd help.'

Mm. 'Are the whole family coming here?' I had visions of feeding a whole family hiding in one of the bedrooms. Thinking of bedrooms, I wondered how long they would be here, how I could sleep them. Perhaps the mother would take over the cooking so I can still go to work.

'I think it will be just Abdul. I told him where we hide the spare key, Mum, so he can just turn up.'

'You sure this is on the level? The key is supposed to be secret. I'll have to change the hiding place. Who else knows about it?'

I now had visions of Abdul and his family safe and warm inside, the mother cooking and the rest of them watching television and people with guns or huge curved knives bombarding our house to seek revenge for something unknown. Suddenly I felt I was on the set of Ali Baba or Aladdin. 'No one, Mum. We can't see him get hurt, can we? I think they're all working out places of safety.'

Christ. 'Have they been to the police?'

'They can't do anything. They can't act on threats, only actions.'

'Look, I'm sorry for Abdul and his family's problems, but I am now concerned for you.'

The boy turned up on Saturday afternoon, dropped outside by a Mercedes with blackened windows. He sat closeted with No.1 in his room apparently playing Mario Brothers games and listening to music. A few hours later he used our phone and another car picked him up outside. He left after saying, "Thank you" and that appeared to be the end of that.

I didn't know who the boy was at the time but it all fell into place a bit later.

While I worked at the bank there was an account of a travel agent. The proprietor occasionally came to the branch himself but mainly sent an employee. The employee was quiet and barely moved a facial muscle: he pushed the paying-in book across the desk and the money in a white cloth bag. The cashier, occasionally me, counted the notes, stamped the receipt and pushed it back. I always smiled and said, "Thank you", to everyone, the straight-faced gofer was no exception.

One day a large cheque for Pakistan International Airways was presented in the daily clearing but there were insufficient funds in the travel agent's account to pay it. Someone called the shop and warned him. He asked us to wait till later in the afternoon. This was a serious thing as it was feared that the airline would bankrupt him if the cheque was dishonoured. Large concerns don't thrive on generosity.

About five minutes before closing time the travel agent and his assistant came into the branch. Each carried a bag full of money. If it had been a stack of notes it would have been easier but each bag held little packs and bundles and envelopes. A few extra clerks were called to the counter to help count them all and finally they were all counted and listed. The enormous total was entered on the paying in slip and the cheque was paid. His crisis had been averted and he now owed hundreds of people a debt of gratitude and each individual donor from his mosque a differing sum.

The airline needed paying in regular instalments. They would periodically round up the total and issue him with an account statement which then had to be paid by a certain date. We wondered what would happen next time, as he would have twice the amount to find. He seemed to sort it all out while I was at that branch because the reprieve gained by the last minute frantic payment was not repeated. I suppose we didn't know what went on behind the walls of the travel agency office.

I hadn't known the identity of the school friend at the time but at parents' evening at school I saw the travel agent and he was Abdul's father. He apparently knew all about us though.

He thanked me for taking his son in a few months earlier and asking no questions: he said his problems had been sorted out. I no longer worked at the bank but heard that when the next large cheque arrived there was no assistance from fellow worshippers and the cheque was returned. The travel agency closed, I believe the house was sold and the family returned to Pakistan, almost in disgrace. It's sad when a business fails and the family is disrupted and in this case transported overseas to a country of origin but in Abdul's case completely unknown area and way of life.

I knew I would have hidden the whole family. I didn't know the details. He may have been a thieving villain but I knew he had worked hard for twenty years and they had a nice home and nice manners. He always presented the branch with a case of table wine at Christmas to be shared out. I wondered what happened to Abdul and if he turned out all right after the drastic disturbance at a formative age, on the cusp of adolescence when long-term associations are made and deep friendships formed.

We called round to the concrete works and saw the new batching plant in action. There was now a small fleet of ready mixed concrete delivery vehicles and they seemed to be regularly coming and going, as well as trucks from quarries bringing the sand and gravel to replenish the stocks. The process seemed to work like a giant conveyor belt and was gradually being transformed into an automatic fill with one instruction from the office and as if by magic, the separate components travelled along their respective chutes into the ever-revolving mixer. While this was taking place at the filling station the driver would be signing in the office and sometimes paying for the goods. Lee now wanted to develop another area of the land into a double row of industrial units, five separate units with a large turning and parking area and facing them an identical row. They talked and Chris began to sketch his thoughts.

We already had map extracts of the land and I had a library of catalogues to thumb through for ideas and inspiration. Chris discussed his thoughts with our lovely draftswoman, who set to work to produce our designs. The walls structure was of blockwork and the external walls, fronts and rear had rendered panels of cladding surfaces. The metal automatic up and over doors matched in appearance and colour the corrugated roof panels and pedestrian entrance doors. The window frames at high level were of powder coated aluminium. Beneath the roof internally an expensive, new product was installed to allow the buildings two hours' resistance in case of fire. At the back of the building a metal balcony was constructed to each unit and stairs led down to an alley at the rear to provide an escape route for workers if a blaze started.

There was very little resistance from the planners and apart from discussions about the chosen colours of the metal roof claddings, the relevant permissions were granted.

The site owner, our young concrete mogul, acted as the building contractor and foreman and organised the building site from inception to completion of the small estate. We went to the site from time to time and when finally completed we prepared a lease plan of each separate unit as they were let out to various trades, consisting of storage mainly of car parts, decorating and building products, electronics, clothing for the market trade, stationery and dried foods.

Our children helped as usual and took a keen interest in the design and construction and the overall atmosphere of the concrete batching, all the powerful motor vehicles, cranes on occasion and general big boys' toys around the place.

**

It was always good to see previous clients call in to say hello and even better if they had another project to ask us for help with. When Graham came in wearing a slightly perplexed face, we waited for his story. He believed his house had started to subside in the front bay area and we both went to his home to have a look.

Sure enough, a gap had appeared between the bottom of the brick dado wall beneath the curved windows and the concrete peripheral apron around. The gap was substantial and had appeared virtually overnight. Inside the front reception room the skirting boards had remained in position, still attached to the front wall but the floor had dropped leaving a void of over half an inch. Poor Lindsay was terribly upset and we got her to make us tea while Chris and I prepared our report.

We advised that the shrubs thriving close to the bay were removed. Laurels and privet are thirsty plants and when we organised trial pits to take soil samples we extracted roots from the pit over a metre deep in the ground and the soil was very dry. The real culprit, however, was an underground rivulet which had been diverted from its course a couple of miles away to make way for a road diversion and although the house basement and cellars had never been flooded by these waters when swollen, the vegetation of the area had grown to rely on the supply and many gradually dried out as the water vanished. Other plants still avidly sought the water they had grown accustomed to and drastic reductions had to be made of growth found to be affecting foundations.

The insurance company insisted on the monitoring that we had installed being watched to see if the ground made a recovery after the plants were reduced, which was usual. A few other houses in the row and opposite began to complain of similar problems and insurers looked into the new course of the diverted stream. The prospect of paying for all these impending claims must have been daunting for them as they would far rather collect the premiums than settle claims. Somehow the powers that be worked with the Highways section and National Rivers and water began to manifest again. We advised the installation of an automatic device in the cellar which would pump out any water collected and divert it into the road drains.

In due course this matter was settled and the handy water pump which actually had been manufactured for use in boats became a device that we specified in places where flooding threatened.

**

We had a visit from David Mozan, who we had not seen since he took the children to the glassworks. No.2 made him a cup of tea and we were all alarmed to see him spoon extra sugar into his cup. 'That's too much sugar,' she told him seriously and he nodded.

'Yes, I know but I like it.'

I thought he looked tired and he admitted he had things on his mind.

No.2 persisted. She had been learning about the destructive properties of sugar in a home and food lesson at school and warned him he could become diabetic. He nodded again. I believe he had already succumbed to this disease but refused to face the consequences.

His hostel was becoming oversubscribed and the local authority continued to send homeless men to the place. From time to time his tenants moved out but there were usually insufficient beds for the needy and he wanted to enlarge the upper floor.

There was a rear section which had a flat felted roof and he reasoned if he built over it, he could form either three rooms or a small dormitory for overnight stays rather than long-term use.

The councils were not keen on a collective room, preferring all the homeless men to have their own space but we argued with them that the Ritz it was not: even a standard hotel it was not. The Salvation Army hostel in London was arranged as a dormitory with a canteen area for breakfast and then the men were obliged to vacate the premises, taking their meagre belongings with them. At night when they settled to sleep they had to keep hold of their bags as unfortunately there was no honour among destitution and thievery was rife.

There will be lockers provided, we suggested, and will enable more people to be accommodated. He got his permission. Behind the main building there was a large area of grass which had been left to provide a garden but David wanted to develop it. We advised him against attempting, it as an area to sit outside was a requirement for all accommodation places, even though it was usually used by men clutching cans or smoking.

He got up to leave and winked at Chris and me. 'Keep a look out in the news. But, I didn't tell you.'

Nothing emanated over the next few days but we had no clue as to the substance of the hint so I bought a few newspapers and we listened on the radio during the day. Finally, it came.

One tiny segment of a national tabloid featured the announcement that three men had been arrested for the murder of a man found dead the previous year. No names were mentioned but we felt sure it was the look-alike Mr Evans from building control they meant. I don't know if these suspects ever went to trial or were convicted. No name was given in the newspaper article.

Several other small extracts mentioned that homes had been raided and people were helping the police in their enquiries for information on the Brink's-Mat robbery after the police received an anonymous tip-off.

Many years later and the police have never got to the bottom of this enormous robbery and much of the gold has never been recovered. The infamous gang believed they were stealing about three million pounds' worth of gold bullion but instead made off, in a heavily weighed down van, with over twenty-six million pounds' worth, including travellers' cheques and diamonds.

The next time we spoke to Jonny Pearson we asked him how various people were, if Del Smith was still out and about and if Jeff Gold with his basement storage was in good health.

He shrugged and professed to know nothing and he probably did know nothing. So many people have been killed, reportedly due to having links with the robbers or the gold or the proceeds of the sale of the gold, being drugs and property that the few with real knowledge probably keep very quiet.

**

Two of the children came home with leaflets about impending school trips which we read and discussed. No.1 was good at art but luckily had not spotted any other tableaux in the forest to attempt to portray: and exceptionally talented at technical drawing which obviously was being polished by the knowledge he was learning with Chris and drawings he was helping to produce, along with experiences of marking out foundations on site. Barcelona had been chosen for the boys, mainly, who showed promise with art, photography, technical drawing and anyone who felt interested in architecture or buildings or wanted to make the number up. He wrinkled his nose and said looking at the crazy cathedral that had been under construction for decades was not really his thing, so wasn't "dead struck."

The trip for No.2 was to stay with a family in Germany. She wanted to go, which surprised me as she had a real suspicion of other people's dads. Her accent when she spoke German, I thought was excellent and she said she wanted to improve it. Apparently, a few of her best friends had elected to go so there was the motive. The journey was by ferry and coach so I think she thought the journey would be a laugh.

Chapter 20

Denny had passed on an acquaintance to us and we worked with him on a private basis, as well as the company he often worked with when they needed assistance.

Tim was a draftsman preparing drawings for all reasons and uses and occasionally needed a beam calculation for his applications and construction. He was good friends with a person who ran a successful company preparing make-overs for pubs, called Pebbles. The venues could be large or small but usually successful. Tim was allowed to use a desk at their company premises and use their facilities as long as he continued to work for the major company whenever needed. From time to time a brewery decided to offload some of their premises and another brewery bought them. Then there would be a frantic time of carrying out dimensional surveys and the talented imaginative architects and technicians at the company would produce their drawings showing completely re-vamped seating arrangements, or dining rooms or outside terraces for use during the better weather. When they needed engineering for a wall to be removed in a bar on an urgent basis, Tim told them of Chris and so started a new intermittent association.

Most of the make-overs involved using the layouts of the existing premises and they were able to change the whole atmosphere and theme of a place by the use of timber cladding, wall coverings and lighting. They would take away the furniture for storage and the pictures and fittings and bring in a completely different range.

They had a comprehensive list of useful people and companies and now we proudly realised that our name had been added to the list when engineering services were required fairly urgently at reasonable cost.

When they were awarded each job to change the building, the drawings were produced and a written specification of works so they could choose the various tradesmen and specialists. Contractors produced estimates and usually the cheapest one was chosen.

The contracts that were drawn up were punitive if the completion times were not adhered to and several times we called around to the site for a final inspection on the last day of the contract, to see last minute painting carried out as others gathered up their equipment for removal and backed out the doors to waiting vans.

The activity during the last couple of days was manic, carpet fitters frantically tacking down the edges while curtains were being hooked up and upholsterers finished off corner sofas and plumbers charged up and down cellar stairs, helping the brewery staff to fit the barrels and get the pressures right. They frequently worked through the night at the end if time was running out and achieved amazing transformations, raising the level of the floor to create interest with small separate sections involving stairs and timber handrails or removing the platforms to open it out again for unhampered vision.

Many public houses started with a public bar and a saloon bar, usually with a wall between. The separating wall often had a chimney breast. This in the days when people went for a drink and the establishments served simple food, workmen in the public bar while the other was for couples and people to sit at small tables for a quiet chat. Everyone could smoke if they wished.

As more pubs started serving more and more food the area for workmen and drinkers shrank, for serving food proved more profitable.

The different breweries owned and controlled many public houses which were contained in groups or chains, the groups used the same menus, the buildings were decorated in the same way with similar set-ups and furnishings. Pictures on the walls had the same themes, country scenes with horses and animals, or ornaments or pictures of pop stars or film stars.

On occasions, part of a wall had been removed during a refurbishment contract and later they would ask for the rest to be taken out, this requiring a steel beam to support the upper floor. The object of some of these exercises was to enable the bar staff to have clear views of the entire pub.

Nooks and private little crannies had to be eliminated to prevent illegal activities carrying on. Any shaded corner due to a small jutting area, once regarded as cool and tasteful or private, was now to be removed to prevent secretive trading of drugs. The landlord or landlady along with bar staff if found to be allowing drug dealing or use would be seriously penalised and the breweries were keen to make their properties as free of blind spots as possible.

Over the years, we visited properties and assisted with a drawing or an engineering project and then perhaps years later, after the breweries had one of their bulk sales, we would go again for more changes to a place we knew would be transferred into a different chain with different ideas.

Usually the landlords were keen to have the works carried out, especially if the carpets and furnishings had worn and frayed. They joined enthusiastically with the meetings with the brewery representative and the designers and when they lodged on the premises, in the rooms above, were on the spot to hover downstairs keeping an eye on the progress. These branches were the popular ones with established clientèle and management knew their regulars would flock back once re-opened, eager to try the new menus and perhaps the new beers.

Some complained. They said they would be expected to increase the takings once the works had been finished and said they were worried they would lose their jobs if they couldn't keep to the targets. They were expected to make the place successful by inventing gimmicks, games and form teams to play rivals. It seemed that when the breweries spent money sprucing up the place the bar staff, principally the manager, were obliged to claw it back in higher sales.

I remember several individuals moaning that well-heeled punters couldn't be dragged inside off the streets.

Rarely were the living quarters given the same lavish care and the standards upstairs sometimes would have shocked the customers downstairs if they could see the state of the bathrooms and bed linens.

As we drive about nowadays we frequently see a building which we had contributed work to in the past and now become something completely different: converted to flats, extended and converted or now a thriving Indian or Chinese Restaurant, a fast-food venue or occasionally a country house. I wonder what became of the staff.

**

We occasionally drew flats schemes or simpler extensions for a builder that I had met while working as a bank cashier. He came in to cash a cheque and I went around the back to look up the account, to confirm that the funds were sufficient and if she had made arrangements to allow a builder to obtain cash. The answer to both queries was ascertained and I went back to the front to count out the money. During the transaction, we had a conversation. As soon as Chris had decided to go out on a limb to start our business I accosted every person who wore overalls or looked remotely like they came from a building site or wielded tools or paintbrushes to promote him. 'Hello, are you a building contractor?'

'You look like you're busy. Are you a plasterer?'

'Where do you work, the local builders' merchants?'

'Do you know a person who prepares plans?'

We became fairly friendly. When we had been left in dire straits by the rogue builders the previous year, he sent his son and a worker to finish off the shower room for us and he owned the holiday place that we borrowed in Nerja, Southern Spain.

He had converted a three-storey building in Stamford Hill before he met us. During the work, he had become acquainted with the next door neighbours who lived on the two upper floors and ran a furniture shop on the ground floor level. The furniture was just beds and chairs for elderly folk and they supplied residential care homes as well as individual sales.

The proprietors were a middle-aged woman and her son. I presume that the husband had died and not run off, as there were photos of him in the main bedroom and living rooms.

The mother was strident and dominant. The son was dapper, subservient and spoilt. He endured the patronising regime of being the assistant to her leadership and remained living in the rooms above the shop, presumably because she showered him with financial rewards and turned a blind eye to his adventures. He owned a very fast sports car and a powerboat. Weekends saw him on the Isle of Wight or Lymington with other boat people, or racing and hobnobbing with enthusiasts at meetings and we spotted his picture in the paper a few times and once saw his shiny red racing boat in a glossy magazine with a short article including comments from him. He must have met and mixed with eligible women and we thought his mother would have eaten them for breakfast. At any rate, he was in his thirties and very much single.

He had been attempting to get her to sell the business, which was extremely successful, relying more on bulk orders than the odd armchair sale and converting the building into three sizeable flats, as next door had done for very lucrative sales. I believe they already owned a small flat on the coast which he possibly used during his water sports pursuits and intended to either move into permanently or install her there.

How he gritted his teeth and endured her negative comments each time he ventured a suggestion is known only to him. I know my own offspring at their ages at the time would have rebelled if I had taken that attitude and tone to them.

We went a few times, measuring and preparing schemes for discussion and the builder carried out a few things which would help their conversion application should this ever get to happen, like widen the rear entrance for car parking and install a ground floor disabled WC. The ground floor had enormous shop windows to the front and side, which would be the most challenging aspect to change as planners, in their wisdom, sometimes enforced their subjective views and insisted on retaining the existing elevation for posterity, showing that originally the property had been a shop. Sometimes they enforced that the shop sign had to remain. Sometimes the unit when completed looked ridiculous in my opinion, having seven feet tall windows along the entire wall, where thick dark curtains had been hung for privacy and a bid to prevent heat loss which gave an old fashioned creepy appearance. I expected to see Christopher Lee flashing his fangs or Boris Karloff as the first Frankenstein's monster, peering around the edge of the drapes.

We drew an extension and a conservatory for the builder's own house too and met the rest of his family.

Sadly, the eldest son of this lovely man died. He had been hooked on drugs and battled constantly to wean himself off them. His marriage had broken up and he lost his children because his wife had refused to suffer his behaviour and constant relapses and he had returned to his parents' home, where he lived in the garden gym trying and failing to get clean. After two weeks of remaining free he went for a drink with some friends and they ended up in a club. He bought a packet of something and used it, costing him a fiver and his life. The police said later that the cocaine had been mixed with Vim, a strong cleaning powder. His parents who had tried so hard to help him and were encouraged by each day of abstinence found him lying on the floor of their garden room, covered in hideous vomit.

Our children had met him and liked him when he fixed the shower and were saddened by the news. They were all young enough to regard drugs in name and substance as horrific and frightening and I hoped they would never be tempted to try and even worse, enjoy the effect and include them in their recreational lifestyle

I threw myself into organising our Easter camping trip and began buying packets and tins of food and thinking of a few outings, determined to make the most of our family life while they still enjoyed spending time with us.

**

The first time that we met Portia it was to help her retain her garden walls. Her house was at the beginning of a new road on a large housing estate. It was all open plan; the road was flanked on each side by pavements. The driveways and garden paths all led from the pavements. There was no sign of a fence or dividing wall to the front layout anywhere apart from

Portia's one metre high solid wall and tiny mock Roman pillars fixed along the top. The whole was painted white and actually looked attractive. We submitted her formal application to retain her walls and sent a letter pointing out that her house did not in reality start at the beginning of the road but had been offset, allowing the plot to spread over the entire corner and it was the only detached house to be completed with a rendered surface, being painted white to all the other semi's plain brickwork.

The appearance of the earlier established dwellings along the perpendicular road was more like hers and they too had low ornamental walls. This would be a case of common sense versus obstinate recalcitrance. The decision when it arrived was to allow her to keep the walls but to remove the ornamental finish. Who said there was no compromise?

While at her home we met her son, who was doing his homework. She told us a horrendous tale which sounded like a film subject and were unable to verify.

Her husband, we were told, was Nigerian, as she was. He was a qualified architect and had been practising in this country when he met and married her. She had been in her village a princess, reportedly, but she gave it all up to marry him. They had three children and after some years he decided to return to their homeland.

Off they went and began a new life somewhere in Africa. Somehow along the way she trained and became a nurse, a midwife and child psychologist, we were not told where the training occurred. We just sat on her sofa and listened.

After a while he changed in his personality and treatment of her and life became unbearable. She said he had taken another, younger wife, as his religion allowed him to do and the younger woman was rude, violent and generally unpleasant to her and her children. She wanted to leave him. In a sort of setting that resembled Sally Fields's portrayal of a maltreated wife in the book and film titled *Not without my daughter* she made her escape back to England but only managing to take the youngest child with her. At the time of our meeting this had occurred about five years earlier and she still hadn't been allowed access to the other two, older children, although she professed to occasionally speak with them on the telephone.

She longed to meet with them again and was trying to arrange a rendezvous in Paris.

I don't know if he sent her money or whether she had her own, but according to the story of her flight she escaped with barely the coat on her back and change in her pocket, but had purchased her own home as well as several others and was still in her forties.

The other two buildings needed floor plans for fire certificates, which we prepared for her. These two buildings were apparently used as children's homes and staffed by her sister, who was a part-time nurse at the local hospital and various other helpers.

She asked Chris to look at a large, three-storey residential house in South West London which she had seen in an auction and wanted to buy. Chris went to look at it and saw that it was distorted. The right-hand side of the building sloped distinctly downwards and the floors were at varying degrees of level. He advised her to leave it as it was severely damaged but he was too late. She had forgotten that she had placed a deposit on it several days before the auction, which meant that she was lawfully obliged to complete on the purchase. Once she received all the papers it could be seen that underpinning had been carried out which had stabilised the movement, but no remedial works to attempt to straighten the floors. She reasoned that once it had been decorated and furnished, the girls she would take into her care wouldn't notice the slalom in the hallway. They would be grateful for her shelter.

We prepared floor plans, which also showed additional walls which she had had installed across the large front rooms to create two smaller rooms.

In those years, we probably met a dozen times.

Suddenly her children's homes were all closed. She or a staff member had been accused by one of the girls of an improper act, this could have been an action or verbal abuse, we never knew. When we saw her next she was surrounded by legal books and was preparing her defence. She intended to represent herself. We never knew the outcome of this apart from learning that her houses had evolved into HMOs.

This lady either had a vivid imagination and an uncanny ability to earn a lot of money, or the whole kit and caboodle was true, but she was the only person I ever met who bought their own home, apparently single handed and on a nurse or midwife's salary, owned at least four other places that we were aware of, ran a very expensive car and privately educated her son. She employed staff as well as travelled all over Europe and had a penchant for Florida during the winter, leaving a housekeeper to look after the teenager during her travels.

**

Easter approached and No.2 was off to Germany for a week while the two boys remained with us. We had arranged to meet Chris's sister and family in Kent with the campervan. The weather was reasonable and the long-range forecast promised some sunshine.

No.1 helped Chris when he went around the sites and practised his drawing skills back in the office. No.3 also went sometimes with Chris and Denny and practised his Jamaican accent, which Denny lapsed into when conversing with some of his friends and clients.

It was time to take her to the school which looked strangely empty at five in the morning to meet the rest of the party and wave her off on the coach. They were all excited.

She had Sterling and Deutschmarks in her purse to spend and was looking forward to meeting her host family, who had twin daughters. During the week, there would be a couple of link ups with the teachers who had gone with them on the trip and a chance to visit shops in order to buy souvenirs.

The time came to return to school to collect her from the playground where there was a great cheer when the coach swung through the gates. I thought the general atmosphere over excited and childlike, they had only been away for a week and to Germany not the Andes or deep Peru. But early mornings never did agree with me.

She waved enthusiastically at me as she came down the coach steps and went around the side of the coach to collect her case. One of the teachers approached me and I instantly felt unnerved. She was looking a bit anxious and I straightened my grin and waited for her words. 'Hello,

Chris,' the teachers sometimes called us by our Christian names. 'Nothing for you to worry about.'

Instantly this invokes worry. 'Your No.2 had her purse stolen.'

Ever since she had been about four and given a purse or bag with her own money, she had routinely lost it. It had become a habit. 'How did she manage? Do we owe you money?'

'We had a collection. Everybody contributed a small amount which they didn't miss and it replaced the pocket money she lost.'

'That's so kind. Thank you and thanks to everybody who put in the whip. At least she had some money to spend.'

Feeling "ever so 'umble" and embarrassed and wanting to make a hasty retreat, I then got accosted by her German teacher. He told me that no blame had been apportioned to No.2 but two of the girls had let themselves and the school down badly by stealing. One of them had been her own best friend, who had tried to avert the blame when she realised she had been spotted by sliding the loot into No.2's carrier bag. Fortunately, the charade had been witnessed and the correct culprit identified. Profuse apologies had been made in Germany, the girls had been severely lectured and of course their mothers were informed.

I felt sick that this unfortunate incident had clouded the whole break and couldn't help wondering who had stolen her purse.

The school friend had been going through an upsetting time at home so some excuses were made for her behaviour and I know her mother was devastated, I never knew the other girl involved, she may have been German.

Once we arrived home we sorted out replacement clean clothes ready to take to join Chris and the boys in Kent and lost no time in taking the motorway to Folkestone where everyone was waiting for us. We all marched off to the local shops where we bought a selection of seafood and followed it up with pizza. There was a lot of catching up to do with our family alone and the cousins hadn't met in weeks.

For this reason, we allowed them to rearrange their sleeping places, the younger ones sleeping in the static caravan and No.1 and the others using our awning which for some odd reason, they thought was cool. 'We can have grown-up conversations without them eavesdropping.'

'Yeah, they interrupt, gets on your nerves.'

We would have the inside of our camper van to sleep in later, oh goody, and spend the evening drinking and chatting in the bigger, more comfortable one.

The younger ones had gone into their section at the back and No.1 and No.3 were chatting with their cousins. We opened a bottle to share and relax together at last.

After about an hour we took more drinks out to the awning and Stella had made a lasagne for a late supper, which was appreciated.

I went to the bedroom end of the caravan where the young ones were laughing about something a little bit naughty, I think, and was about to push the door open to ask if they wanted a chocolate drink when I heard No.3 tell the others, 'Something awful happened to me a little while ago. I haven't told mum and dad yet.'

I waited, as I didn't want to ruin his sentence, but then was obliged to wait outside as the story began. 'Dad picked No.2 and me up from school and we went to a leather warehouse to talk about their drawings. The owner and the workers all spoiled us, probably felt they had to in front of Dad, but the owner made a big thing of sending someone out to get us cakes. We sat on the edge of the room and Dad and the owner went into his office to talk.

'The guy came back with two cream doughnuts, they were huge. Then they got on with the packing they were doing and left us by the desk but they could see us. So, we had a great big cake each and the cream was oozing everywhere, so we started eating them. We were bored and hated going there. We didn't like the smell of the leather and we couldn't understand what the workers said. They didn't like us really, they just had to be polite and friendly because their boss was there, and Dad, of course.

'So, we started pulling faces at each other, you know opening our mouths and showing all the cake and cream inside and laughing. Then we pretended to heave and were doing all the actions, even made the noises and the workers looked at us like we were crazy. Then a great big blob of cream fell on the floor and we were giggling like mad. I had cream all over my chin where I was laughing so much and thought I'd better try to wipe the floor, so I stuffed a bit more of my cake in my mouth and couldn't find any tissues so I wiped my hand on the blob but it just smeared into a bigger patch.'

'What was No 2 doing?' Good question, I thought, still listening at the door.

'She was rolling on the floor in fits of laughter.'

I listened to the rest of the sorry tale and thought about his story. As it unfolded it was like a well-rehearsed farce.

Apparently, No.2 was hysterical with mirth so he tried to clear it up alone. Holding half his cake in one hand and mopping up cream in the other, he turned around looking for a remnant of cloth or hanky and bumped into a rack of coats and jackets behind him, ready for the workers to pack up. His cream-covered hand held at right angles from his body ploughed right into the brand-new clothes and spread the cream along a short row of their hems. This of course horrified him but just made No.2 worse, as by now she was doubled up, saying she was going to wet herself. The workers apparently stopped packing and watched her, perplexed, as No.3 was hidden behind the rack of garments and luckily, they couldn't see what was going on.

At this point, he had one cream-covered hand, a partially eaten doughnut and several coats with smeared hems. He tried to clean the coats by rubbing his elbow across, thinking Mum would rather clean his blazer than a load of new coats but managed to damage a different section from the uneaten cake in his hand. Looking at his sister for aid only made things worse, as she was still convulsed with tears running down her face.

He knew by the smell escaping from a door at the side that a WC for the workers existed and crept in there. It smelt even worse inside but the leaking tap at least washed his hands and, grabbing a heap of paper that he hoped was clean, he went back to the room and began wiping the coats down just in time before the owner and his father came out of the office.

He thought he'd made a reasonable job of wiping the cream off, he told them but I wondered whether the grease would have stained the leather. It seemed that No.3 may have affected six or seven jackets and I began to wonder if that was the reason that the last cheque bounced and he refused to take our calls. I asked Chris later if he had known of a cream cake incident at the warehouse and he said he knew something had happened because No.3 looked guilty and No.2 was red and bleary eyed. I decided I would keep him in the dark.

All too soon the camping trip was over and we packed up and drove home. While I went shopping with Nos.2 and 3 the next day, Chris drove about a mile in the camper van and sold it to the car sales outfit that promised to buy anything on the spot, whatever the condition was. Stuffing the cheque in his pocket he walked back home and got on with tidying the garage.

When we all got back and noticed the missing yellow and white van he looked quite casual. 'It's damp in there, the bed's hard, the seats are hard, the sink's naff and I don't want any more backache trying to cook breakfast. The damn thing's gone.'

The end of one episode and on with all the others.